AF512573

FINANCIAL ECONOMICS: TEXTS AND CASES

FINANCIAL ECONOMICS: TEXTS AND CASES

By

Nishant K. Shukla

CYBER TECH PUBLICATIONS
4264/3, Ansari Road, Daryaganj, New Delhi-110002 (India)
Ph.: 011-23244078. Fax: 011-23280028
E-Mail: cyberpublicationsdelhi@yahoo.com

FINANCIAL ECONOMICS: TEXTS AND CASES

Nishant K. Shukla

© Reserved

Edition 2026

All rights reserved. No part of this publication may be reproduced, stored in a retrieval system or transmitted, in any form or by any means, electronic, mechanical, photo copying, recording or otherwise, without the prior permission of the publisher.

Published by :

G.S. Rawat for **Cyber Tech Publications**
4264/3, Ansari Road, Daryaganj, New Delhi-110002 (India)
Ph.: 011-23244078. Fax: 011-23280028
E-Mail: cyberpublicationsdelhi@yahoo.com

Printed at : **Amit Enterprises**, Maujpur, Delhi, (9810878184)

Preface

Financial economics is the branch of economics concerned with resource allocation over time. It is further distinguished from other branches of economics by its concentration on monetary activities, in which money of one type or another is likely to appear on both sides of a trade.

Financial economics tends to deal with the workings of financial markets, such as the stock market, and the financing of companies, and includes the following subject areas: Budgeting, saving, investing, borrowing, lending, insuring, hedging, diversifying, and asset management. Because the future is never known with certainty, a central concern of financial economics is the impact of uncertainty on resource allocation. Financial economics is based on several assumptions - chief amongst these, that financial decision makers are rational. However, recently, researchers in Experimental economics and Experimental finance have challenged this assumption empirically. Further, these assumptions are challenged - theoretically - by Behavioral finance, a discipline primarily concerned with the rationality, or lack thereof, of economic agents.

Other common assumptions include market prices following a random walk, or asset returns being normally distributed. Empirical evidence suggests that these assumptions may not hold, and in practice, traders and analysts, and particularly risk managers, frequently modify the standard models.

In this book I have tried my best to bring all the concerned issues and facts of the field in text with relevant examples wherever necessary. Hope that readers will find it informative and valuable.

Suggestions and complaints are always welcome.

—*Author*

Contents

1

INTRODUCTION

Financial economics is the branch of economics concerned with resource allocation over time. It is further distinguished from other branches of economics by its "concentration on monetary activities", in which "money of one type or another is likely to appear on both sides of a trade" .

The questions addressed by the discipline are typically framed in terms of "time, uncertainty, options and information".

- *Time:* money now is traded for money in the future.
- *Uncertainty (or risk):* The amount of money to be transferred in the future is uncertain.
- *Options:* one party to the transaction can make a decision at a later time that will affect subsequent transfers of money.
- *Information:* knowledge of the future can reduce, or possibly eliminate, the uncertainty associated with future monetary value (FMV).

SUBJECT MATTER

Given its scope, as above, financial economics tends to deal with the workings of financial markets, such as the stock market, and the financing of companies, and includes the following subject areas: Budgeting, saving, investing, borrowing, lending, insuring, hedging, diversifying, and asset management. Because the future is never known with certainty, a central concern of financial economics is the impact of uncertainty on resource allocation.

Financial economics thus attempts to answer questions such as:

- How are the prices of financial assets determined (stocks, bonds, currencies, and commodities)?
- What are the effects of a company choosing different methods of financing its operations, such as issuing shares or borrowing?
- What portfolio of assets should an investor hold in order to best meet his/her objectives?

ASSUMPTIONS

Financial economics is based on several assumptions-chief amongst these, that financial decision makers are rational (see Homo economicus; Efficient market hypothesis). However, recently, researchers in Experimental economics and Experimental finance have challenged this assumption empirically. Further, these assumptions are challenged-theoretically-by Behavioral finance, a discipline primarily concerned with the rationality, or lack thereof, of economic agents.

Other common assumptions include market prices following a random walk, or asset returns being normally distributed. Empirical evidence suggests that these assumptions may not hold, and in practice, traders and analysts, and particularly risk managers, frequently modify the "standard models".

RISK-FREE INTEREST RATE

The risk-free interest rate is the interest rate that it is assumed can be obtained by investing in financial instruments with no default risk. However, the financial instrument can carry other types of risk, e.g. market risk (the risk of changes in market interest rates), liquidity risk (the risk of being unable to sell the instrument for cash at short notice without significant costs) etc.

Though a truly "risk-free" asset exists only in theory, in practice most professionals and academics use short-dated government bonds of the currency in question. For USD investments, usually US Treasury bills are used, while a common choice for EUR investments are German government bills or Euribor rates. Those securities are considered to be risk-free because the likelihood of these governments defaulting is extremely low, and because the short maturity of the bill protects the investor from interest-rate risk that is present in all fixed rate bonds (if interest rates go up soon after the bill is purchased, the investor will miss out on a fairly small amount of interest before the bill matures and can be reinvested at the new interest rate).

Since this interest rate can be obtained with no risk, it is implied that any additional risk taken by an investor should be rewarded with an interest rate higher than the risk-free rate (on an after-tax basis, which may be achieved with preferential tax treatment; some local government US bonds give below the risk-free rate).

The risk-free interest rate is thus of significant importance to modern portfolio theory in general, and is an important assumption for rational pricing. It is also a required input in financial calculations, such as the Black-Scholes formula for pricing stock options. Note that some finance and economic theory assumes that market participants can borrow at the risk free rate; in practice, of course, very few borrowers have access to finance at the risk free rate.

One explanation for the assumption that no default risk exists is due to the nature of government debt. For a fiat currency, the government retains the theoretical capacity to print as much of that currency as will be required to pay its own debts (in that currency). In this case, true default is theoretically impossible: owners of government debt can always be paid, but with money that may have substantially lower value. Rather than reflecting the default risk of the government, the risk-free interest rate therefore reflects the likelihood that the government will print money to pay its debts, thereby debasing the currency. Note that this does not apply to currencies such as the Euro where no individual government has the authority to print currency. Of course, many countries have other measures and institutions (such as theoretically independent central banks) to reduce the likelihood of such an occurrence. An alternative interpretation is that, while no investment is truly free of risk, scenarios in which a major government with a long track record of stability defaults on its obligations are so far outside what is known that one cannot make quantitative statements about their chances of happening, and therefore it is simply not feasible to include them in financial planning.

A German circa 1904 deciding whether to purchase long-term bonds issued by the German government could scarcely have been able to anticipate a World War followed by hyperinflation.

SHORT RATE MODEL

In the context of interest rate derivatives, a short rate model is a mathematical model that describes the future evolution of interest rates by describing the future evolution of the short rate.

The Short Rate

The short rate, usually written *rt* is the (annualized) interest rate at which an entity can borrow money for an infinitesimally short period of time from time *t*. Specifying the current short rate does not specify the entire yield curve. However no-arbitrage arguments show that, under some fairly relaxed technical conditions, if we model the evolution of r_t as a stochastic process under a risk-neutral measure Q then the price at time *t* of a zero-coupon bond maturing at time T is given by

$$P(t,T) = E\left[\exp\left(-\int_t^T \gamma_s ds\right)\middle| Ft\right]$$

where F is the natural filtration for the process. Thus specifying a model for the short rate specifies future bond prices. This means that instantaneous forward rates are also specified by the usual formula

$$f(t,T) = -\frac{\partial}{\partial T}\ln(P(t,T)).$$

And its third equivalent, the yields are given as well.

Particular Short-rate Models

Throughout this section W_t represents a standard Brownian motion and dW_t its differential.

1. The Rendleman-Bartter model models the short rate as

   $$dt_t = \theta r_t dt + \sigma r_t dW_t$$

2. The Vasicek model models the short rate as

   $$dr_t = a(b - r_t)dt + \sigma dW_t$$

3. The Ho-Lee model models the short rate as

   $$dr_t = \theta_t dt + \sigma dW_t$$

4. The Hull-White model (also called the extended Vasicek model sometimes) posits $dr_t = (\theta_t - \alpha r_t)dt + \sigma_t dW_t$. In many presentations one or more of the parameters θ, α and σ are not time-dependent. The process is called an Ornstein-Uhlenbeck process.
5. The Cox-Ingersoll-Ross model supposes

   $$dr_t = (\theta_t - \alpha r_t)dt + \sqrt{r_t}\sigma_t dW_t$$

6. In the Black-Karasinski model a variable X_t is assumed to follow an Ornstein-Uhlenbeck process and r_t is assumed to follow $r_t = \exp X_t$.

Besides the above one-factor models, there are also multi-factor models of the short rate, among them the best known are Longstaff and Schwartz two factor model and Chen three factor model (also called "stochastic mean and stochastic volatility model"):

1. The Longstaff-Schwartz model supposes the short rate dynamics is given by the following two equations:

   $$dX_t = (\theta_t - Y_t)dt + \sqrt{X_t}\sigma_t dW_t,$$

   $$dY_t = (\zeta_t - Y_t)dt + \sqrt{Y_t}\sigma_t dW_t.$$

2. The Chen model models the short rate, also called stochastic mean and stochastic volatility of the short rate, is given by:

$$dr_t = (\theta_t - \alpha_t)dt + \sqrt{r_t}\sigma_t dW_t.$$

$$d\alpha_t = (\zeta_t - \alpha_t)dt + \sqrt{\alpha_t}\sigma_t dW_t.$$

$$d\sigma_t = (\beta_t - \sigma_t)dt + \sqrt{\sigma_t}\eta_t dW_t.$$

REAL INTEREST RATE

The "real interest rate" is the effective interest rate minus the inflation rate. Since the inflation rate over the course of a loan is not known initially, volatility in inflation represents a risk to both the lender and the borrower.

EXPLANATION OF THE CONCEPT

Risks

In economics and finance, an individual who lends money for repayment at a later point in time expects to be compensated for the time value of money, or not having the use of that money while it is lent. In addition, they will want to be compensated for the risks of having less purchasing power when the loan is repaid. These risks are systematic risks, regulatory risks and inflation risks. The first includes the possibility that the borrower will default or be unable to pay on the originally agreed upon terms, or that collateral backing the loan will prove to be less valuable than estimated. The second includes taxation and changes in the law which would prevent the lender from collecting on a loan or having to pay more in taxes on the amount repaid than originally estimated. The third takes into account that the money repaid may not have as much buying power from the perspective of the lender as the money originally lent, that is inflation, and may include fluctuations in the value of the currencies involved.

Nominal interest rates include all three risk factors, plus the time value of the money itself. Real interest rates include only the systematic and regulatory risks and are meant to measure the time value of money. Real rates = Nominal rates minus Inflation and Currency adjustment. The "real interest rate" in an economy is often the rate of return on a risk free investment, such as US Treasury notes, minus an index of inflation, such as the CPI, or GDP deflator.

See Fisher equation $1+r = (1+R)/(1+\pi)$ where r = real interest rate (ex-ante); R = nominal interest rate; π = expected inflation rate.

For example, if somebody lends $1000 for a year at 10 percent, and receives $1100 back at the end of the year, this represents a 10 percent increase in his purchasing power if prices for the average goods and services that he buys are unchanged from what they were at the beginning of the year. However, if the prices of the food, clothing, housing, and other things that he wishes to purchase have increased 20 percent over this period, he has in fact suffered a real loss of about 10 percent in his purchasing power.

The inflation rate will not be known in advance. People often base their expectation of future inflation on an average of inflation rates in the past, but this gives rise to errors. The real interest rate ex post may turn out to be quite different from the real interest rate that was expected in advance. Borrowers hope to repay in cheaper money in the future, while lenders hope to collect on more expensive money. When inflation and currency risks are underestimated by lenders, then they will suffer a net reduction in buying power, when inflation and currency risks are over-estimated by borrowers, they will suffer a net reduction in buying power.

The complexity increases for bonds issued for a long term, where the average inflation rate over the term of the loan may be subject to a great deal of uncertainty. In response to this, many governments have issued real return bonds (also known as inflation indexed, in which the principle value and coupon rises each year with the rate of inflation, with the result that the interest rate on the bond is a real interest rate.

The expected real interest rate can vary considerably from year to year. The real interest rate on short term loans is strongly influenced by the monetary policy of central banks.

The real interest rate on longer term bonds tends to be more market driven, and in recent decades, with globalized financial markets, the real interest rates in the industrialized countries have become increasingly correlated. Real interest rates have been low by historical standards since 2000, due to a combination of factors, including relatively weak demand for loans by corporations, plus strong savings in newly industrializing countries in Asia. The latter has offset the large borrowing demands by the US Federal Government, which might otherwise have put more upward pressure on real interest rates.

Related is the concept of "risk adjusted return", which is the rate of return minus the risks as measured against the least risk investment available. Thus if a loan is made at 15% with an inflation rate of 5% and 10% in risks associated with default or problems repaying, then the "risk adjusted" rate of return on the investment is 0%.

Significance in Economic Theory

Economics relies on measurable variables, chiefly price and objectively measurable production. Since production is "real", while prices are relative to the general price level, in order to compare an economy at two points in time, nominal price variables must be converted into "real" variables. For example, the number of people on payrolls represents a "real" variable, as does the number of hours worked. But in order to measure productivity, the nominal prices of the goods and services that labor produces must be converted to the "real" purchasing power. To do this requires adjusting prices for inflation.

The same is true of investment. Investment produces real gains in efficiency, and purchases productive capacity-factories, machines and so on-which is also real. To find the return on this capital, it is necessary to subtract the increases in its nominal value that are the result of increases in the general level of prices. To do this means subtracting the inflation rate from the nominal rate of return. For example, a portfolio of stocks that returns 10%, when inflation is running at 4% has a 6% real rate of return.

The real interest rate is used in various economic theories to explain such phenomena as the capital flight, business cycle and fluctuations in the stock market. When the real rate of interest is high, that is demand for credit is high, then money will, all other things being equal, move from consumption to savings. Conversely, when the real rate of interest is low, demand will move from savings, to investment and consumption. Different economic theories, beginning with the work of Knut Wicksell have had different explanations of the effect of rising and falling real interest rates. Also, international capital moves to countries that offer higher real rates of interest from countries that offer low or negative real rates of interest.

Related to this concept is the idea of a "natural rate of interest", that is, the expected return on savings and capital invested.

TIME VALUE OF MONEY

The time value of money is the premise that an investor prefers to receive a payment of a fixed amount of money today, rather than an equal amount in the future, all else being equal.

In other words, the present value of a certain amount a of money is greater than the present value of the right to receive the same amount of money time t in the future. This is because the amount a could be deposited in an interest-bearing bank account (or otherwise invested) from now to time t and yield interest.

Consequently, lenders acting at arm's length demand interest payments for use of their financial capital. Additional motivations for demanding interest are to compensate for the risk of borrower default and the risk of inflation, as well as other, more technical considerations.

All of the standard calculations are based on the most basic formula, the present value of a future sum, "discounted" to a present value. For example, a sum of FV to be received in one year is discounted (at the appropriate rate of R) to give a sum of PV at present.

Some standard calculations based on the time value of money are:

Present Value (PV) of an amount that will be received in the future.

Future Value (FV) of an amount invested (such as in a deposit account) now at a given rate of interest.

Present Value of an Annuity (PVA) is the present value of a stream of (equally-sized) future payments, such as a mortgage.

Future Value of an Annuity (FVA) is the future value of a stream of payments (annuity), assuming the payments are invested at a given rate of interest.

Present Value of a Perpetuity is the value of a regular stream of payments that lasts "forever", or at least indefinitely.

Calculations

There are several basic equations that represent the equalities listed above. The solutions may be found using (in most cases) a financial calculator or other means.

For any of the equations below, the formulae may also be rearranged to determine one of the other unknowns. In the case of the standard annuity formula, however, there is no closed-form algebraic solution for the interest rate (although financial calculators can readily determine solutions).

These equations are frequently combined for particular uses. For example, bonds can be readily priced using these equations. A typical coupon bond is composed of two types of payments: a stream of coupon payments similar to an annuity, and a lump-sum return of capital at the end of the bond's maturity-that is, a future payment. The two formulas can be combined to provide a present value for the bond.

An important note is that the interest rate r is the interest rate for the relevant period. For an annuity that makes one payment per year, r will be the annual interest rate. For an income or payment stream with a different payment schedule, the interest rate must be converted into the relevant periodic interest rate, for example, a monthly rate for a mortgage with monthly payments. See compound interest for details on converting between different periodic interest rates.

The rate of return in the calculations can be either the variable solved for, or a predefined variable that measures a discount rate, interest, inflation, rate of return, cost of equity, cost of debt or any number of other analogous concepts. The choice of the appropriate rate is critical to the exercise, and choice of the wrong discount rate can make the results meaningless. In most cases, however, the mathematics are similar, if not identical.

For calculations of annuities, you must decide whether the payments are made at the beginning of each time period, or (as in the formulas given) at the end. The calculator you use will allow the input somehow.

FORMULAS

Present Value of a Future Sum

The present value formula is the core formula for the time value of money; each of the other formulae is derived from this formula. For example, the annuity formula is the sum of a series of present value calculations.

- The present value (PV) formula has four variables, each of which can be solved for:

   1. PV is the value at time = 0
   2. FV is the value at time = n
   3. r is the rate at which the amount will be compounded each period
   4. n is the number of periods

$$PV = \frac{FV}{(1+r)^n}$$

Future value of a present sum:

- The future value (FV) formula is similar and uses the same variable.

$$FV = PV.(1+r)^n$$

Present Value of an Annuity

- The present value of an annuity (PVA) formula has four variables, each of which can be solved for:

1. PVA the value of the annuity at time = 0
2. A the value of the individual payments in each compounding period
3. r equals the interest rate that would be compounded for each period of time
4. n is the number of payment periods.

$$PV(A) = A.\frac{1-\dfrac{1}{(1+r)^n}}{r}$$

Future Value of an Annuity

- The future value of an annuity (FVA) formula has four variables, each of which can be solved for:

1. FV(A) the value of the annuity at time = n
2. A the value of the individual payments in each compounding period
3. r equals the interest rate that would be compounded for each period of time
4. n is the number of payment periods.

$$FV(A) = A.\frac{(1+r)^n - 1}{r}$$

Present Value of a Growing Annuity

Similar to the formula for an annuity, the present value of a growing annuity (PVGA) uses the same variables with the addition of G as the rate of growth of the annuity (A is the annuity payment in the first period).

This is a calculation that is rarely provided for on financial calculators.

$$PV = \frac{A}{(r-g)}\left[1-\left(\frac{1+g}{1+r}\right)^n\right]$$

Present Value of a Perpetuity

The PV of a perpetuity (a perpetual annuity) formula is simple division.

$$PV(P) = \frac{A}{r}$$

Present Value of a Growing Perpetuity

When the perpetual annuity payment grows at a fixed rate (g) the value is theoretically determined according to the following formula. In practice, there are few securities with precisely these characteristics, and the application of this valuation approach is subject to various qualifications and modifications. Most importantly, it is rare to find a growing perpetual annuity with fixed rates of growth and true perpetual cash flow generation. Despite these qualifications, the general approach may be used in valuations of real estate, equities, and other assets. True.

$$PVGP = \frac{A}{(r-g)}$$

DERIVATIONS

Annuity Derivation

The formula for the future value of a regular stream of future payments (an annuity) is derived from a sum of the formula for future value of a single future payment, as below, where C is the payment amount and n the time period.

A single payment C at future time i has the following future value at future time n:

$$FV = C(1+r)^{n-i}$$

Summing over all payments from time 1 to time n, then reversing the order of terms and substituting k = n - i:

$$FVA = \sum_{i=1}^{n} C(1+r)^{n-i} = \sum_{k=0}^{n=1} C(1+r)^{k}$$

Note that this is a geometric series, with the initial value being a = C, the multiplicative factor being 1 + r, with n terms. Applying the formula for geometric series, we get

$$FVA = \frac{C\left(1-(1+r)^n\right)}{1-(1+r)} = \frac{C\left((1+r)^n - 1\right)}{r}$$

The present value of the annuity (PVA) is obtained by simply dividing by (1 + *r*)*n*:

$$PVA = \frac{FVA}{(1+r)^n} = \frac{C}{r}\left(1 - \frac{1}{(1+r)^n}\right)$$

Another simple and intuitive way to derive the future value of an annuity is to consider an endowment, whose interest is paid as the annuity, and whose principal remains constant. The principal of this hypothetical endowment can be computed as that whose interest equals the annuity payment amount:

Principal × r = C

Principal = C / r

Note that no money enters or leaves the combined system of endowment principal + accumulated annuity payments, and thus the future value of this system can be computed simply via the future value formula:

$FV = PV(1 + r)^n$

Initially, before any payments, the present value of the system is just the endowment principal (PV = C / r). At the end, the future value is the endowment principal (which is the same) plus the future value of the total annuity payments (FV = C / r + FVA). Plugging this back into the equation:

$$\frac{C}{r} + FVA = \frac{C}{r}(1+r)^n$$

$$FVA = \frac{C}{r}\left((1+r)^n - 1\right)$$

Perpetuity Derivation

Without showing the formal derivation here, the perpetuity formula is derived from the annuity formula. Specifically, the term:

$$\left(1-\frac{1}{(1+r)^n}\right)$$

can be seen to approach the value of 1 as n grows larger. At infinity, it is equal to 1, leaving $\frac{C}{r}$ as the only term remaining.

Examples

Example 1: Present Value

One hundred euros to be paid 1 year from now, where the expected rate of return is 5% per year, is worth in today's money:

$$P = F \times (P/F) = F \times \frac{1}{(1+r)^n} = \frac{100}{1.05} = 95.23$$

So the present value of □100 one year from now at 5% is □95.23.

Example 2: Present Value of an Annuity-solving for the Payment Amount

Consider a 10 year mortgage where the principal amount P is $200,000 and the annual interest rate is 6%.

The number of monthly payments is

n = 10 years × 12 months per year = 120 months

and the monthly interest rate is

$$r = \frac{6\% \text{ per year}}{12 \text{ months per year}} = 0.5\% \text{ per month}$$

The annuity formula for (A/P) calculates the monthly payment:

$$A = P \times (A/P) = P \times \frac{r(1+r)^n}{(1+r)^n - 1}$$

$$= \$200,000 \times \frac{0.005(1.005)^{120}}{(1.005)^{120} - 1}$$

$$= \$200,000 \times 0.01110205 = \$2,220.41 \text{ per month}$$

Example 3: Solving for the period needed to double money

Consider a deposit of $100 placed at 10% (annual). How many years are needed for the value of the deposit to double to $200?

Using the algebraic identity that if:

$x = b^y$

then

$$y = \frac{\ln(x)}{\ln(b)}$$

The present value formula can be rearranged such that:

$$y = \frac{\ln\left(\frac{FV}{PV}\right)}{\ln(1+r)} = \frac{\ln\left(\frac{200}{100}\right)}{\ln(1.10)} = \frac{0.693}{0.0953} = 7.27(\text{Years})$$

This same method can be used to determine the length of time needed to increase a deposit to any particular sum, as long as the interest rate is known.

For the period of time needed to double an investment, the Rule of 72 is a useful shortcut that gives a reasonable approximation of the time period needed.

Example 4: What return is needed to double money?

Similarly, the present value formula can be rearranged to determine what rate of return is needed to accumulate a given amount from an investment. For example, \$100 is invested today and \$200 return is expected in five years; what rate of return (interest rate) does this represent?

The present value formula restated in terms of the interest rate is:

$$r = \left(\frac{FV}{PV}\right)^{\frac{1}{n}} - 1 = \left(\frac{200}{100}\right)^{\frac{1}{5}} - 1 = 2^{0.20} - 1 = 0.15 = 15\%$$

Example 5: Calculate the value of a regular savings deposit in the future.

To calculate the future value of a stream of savings deposit in the future requires two steps, or, alternatively, combining the two steps into one large formula. First, calculate the present value of a stream of deposits of \$1,000 every year for 20 years earning 7% interest:

$$PVA = A.\frac{1 - \frac{1}{(1+r)^n}}{r} = 100.\frac{1 - \frac{1}{(1+.07)^{20}}}{.07}$$

$$= 1000.\frac{1 - 0.258}{.07} = 1000 * 10.594 = \$10,594$$

This does not sound like very much, but remember-this is future money discounted back to its value today; it is understandably lower. To calculate the future value (at the end of the twenty-year period):

$$FV = PV(1+r)^n = \$10,594 * (1+.07)^{20}$$

$$= \$10,594 * 3.87 = \$40,995$$

These steps can be combined into a single formula:

$$FV = A.\frac{1 - \frac{1}{(1+r)^n}}{r}.(1+r)^n = A.\frac{(1+r)^n - 1}{r}$$

Example 6: Price/earnings (P/E) ratio

It is often mentioned that perpetuities, or securities with an indefinitely long maturity, are rare or unrealistic, and particularly those with a growing payment. In fact, many types of assets have characteristics that are similar to perpetuities. Examples might include income-oriented real estate, preferred shares, and even most forms of publicly-traded stocks. Frequently, the terminology may be slightly different, but are based on the fundamentals of time value of money calculations. The application of this methodology is subject to various qualifications or modifications, such as the Gordon growth model.

For example, stocks are commonly noted as trading at a certain price/earnings ratio. The P/E ratio is easily recognized as a variation on the perpetuity or growing perpetuity formulae-save that the P/E ratio is usually cited as the inverse of the "rate" in the perpetuity formula. If we substitute for the time being: the price of the stock for the present value; the earnings per share of the stock for the cash annuity; and, the discount rate of the stock for the interest rate, we can see that:

$$\frac{P}{E}=\frac{1}{r}=\frac{PV}{A}$$

And in fact, the P/E ratio is analogous to the inverse of the interest rate (or discount rate).

$$\frac{1}{P/E}=r$$

Of course, stocks may have increasing earnings. The formulation above does not allow for growth in earnings, but to incorporate growth, the formula can be restated as follows:

$$\frac{P}{E}=\frac{1}{(r-g)}$$

If we wish to determine the implied rate of growth (if we are given the discount rate), we may solve for g:

$$g=r-\frac{E}{P}$$

Time Value of Money Formulae with Continuous Compounding

Rates are sometimes converted into the continuous compound interest rate equivalent because the continuous equivalent is more convenient (for example, more easily differentiated). Each of the formulae above may be restated in their continuous equivalents. For example, the present value of a future payment can be restated in the following way, where e is the base of the natural logarithm:

$$PV = FVe^{-rn}$$

See below for formulaic equivalents of the time value of money formulae with continuous compounding.

Present value of an annuity

$$PV = \frac{A\left(1 - e^{-rn}\right)}{e^{r} - 1}$$

Present value of a perpetuity

$$PV = \frac{A}{e^{r} - 1}$$

Present value of a growing annuity

$$PV = \frac{A\left(1 - e^{-(r-g)n}\right)}{e^{(r-g)} - 1}$$

Present value of a growing perpetuity

$$PV = \frac{A}{e^{(r-g)} - 1}$$

FISHER SEPARATION THEOREM

The Fisher separation theorem in economics asserts that the objective of a firm will be the maximization of its present value, regardless of the preferences of its owners. The theorem therefore separates management's "productive opportunities" from the entrepreneur's "market opportunities". It was proposed by-and is named after-the economist Irving Fisher.

The Fisher Separation Theorem states that:

- the firm's investment decision is independent of the preferences of the owner;
- the investment decision is independent of the financing decision.
- the value of a capital project (investment) is independent of the mix of methods-equity, debt, and/or cash-used to finance the project.

Fisher showed the above as follows:

1. The firm can make the investment decision-i.e. the choice between productive opportunities-that maximizes its present value, independent of its owner's investment preferences.
2. The firm can then ensure that the owner achieves his optimal position in terms of "market opportunities" by funding its investment either with borrowed funds, or internally as appropriate.

2

Corporate Finance

INTRODUCTION

Corporate finance is an area of finance dealing with the financial decisions corporations make and the tools and analysis used to make these decisions. The primary goal of corporate finance is to enhance corporate value while reducing the firm's financial risks. Equivalently, the goal is to maximize the corporations' return to capital. Although it is in principle different from managerial finance which studies the financial decisions of all firms, rather than corporations alone, the main concepts in the study of corporate finance are applicable to the financial problems of all kinds of firms.

The discipline can be divided into long-term and short-term decisions and techniques. Capital investment decisions are long-term choices about which projects receive investment, whether to finance that investment with equity or debt, and when or whether to pay dividends to shareholders. On the other hand, the short term decisions can be grouped under the heading "Working capital management".

This subject deals with the short-term balance of current assets and current liabilities; the focus here is on managing cash, inventories, and short-term borrowing and lending (such as the terms on credit extended to customers).

The terms Corporate finance and Corporate financier are also associated with investment banking. The typical role of an investment banker is to evaluate investment projects for a bank to make investment decisions.

CAPITAL INVESTMENT DECISIONS

Capital investment decisions are long-term corporate finance decisions relating to fixed assets and capital structure. Decisions are based on several inter-related criteria. Corporate management seeks to maximize the value of the firm by investing in projects which yield a positive net present value when valued using an appropriate discount rate. These projects must also be financed appropriately. If no such opportunities exist, maximizing shareholder value dictates that management return excess cash to shareholders. Capital investment decisions thus comprise an investment decision, a financing decision, and a dividend decision.

THE INVESTMENT DECISION

Management must allocate limited resources between competing opportunities ("projects") in a process known as capital budgeting. Making this capital allocation decision requires estimating the value of each opportunity or project: a function of the size, timing and predictability of future cash flows.

PROJECT VALUATION

In general, each project's value will be estimated using a discounted cash flow (DCF) valuation, and the opportunity with the highest value, as measured by the resultant net present value (NPV) will be selected (see Fisher separation theorem). This requires estimating the size and timing of all of the incremental cash flows resulting from the project. These future cash flows are then discounted to determine their present value (see Time value of money). These present values are then summed, and this sum net of the initial investment outlay is the NPV.

The NPV is greatly influenced by the discount rate. Thus selecting the proper discount rate-the project "hurdle rate"-is critical to making the right decision. The hurdle rate is the minimum acceptable return on an investment-i.e. the project appropriate discount rate. The hurdle rate should reflect the riskiness of the investment, typically measured by volatility of cash flows, and must take into account the financing mix.

Managers use models such as the CAPM or the APT to estimate a discount rate appropriate for a particular project, and use the weighted average cost of capital (WACC) to reflect the financing mix selected. (A common error in choosing a discount rate for a project is to apply a WACC that applies to the entire firm. Such an approach may not be appropriate where the risk of a particular project differs markedly from that of the firm's existing portfolio of assets.)

In conjunction with NPV, there are several other measures used as (secondary) selection criteria in corporate finance. These are visible from the DCF and include payback, IRR, Modified IRR, equivalent annuity, capital efficiency, and ROI.

VALUING FLEXIBILITY

In many cases, for example R&D projects, a project may open (or close) paths of action to the company, but this reality will not typically be captured in a strict NPV approach. Management will therefore (sometimes) employ tools which place an explicit value on these options. So, whereas in a DCF valuation the most likely or average or scenario specific cash flows are discounted, here the "flexible and staged nature" of the investment is modelled, and hence "all" potential payoffs are considered. The difference between the two valuations is the "option value" inherent in the project.

The two most common tools are Decision Tree Analysis (DTA) and Real options analysis:

- The DTA approach attempts to capture flexibility by incorporating likely events and consequent management decisions into the valuation. In the decision tree, each management decision in response to an "event" generates a "branch" or "path" which the company could follow. (For example, management will only proceed with stage 2 of the project given that stage 1 was successful; stage 3, in turn, depends on stage 2. In a DCF model, on the other hand, there is no "branching"-each scenario must be modelled separately.) The highest value path (probability weighted) is regarded as representative of project value

- The real options approach is used when the value of a project is contingent on the value of some other asset or underlying variable. (For example, the viability of a mining project is contingent on the price of gold; if the price is too low, management will abandon the mining rights, if sufficiently high, management will develop the ore body. Again, a DCF valuation would capture only one of these outcomes.) Here, using financial option theory as a framework, the decision to be taken is identified as corresponding to either a call option or a put option-valuation is then via the Binomial model or, less often for this purpose, via Black Scholes; see Contingent claim valuation. The "true" value of the project is then the NPV of the "most likely" scenario plus the option value.

THE FINANCING DECISION

Achieving the goals of corporate finance requires that any corporate investment be financed appropriately. As above, since both hurdle rate and cash flows (and hence the riskiness of the firm) will be affected, the financing mix can impact the valuation. Management must therefore identify the "optimal mix" of financing-the capital structure that results in maximum value. (See Balance sheet, WACC, Fisher separation theorem; but, see also the Modigliani-Miller theorem.)

The sources of financing will, generically, comprise some combination of debt and equity. Financing a project through debt results in a liability that must be serviced-and hence there are cash flow implications regardless of the project's success. Equity financing is less risky in the sense of cash flow commitments, but results in a dilution of ownership and earnings. The cost of equity is also typically higher than the cost of debt (see CAPM and WACC), and so equity financing may result in an increased hurdle rate which may offset any reduction in cash flow risk. Management must also attempt to match the financing mix to the asset being financed as closely as possible, in terms of both timing and cash flows.

One of the main theories of how firms make their financing decisions is the Pecking Order Theory, which suggests that firms avoid external financing while they have internal financing available and avoid new equity financing while they can engage in new debt financing at reasonably low interest rates. Another major theory is the Trade-Off Theory in which firms are assumed to trade-off the Tax Benefits of debt with the Bankruptcy Costs of debt when making their decisions. One last theory about this decision is the Market timing hypothesis which states that firms look for the cheaper type of financing regardless of their current levels of internal resources, debt and equity.

THE DIVIDEND DECISION

In general, management must decide whether to invest in additional projects, reinvest in existing operations, or return free cash as dividends to shareholders. The dividend is calculated mainly on the basis of the company's unappropriated profit and its business prospects for the coming year. If there are no NPV positive opportunities, i.e. where returns exceed the hurdle rate, then management must return excess cash to investors- these free cash flows comprise cash remaining after all business expenses have been met. (This is the general case, however there are exceptions. For example, investors in a "Growth stock", expect that the company will, almost by definition, retain earnings so as to fund growth internally. In other cases, even though an opportunity is currently NPV negative, management may consider "investment flexibility" / potential payoffs and decide to retain cash flows).

Management must also decide on the form of the distribution, generally as cash dividends or via a share buyback. There are various considerations: where shareholders pay tax on dividends, companies may elect to retain earnings, or to perform a stock buyback, in both cases increasing the value of shares outstanding; some companies will pay "dividends" from stock rather than in cash. Today it is generally accepted that dividend policy is value neutral.

WORKING CAPITAL MANAGEMENT

Decisions relating to working capital and short term financing are referred to as working capital management. These involve managing the relationship between a firm's short-term assets and its short-term liabilities. The goal of Working capital management is to ensure that the firm is able to continue its operations and that it has sufficient cash flow to satisfy both maturing short-term debt and upcoming operational expenses.

Decision Criteria

By definition, Working capital management entails short term decisions-generally, relating to the next one year period-which are "reversible". These decisions are therefore not taken on the same basis as Capital Investment Decisions (NPV or related, as above) rather they will be based on cash flows and/ or profitability.

- One measure of cash flow is provided by the cash conversion cycle-the net number of days from the outlay of cash for raw material to receiving payment from the customer. As a management tool, this metric makes explicit the inter-relatedness of decisions relating to inventories, accounts receivable and payable, and cash. Because this number effectively corresponds to the time that the firm's cash is tied up in operations and unavailable for other activities, management generally aims at a low net count.
- In this context, the most useful measure of profitability is Return on capital (ROC). The result is shown as a percentage, determined by dividing relevant income for the 12 months by capital employed; Return on equity (ROE) shows this result for the firm's shareholders. Firm value is enhanced when, and if, the return on capital, which results from working capital management, exceeds the cost of capital, which results from capital investment decisions as above. ROC measures are therefore useful as a management tool, in that they link short-term policy with long-term decision making.

MANAGEMENT OF WORKING CAPITAL

Guided by the above criteria, management will use a combination of policies and techniques for the management of working capital. These policies aim at managing the current assets (generally cash and cash equivalents, inventories and debtors) and the short term financing, such that cash flows and returns are acceptable.

- *Cash Management:* Identify the cash balance which allows for the business to meet day to day expenses, but reduces cash holding costs.
- *Inventory Management:* Identify the level of inventory which allows for uninterrupted production but reduces the investment in raw materials-and minimizes reordering costs-and hence increases cash flow; see Supply chain management; Just In Time (JIT); Economic order quantity (EOQ); Economic production quantity (EPQ).
- *Debtors Management:* Identify the appropriate credit policy, i.e. credit terms which will attract customers, such that any impact on cash flows and the cash conversion cycle will be offset by increased revenue and hence Return on Capital (or vice versa); see Discounts and allowances.
- *Short Term Financing:* Identify the appropriate source of financing, given the cash conversion cycle: the inventory is ideally financed by credit granted by the supplier; however, it may be necessary to utilize a bank loan (or overdraft), or to "convert debtors to cash" through "factoring".

FINANCIAL RISK MANAGEMENT

Risk management is the process of measuring risk and then developing and implementing strategies to manage that risk. Financial risk management focuses on risks that can be managed ("hedged") using traded financial instruments (typically changes in commodity prices , interest rates, foreign exchange rates and stock prices). Financial risk management will also play an important role in cash management.

This area is related to corporate finance in two ways. Firstly, firm exposure to business risk is a direct result of previous

Investment and Financing decisions. Secondly, both disciplines share the goal of creating, or enhancing, firm value. All large corporations have risk management teams, and small firms practice informal, if not formal, risk management. Derivatives are the instruments most commonly used in Financial risk management.

Because unique derivative contracts tend to be costly to create and monitor, the most cost-effective financial risk management methods usually involve derivatives that trade on well-established financial markets.

These standard derivative instruments include options, futures contracts, forward contracts, and swaps.

RELATIONSHIP WITH OTHER AREAS IN FINANCE

Investment Banking

Use of the term "corporate finance" varies considerably across the world. In the United States it is used, as above, to describe activities, decisions and techniques that deal with many aspects of a company's finances and capital.

In the United Kingdom and Commonwealth countries, the terms "corporate finance" and "corporate financier" tend to be associated with investment banking-i.e. with transactions in which capital is raised for the corporation.

Personal and Public Finance

Corporate finance utilizes tools from almost all areas of finance. Some of the tools developed by and for corporations have broad application to entities other than corporations, for example, to partnerships, sole proprietorships, not-for-profit organizations, governments, mutual funds, and personal wealth management.

But in other cases their application is very limited outside of the corporate finance arena. Because corporations deal in quantities of money much greater than individuals, the analysis has developed into a discipline of its own. It can be differentiated from personal finance and public finance.

MODIGLIANI-MILLER THEOREM

The Modigliani-Miller theorem (of Franco Modigliani, Merton Miller) forms the basis for modern thinking on capital structure.

The basic theorem states that, in the absence of taxes, bankruptcy costs, and asymmetric information, and in an efficient market, the value of a firm is unaffected by how that firm is financed. It does not matter if the firm's capital is raised by issuing stock or selling debt. It does not matter what the firm's dividend policy is.

Propositions

The theorem is made up of two propositions which can also be extended to a situation with taxes. Consider two firms which are identical except for their financial structures. The first (Firm U) is unlevered: that is, it is financed by equity only. The other (Firm L) is levered: it is financed partly by equity, and partly by debt. The Modigliani-Miller theorem states that the value of the two firms is the same.

Without Taxes

Proposition I: $V_U = V_L$ where V_U is the value of an unlevered firm = price of buying a firm composed only of equity, and V_L is the value of a levered firm = price of buying a firm that is composed of some mix of debt and equity.

To see why this should be true, suppose an investor is considering buying one of the two firms U or L. Instead of purchasing the shares of the levered firm L, he could purchase the shares of firm U and borrow the same amount of money B that firm L does. The eventual returns to either of these investments would be the same.

Therefore the price of L must be the same as the price of U minus the money borrowed B, which is the value of L's debt. This discussion also clarifies the role of some of the theorem's assumptions. We have implicitly assumed that the investor's cost of borrowing money is the same as that of the firm, which need not be true in the presence of asymmetric information or in the absence of efficient markets.

Proposition II:

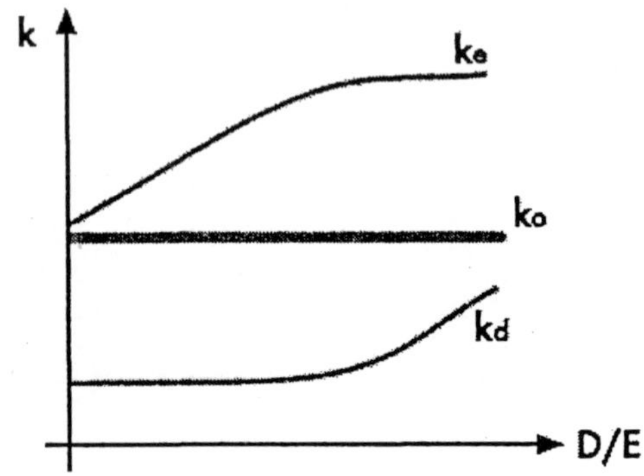

Proposition II with risky debt. As leverage (D/E) increases, the WACC stays constant.

$$y = c_0 + \frac{D}{E}(c_0 - b)$$

- y is the required rate of return on equity, or cost of equity.
- c0 is the cost of capital for an all equity firm.
- b is the required rate of return on borrowings, or cost of debt.
- D / E is the debt-to-equity ratio.

This proposition states that the cost of equity is a linear function of the firm's debt to equity ratio. A higher debt-to-equity ratio leads to a higher required return on equity, because of the higher risk involved for equity-holders in a company with debt. The formula is derived from the theory of weighted average cost of capital. These propositions are true assuming the following assumptions:

- no taxes exist,
- no transaction costs exist, and
- individuals and corporations borrow at the same rates.

These results might seem irrelevant (after all, none of the conditions are met in the real world), but the theorem is still taught and studied because it tells us something very important.

That is, if capital structure matters, it is precisely because one or more of the assumptions is violated. It tells us where to look for determinants of optimal capital structure and how those factors might affect optimal capital structure.

With Taxes

Proposition I:

$$V_L = V_U + T_C D$$

where

- V_L is the value of a levered firm.
- V_U is the value of an unlevered firm.
- $T_C D$ is the tax rate (T_C) x the value of debt (D)

This means that there are advantages for firms to be levered, since corporations can deduct interest payments. Therefore leverage lowers tax payments. Dividend payments are non-deductible.

Proposition II:

$$y = c_0 + \frac{D}{E}(c_0 - b)(1 - T_C)$$

where

- y is the required rate of return on equity, or cost of equity.
- c_0 is the cost of capital for an all equity firm.
- b is the required rate of return on borrowings, or cost of debt.
- D/E is the debt-to-equity ratio.
- T_c is the tax rate.

The same relationship as earlier described stating that the cost of equity rises with leverage, because the risk to equity rises, still holds. The formula however has implications for the difference with the WACC.

The following assumptions are made in the propositions with taxes:

- corporations are taxed at the rate T_C on earnings after interest,
- no transaction cost exist, and
- individuals and corporations borrow at the same rate

Miller and Modigliani published a number of follow-up papers discussing some of these issues.

The theorem first appeared in: F. Modigliani and M. Miller, "The Cost of Capital, Corporation Finance and the Theory of Investment," American Economic Review (June 1958).

ARBITRAGE

In economics and finance, arbitrage is the practice of taking advantage of a price differential between two or more markets: a combination of matching deals are struck that capitalize upon the imbalance, the profit being the difference between the market prices. When used by academics, an arbitrage is a transaction that involves no negative cash flow at any probabilistic or temporal state and a positive cash flow in at least one state; in simple terms, a risk-free profit. A person who engages in arbitrage is called an arbitrageur. The term is mainly applied to trading in financial instruments, such as bonds, stocks, derivatives, commodities and currencies. Search Arbitrage is also another way of leveraging online advertising using this market theory.

If the market prices do not allow for profitable arbitrage, the prices are said to constitute an arbitrage equilibrium or arbitrage free market. An arbitrage equilibrium is a precondition for a general economic equilibrium.

Statistical arbitrage is an imbalance in expected values. A casino has a statistical arbitrage in almost every game of chance that it offers.

Conditions for Arbitrage

Arbitrage is possible when one of three conditions is met:

1. The same asset does not trade at the same price on all markets ("the law of one price").

2. Two assets with identical cash flows do not trade at the same price.
3. An asset with a known price in the future does not today trade at its future price discounted at the risk-free interest rate (or, the asset does not have negligible costs of storage; as such, for example, this condition holds for grain but not for securities).

Arbitrage is not simply the act of buying a product in one market and selling it in another for a higher price at some later time. The transactions must occur simultaneously to avoid exposure to market risk, or the risk that prices may change on one market before both transactions are complete. In practical terms, this is generally only possible with securities and financial products which can be traded electronically.

In the most simple example, any good sold in one market should sell for the same price in another. Traders may, for example, find that the price of wheat is lower in agricultural regions than in cities, purchase the good, and transport it to another region to sell at a higher price. This type of price arbitrage is the most common, but this simple example ignores the cost of transport, storage, risk, and other factors. "True" arbitrage requires that there be no market risk involved. Where securities are traded on more than one exchange, arbitrage occurs by simultaneously buying in one and selling on the other.

Examples

- Suppose that the exchange rates (after taking out the fees for making the exchange) in London are £5 = $10 = ¥1000 and the exchange rates in Tokyo are ¥1000 = £6 = $12. Converting ¥1000 to $12 in Tokyo and converting that $12 into ¥1200 in London, for a profit of ¥200, would be arbitrage. In reality, this "triangle arbitrage" is so simple that it almost never occurs. But more complicated foreign exchange arbitrages, such as the spot-forward arbitrage (see interest rate parity) are much more common.
- One example of arbitrage involves the New York Stock Exchange and the Chicago Mercantile Exchange. When

the price of a stock on the NYSE and its corresponding futures contract on the CME are out of sync, one can buy the less expensive one and sell the more expensive. Because the differences between the prices are likely to be small (and not to last very long), this can only be done profitably with computers examining a large number of prices and automatically exercising a trade when the prices are far enough out of balance. The activity of other arbitrageurs can make this risky. Those with the fastest computers and the smartest mathematicians take advantage of series of small differentials that would not be profitable if taken individually.

- Economists use the term "global labor arbitrage" to refer to the tendency of manufacturing jobs to flow towards whichever country has the lowest wages per unit output at present and has reached the minimum requisite level of political and economic development to support industrialization. At present, many such jobs appear to be flowing towards China, though some which require English are going to India.
- Sports arbitrage-numerous internet bookmakers offer odds on the outcome of the same event. Any given bookmaker will weight their odds so that no one customer can cover all outcomes at a profit against their books. However, in order to remain competitive their margins are usually quite low. Different bookmakers may offer different odds on the same outcome of a given event; by taking the best odds offered by each bookmaker, a customer can under some circumstances cover all possible outcomes of the event and lock a small risk-free profit, known as a Dutch book. This profit would typically be between 1% and 5% but can be much higher. One problem with sports arbitrage is that bookmakers sometimes make mistakes and this can lead to an invocation of the 'palpable error' rule, which most bookmakers invoke when they have made a mistake by offering or posting incorrect odds. As bookmakers become more proficient, the odds of making an 'arb' usually last for less than an hour and typically only a few minutes.

Furthermore, huge bets on one side of the market also alert the bookies to correct the market.

- Exchange-traded fund arbitrage-Exchange Traded Funds allow authorized participants to exchange back and forth between shares in underlying securities held by the fund and shares in the fund itself, rather than allowing the buying and selling of shares in the ETF directly with the fund sponsor. ETFs trade in the open market, with prices set by market demand. An ETF may trade at a premium or discount to the value of the underlying assets. When a significant enough premium appears, an arbitrageur will buy the underlying securities, convert them to shares in the ETF, and sell them in the open market. When a discount appears, an arbitrageur will do the reverse. In this way, the arbitrageur makes a low-risk profit, while fulfilling a useful function in the ETF marketplace by keeping ETF prices in line with their underlying value.
- Some types of hedge funds make use of a modified form of arbitrage to profit. Rather than exploiting price differences between identical assets, they will purchase and sell securities, assets and derivatives with similar characteristics, and hedge any significant differences between the two assets. Any difference between the hedged positions represents any remaining risk (such as basis risk) plus profit; the belief is that there remains some difference which, even after hedging most risk, represents pure profit. For example, a fund may see that there is a substantial difference between U.S. dollar debt and local currency debt of a foreign country, and enter into a series of matching trades (including currency swaps) to arbitrage the difference, while simultaneously entering into credit default swaps to protect against country risk and other types of specific risk.

Price Convergence

Arbitrage has the effect of causing prices in different markets to converge. As a result of arbitrage, the currency exchange rates, the price of commodities, and the price of securities in different markets tend to converge to the same prices, in all markets, in each category. The speed at which prices converge is a measure of market efficiency. Arbitrage tends to reduce price discrimination by encouraging people to buy an item where the price is low and resell it where the price is high, as long as the buyers are not prohibited from reselling and the transactions cost of buying, holding and reselling are small relative to the difference in prices in the different markets.

Arbitrage moves different currencies toward purchasing power parity. As an example, assume that a car purchased in America is cheaper than the same car in Canada. Canadians would buy their cars across the border to exploit the arbitrage condition. At the same time, Americans would buy US cars, transport them across the border, and sell them in Canada. Canadians would have to buy American Dollars to buy the cars, and Americans would have to sell the Canadian dollars they received in exchange for the exported cars. Both actions would increase demand for US Dollars, and supply of Canadian Dollars, and as a result, there would be an appreciation of the US Dollar. Eventually, if unchecked, this would make US cars more expensive for all buyers, and Canadian cars cheaper, until there is no longer an incentive to buy cars in the US and sell them in Canada. More generally, international arbitrage opportunities in commodities, goods, securities and currencies, on a grand scale, tend to change exchange rates until the purchasing power is equal.

In reality, of course, one must consider taxes and the costs of travelling back and forth between the US and Canada. Also, the features built into the cars sold in the US are not exactly the same as the features built into the cars for sale in Canada, due, among other things, to the different emissions and other auto regulations in the two countries. In addition, our example assumes that no duties have to be paid on importing or exporting cars from the USA to Canada. Similarly, most assets exhibit (small) differences between countries, and transaction costs, taxes, and other costs provide an impediment to this kind of arbitrage.

Similarly, arbitrage affects the difference in interest rates paid on government bonds, issued by the various countries, given the expected depreciations in the currencies, relative to each other (see interest rate parity).

Risks

Arbitrage transactions in modern securities markets involve fairly low risks. Generally it is impossible to close two or three transactions at the same instant; therefore, there is the possibility that when one part of the deal is closed, a quick shift in prices makes it impossible to close the other at a profitable price. There is also counter-party risk, that the other party to one of the deals fails to deliver as agreed; though unlikely, this hazard is serious because of the large quantities one must trade in order to make a profit on small price differences. These risks become magnified when leverage or borrowed money is used.

Another risk occurs if the items being bought and sold are not identical and the arbitrage is conducted under the assumption that the prices of the items are correlated or predictable. In the extreme case this is risk arbitrage, described below. In comparison to the classical quick arbitrage transaction, such an operation can produce disastrous losses.

Competition in the marketplace can also create risks during arbitrage transactions. As an example, if one was trying to profit from a price discrepancy between IBM on the NYSE and IBM on the London Stock Exchange, they may purchase a large number of shares on the NYSE and find that they cannot simultaneously sell on the LSE. This leaves the arbitrageur in an unhedged risk position.

In the 1980s, risk arbitrage was common. In this form of speculation, one trades a security that is clearly undervalued or overvalued, when it is seen that the wrong valuation is about to be corrected by events. The standard example is the stock of a company, undervalued in the stock market, which is about to be the object of a takeover bid; the price of the takeover will more truly reflect the value of the company, giving a large profit to those who bought at the current price-if the merger goes through as predicted. Traditionally, arbitrage transactions in the securities markets involve high speed and low risk. At some moment a price difference exists, and the problem is to execute two or three balancing transactions while the difference persists (that is, before the other arbitrageurs act). When the transaction involves a delay of weeks or months, as above, it may entail considerable risk if borrowed money is used to magnify the reward through leverage. One way of reducing the risk is through the illegal use of inside information, and in fact risk arbitrage with regard to leveraged buyouts was associated with some of the famous financial scandals of the 1980s such as those involving Michael Milken and Ivan Boesky.

TYPES OF ARBITRAGE

Merger Arbitrage

Also called risk arbitrage, merger arbitrage generally consists of buying the stock of a company that is the target of a takeover while shorting the stock of the acquiring company.

Usually the market price of the target company is less than the price offered by the acquiring company. The spread between these two prices depends mainly on the probability and the timing of the takeover being completed as well as the prevailing level of interest rates.

The bet in a merger arbitrage is that such a spread will eventually be zero, if and when the takeover is completed. The risk is that the deal "breaks" and the spread massively widens.

Municipal Bond Arbitrage

Also called municipal bond relative value arbitrage, municipal arbitrage, or just muni arb, this hedge fund strategy involves one of two approaches.

Generally, managers seek relative value opportunities by being both long and short municipal bonds with a duration-neutral book. The relative value trades may be between different issuers, different bonds issued by the same entity, or capital structure trades referencing the same asset (in the case of revenue bonds). Managers aim to capture the inefficiencies arising from the heavy participation of non-economic investors (i.e., high income "buy and hold" investors seeking tax-exempt income) as well as the "crossover buying" arising from corporations' or individuals' changing income tax situations (i.e., insurers switching their munis for corporates after a large loss as they can capture a higher after-tax yield by offsetting the taxable corporate income with underwriting losses). There are additional inefficiencies arising from the highly fragmented nature of the municipal bond market which has 50,000 issuers and two million outstanding issues in contrast to the Treasury market which has 400 issues and a single issuer.

Second, managers construct leveraged portfolios of AAA-or AA-rated tax-exempt municipal bonds with the duration risk hedged by shorting the appropriate ratio of taxable corporate bonds. These corporate equivalents are typically interest rate swaps referencing Libor or BMA (short for Bond Market Association). The arbitrage manifests itself in the form of a relatively cheap longer maturity municipal bond, which is a municipal bond that yields significantly more than 65% of a corresponding taxable corporate bond. The steeper slope of the municipal yield curve allows participants to collect more after-tax income from the municipal bond portfolio than is spent on the interest rate swap; the carry is greater than the hedge expense. Positive, tax-free carry from muni arb can reach into the double digits. The bet in this municipal bond arbitrage is that, over a longer period of time, two similar instruments--municipal bonds and interest rate swaps--will correlate with each other; they are both very high quality credits, have the same maturity and are denominated in U.S. dollars. Credit risk and duration risk are largely eliminated in this strategy. However, basis risk arises from use of an imperfect hedge, which results in significant, but range-bound principal volatility. The end goal is to limit this principal volatility, eliminating its relevance over time as the high, consistent, tax-free cash flow accumulates. Since the inefficiency is related to government tax policy, and hence is structural in nature, it has not been arbitraged away.

Convertible Bond Arbitrage

A convertible bond is a bond that an investor can return to the issuing company in exchange for a predetermined number of shares in the company.

A convertible bond can be thought of as a corporate bond with a stock call option attached to it.

The price of a convertible bond is sensitive to three major factors:

- interest rate. When rates move higher, the bond part of a convertible bond tends to move lower, but the call option part of a convertible bond moves higher (and the aggregate tends to move lower).
- stock price. When the price of the stock the bond is convertible into moves higher, the price of the bond tends to rise.
- credit spread. If the creditworthiness of the issuer deteriorates (e.g. rating downgrade) and its credit spread widens, the bond price tends to move lower, but, in many cases, the call option part of the convertible bond moves higher (since credit spread correlates with volatility).

Given the complexity of the calculations involved and the convoluted structure that a convertible bond can have, an arbitrageur often relies on sophisticated quantitative models in order to identify bonds that are trading cheap versus their theoretical value.

Convertible arbitrage consists of buying a convertible bond and hedging two of the three factors in order to gain exposure to the third factor at a very attractive price.

For instance an arbitrageur would first buy a convertible bond, then sell fixed income securities or interest rate futures (to hedge the interest rate exposure) and buy some credit protection (to hedge the risk of credit deterioration). Eventually what he'd be left with is something similar to a call option on the underlying stock, acquired at a very low price. He could then make money either selling some of the more expensive options that are openly traded in the market or delta hedging his exposure to the underlying shares.

Depository Receipts

A depository receipt is a security that is offered as a "tracking stock" on another foreign market. For instance a Chinese company wishing to raise more money may issue a depository receipt on the New York Stock Exchange, as the amount of capital on the local exchanges is limited. These securities, known as ADRs (American Depositary Receipt) or GDRs (Global Depositary Receipt) depending on where they are issued, are typically considered "foreign" and therefore trade at a lower value when first released.

However, they are exchangeable into the original security (known as fungibility) and actually have the same value. In this case there is a spread between the perceived value and real value, which can be extracted. Since the ADR is trading at a value lower than what it is worth, one can purchase the ADR and expect to make money as its value converges on the original. However there is a chance that the original stock will fall in value too, so by shorting it you can hedge that risk.

Regulatory Arbitrage

Regulatory arbitrage is where a regulated institution takes advantage of the difference between its real (or economic) risk and the regulatory position. For example, if a bank, operating under the Basel I accord, has to hold 8% capital against default risk, but the real risk of default is lower, it is profitable to securitise the loan, removing the low risk loan from its portfolio. On the other hand, if the real risk is higher than the regulatory risk then it is profitable to make that loan and hold on to it, provided it is priced appropriately.

This process can increase the overall riskiness of institutions under a risk insensitive regulatory regime, as described by Alan Greenspan in his October 1998 speech on The Role of Capital in Optimal Banking Supervision and Regulation.

In economics, regulatory arbitrage (sometimes, tax arbitrage) may be used to refer to situations when a company can choose a nominal place of business with a regulatory, legal or tax regime with lower costs. For example, an insurance company may choose to locate in Bermuda due to preferential tax rates and policies for insurance companies.

This can occur particularly where the business transaction has no obvious physical location: in the case of many financial products, it may be unclear "where" the transaction occurs.

Telecom Arbitrage

Telecom arbitrage companies like Action Telecom UK allow mobile phone users to make international calls for free through certain access numbers. The telecommunication arbitrage companies get paid an interconnect charge by the UK mobile networks and then buy international routes at a lower cost. The calls are seen as free by the UK contract mobile phone customers since they are using up their allocated monthly minutes rather than paying for additional calls. The end effect is telecom arbitrage. This is usually marketed as "free international calls". The profit margins are usually very small. However, with enough volume, enough money is made from the cost difference to turn a profit. This is very similar to Future Phone in the US.

Online Advertising Arbitrage

Online ad services like Yahoo! Search Marketing and Google Adwords allow you to purchase online advertisements which cost you an agreed upon cost per click. These are known as PPC (Pay Per Click) ads. Some ad clicks will cost advertisers $0.01 while some can cost well over $10 depending on the keywords that were associated with the ad. Yahoo and Google both have programs which allow web publishers to place ads on their own websites to make money. Some webmasters will make a website associated with a high paying keyword(s) and place PPC ads on it. Then, they will purchase low cost ads on Yahoo and Google for their websites. The end effect is traffic arbitrage. Low cost traffic is redirected towards pages which contain high paying links. Enough money is made from clicks to cover the traffic cost and turn a profit.

This is not arbitrage as defined above. The owner of the website is simply betting that the income from the affiliate marketing organisation is more than the cost of bringing visitors to the site. The website owner must pay the search engine for each visitor to the website but payment from the affiliate only occurs if the visitor actually clicks onto one of the affiliate advertisements. A classic example might be where each visitor to the site costs the site owner 10 cents but an affiliate marketer will pay the website owner 10 dollars if that visitor clicks through to the target website. In this case if more than 1 in

100 visitors click through then the site makes a profit; and conversely if less than 1 in 100 click through then the site makes a loss. The same theory holds true if the affiliate is the same (or another) search engine.

The Debacle of Long-Term Capital Management

Long-Term Capital Management (LTCM) lost 4.6 billion U.S. dollars in fixed income arbitrage in September 1998. LTCM had attempted to make money on the price difference between different bonds. For example, it would sell U.S. Treasury securities and buy Italian bond futures. The concept was that because Italian bond futures had a less liquid market, in the short term Italian bond futures would have a higher return than U.S. bonds, but in the long term, the prices would converge. Because the difference was small, a large amount of money had to be borrowed to make the buying and selling profitable.

The downfall in this system began on August 17, 1998, when Russia defaulted on its ruble debt and domestic dollar debt. Because the markets were already nervous due to the Asian financial crisis, investors began selling non-U.S. treasury debt and buying U.S. treasuries, which were considered a safe investment. As a result the return on U.S. treasuries began decreasing because there were many buyers, and the return on other bonds began to increase because there were many sellers. This caused the difference between the returns of U.S. treasuries and other bonds to increase, rather than to decrease as LTCM was expecting. Eventually this caused LTCM to fold, and their creditors had to arrange a bail-out. More controversially, officials of the Federal Reserve assisted in the negotiations that led to this bail-out, on the grounds that so many companies and deals were intertwined with LTCM that if LTCM actually failed, they would as well, causing a collapse in confidence in the economic system. Thus LTCM failed as a fixed income arbitrage fund, although it is unclear what sort of profit was realized by the banks that bailed LTCM out.

Etymology

Arbitrage is French and denotes a decision by an arbitrator or arbitration tribunal. (In modern French, "arbitre" usually means referee or umpire). In the sense used here it is first defined in 1704 by Mathieu de la Porte in his treatise "La science des négocians et teneurs de livres" as a consideration of different exchange rates to recognize the most profitable places of issuance and settlement for a bill of exchange ("[U]ne combinaison que l'on fait de plusieurs Changes, pour connoître quelle Place est plus avantageuse pour tirer et remettre").

ARBITRAGE BETTING

Betting arbitrage or sports arbitraging is a particular case of arbitrage arising on betting markets due to either bookmakers' different opinions on event outcomes or plain errors. By placing one bet per each outcome with different betting companies, the bettor can make a profit.

In the bettors' slang an arbitrage is often referred to as an arb. A typical arb is around 2%, often less, however 4%-5% are also normal and during some special events they might reach 20%.

Arbitrage betting is usually done on the web by researching prices (odds) on betting web sites or subscribing to one of the arb-hunting services. As an investment practice, it is not completely risk-free despite the commercially used terms 'no-risk' and risk-free betting. Some of the risks include:

- Price changes midway through the arbitrage bet
- Bookmakers refusing to honour the wager
- Bookmakers unable to remain solvent

It involves relatively large sums of money (stakes are bigger than in normal betting) while another variety, betting investment, means placing relatively small bets systematically on overvalued odds most of which will lose but some win thus making a profit.

Arbitrage in Theory

There are a number of potential arbitrage deals. Below is an explanation of some of them including formulas and risks associated with these arbitrage deals. The table below introduces a number of variables that will be used to formalise the arbitrage models.

Variable	Explanation
s_1	Stake in outcome 1
s_2	Stake in outcome 2
o_1	Odds for outcome 1
o_2	Odds for outcome 2
r_1	Return if outcome 1 occurs
r_2	Return if outcome 2 occurs

Arbitrage using Bookmakers

This type of arbitrage takes advantage of different odds offered by different bookmakers. Assume the following situation:

We consider an event with 2 possible outcomes (e.g. a tennis match-either Federer wins or Henman wins), the idea can be generalized to events with more outcomes, but we use this as an example.

The 2 bookmakers have differing ideas of who have the best chances of winning, they offer the following Fixed-odds gambling on the outcomes of the event

	Bookmaker 1	Bookmaker 2
Outcome 1	1.25	1.43
Outcome 2	3.9	2.85

For an individual bookmaker, the sum of the inverse of all outcomes of an event will always be greater than 1.

$$0_1^{-1} + 0_2^{-1} > 1 \; 0_1^{-1} + 0_2^{-1} > 1$$

As they are in this case: $1.25^{-1} + 3.9^{-1} = 1.056$ and $1.43^{-1} + 2.85^{-1} = 1.051$

The fraction above 1, is the bookmakers return rate, the amount the bookmaker earns on offering bets at some event. Bookmaker 1 will in this example expect to earn 5,6 % on bets on the tennis game. Usually these gaps will be in the order 8 - 12%.

The idea is to find odds at different bookmakers, where the sum of the inverse of all the outcomes are below 1. Meaning that the bookmakers disagree on the chances of the outcomes. This discrepancy can be used to obtain a profit.

For instance if you bet at outcome 1 at bookmaker 2 and outcome 2 at bookmaker 1:

$$1.43^{-1} + 3.9^{-1} = 0.956$$

Placing a bet of 100$ on outcome 1 with bookmaker 2 and a bet of $100 * 1.43 / 3.9 = 36.67 on outcome 2 at bookmaker 1 would ensure the bettee a profit.

In case outcome 1 comes out, you could collect r_1 = $100 * 1.43 = $143 from bookmaker 2. In case outcome 2 comes out, you could collect r_2 = $36.67 * 3.9 = $143 from bookmaker 1. You would have invested $136.67, but have collected $143, a profit of $6.33 (%4.6) no matter the outcome of the event.

So for 2 odds o_1 and o_2, where $0_1^{-1} + 0_2^{-1} > 1$. You wish to place stake s1 at outcome 1, then you should place $s_2 = s_1 * o_1 / o_2$ at outcome 2, to even out the odds, and receive the same return no matter the outcome of the event.

Or in other words, if you have two outcomes a 2/1 and a 3/1, by covering the 2/1 with $500 and the 3/1 with $333, you are guaranteed to win $1000 at a cost of $833, giving a 16% profit. More often profits exists around the 4% mark or less.

In practice it is very hard to find bets with this property and due to the small discrepancies of a few percent (you will be very unlikely to find higher) you will need to invest large sums to receive a profit of any real size. Which can be very dangerous as mentioned in the introduction of this article.

Reducing the risk of human error is vital being that the mathematical formula is sound and only external factor add "risk". Numerous online arbitrage calculator tools exist to help bettors get the math right.

Back-lay Sports Arbitrage

Betting exchanges open up a new range of arbitrage possibilities since it is possible to back as well as lay an event.

Arbitrage using only the back or lay side might occur on betting exchanges. It is in principle the same as the arbitrage using different bookmakers. Arbitrage using back and lay side is possible if a lay bet provides lower odds than a back bet. (Of course, the commission of the bookmaker must be included into calculations.)

Bonus Sports Arbitrage

Many bookmakers offer first time users a sign-up bonus in the range 10 - 200 $ for depositing an initial amount. They typically demand that this amount is wagered a number of times before the bonus can be withdrawn. Bonus sport arbitraging is a form of sports arbitraging where you hedge or back your bets as usual, but since you received the bonus, a small loss can be allowed on each wager (2-5 %), which comes off your profit. In this way the bookmakers wagering demand can be met and the initial deposit and sign up bonus can be withdrawn with little loss.

The advantage over usual betting arbitrage is that it is a lot easier to find bets with an acceptable loss, instead of an actual profit. Since most bookmakers offer these bonuses this can potentially be exploited to harvest the sign up bonuses.

ARBITRAGE PRICING THEORY

Arbitrage pricing theory (APT), in Finance, is a general theory of asset pricing, that has become influential in the pricing of shares.

APT holds that the expected return of a financial asset can be modeled as a linear function of various macro-economic factors or theoretical market indices, where sensitivity to changes in each factor is represented by a factor specific beta coefficient. The model derived rate of return will then be used to price the asset correctly-the asset price should equal the expected end of period price discounted at the rate implied by model. If the price diverges, arbitrage should bring it back into line.

The theory was initiated by the economist Stephen Ross in 1976.

The APT Model

If APT holds, then a risky asset can be described as satisfying the following relation:

$$E(r_j) = r_f + b_{j1}RP_1 + b_{j2}RP_2 + \ldots + b_{jn}RP_n$$

$$r_j = E(r_j) + b_{j1}F_1 + b_{j2}F_2 + \ldots + b_{jn}F_n + \varepsilon_j$$

where

- $E(r_j)$ is the risky asset's expected return,
- RP_k is the risk premium of the factor,
- r_f is the risk-free rate,
- F_k is the macroeconomic factor,
- b_{jk} is the sensitivity of the asset to factor k, also called factor loading,
- and ε_j is the risky asset's idiosyncratic random shock with mean zero.

That is, the uncertain return of an asset j is a linear relationship among n factors. Additionally, every factor is also considered to be a random variable with mean zero.

Note that there are some assumptions and requirements that have to be fulfilled for the latter to be correct: There must be perfect competition in the market, and the total number of factors may never surpass the total number of assets (in order to avoid the problem of matrix singularity),

Arbitrage and the APT

Arbitrage is the practice of taking advantage of a state of imbalance between two (or possibly more) markets and thereby making a risk free profit.

Arbitrage in Expectations

The APT describes the mechanism whereby arbitrage by investors will bring an asset which is mispriced, according to the APT model, back into line with its expected price. Note that under true arbitrage, the investor locks-in a guaranteed payoff, whereas under APT arbitrage as described below, the investor locks-in a positive expected payoff. The APT thus assumes "arbitrage in expectations"-i.e. that arbitrage by investors will bring asset prices back into line with the returns expected by the model portfolio theory.

Arbitrage Mechanics

In the APT context, arbitrage consists of trading in two assets-with at least one being mispriced. The arbitrageur sells the asset which is relatively too expensive and uses the proceeds to buy one which is relatively too cheap.

Under the APT, an asset is mispriced if its current price diverges from the price predicted by the model. The asset price today should equal the sum of all future cash flows discounted at the APT rate, where the expected return of the asset is a linear function of various factors, and sensitivity to changes in each factor is represented by a factor-specific beta coefficient.

A correctly priced asset here may be in fact a synthetic asset-a portfolio consisting of other correctly priced assets. This portfolio has the same exposure to each of the macroeconomic factors as the mispriced asset.

The arbitrageur creates the portfolio by identifying x correctly priced assets (one per factor plus one) and then weighting the assets such that portfolio beta per factor is the same as for the mispriced asset.

When the investor is long the asset and short the portfolio (or vice versa) he has created a position which has a positive expected return (the difference between asset return and portfolio return) and which has a net-zero exposure to any macroeconomic factor and is therefore risk free (other than for firm specific risk). The arbitrageur is thus in a position to make a risk free profit:

Where today's price is too low:

The implication is that at the end of the period the portfolio would have appreciated at the rate implied by the APT, whereas the mispriced asset would have appreciated at more than this rate. The arbitrageur could therefore:

Today:

1 short sell the portfolio

2 buy the mispriced-asset with the proceeds.

At the end of the period:

1 sell the mispriced asset

2 use the proceeds to buy back the portfolio

3 pocket the difference.

Where today's price is too high:

The implication is that at the end of the period the portfolio would have appreciated at the rate implied by the APT, whereas the mispriced asset would have appreciated at less than this rate. The arbitrageur could therefore:

Today:

1 short sell the mispriced-asset

2 buy the portfolio with the proceeds.

At the end of the period:

1 sell the portfolio

2 use the proceeds to buy back the mispriced-asset

3 pocket the difference.

Relationship with the Capital Asset Pricing Model

The APT along with the capital asset pricing model (CAPM) is one of two influential theories on asset pricing. The APT differs from the CAPM in that it is less restrictive in its assumptions.

It allows for an explanatory (as opposed to statistical) model of asset returns. It assumes that each investor will hold a unique portfolio with its own particular array of betas, as opposed to the identical "market portfolio". In some ways, the CAPM can be considered a "special case" of the APT in that the securities market line represents a single-factor model of the asset price, where Beta is exposure to changes in value of the Market.

Additionally, the APT can be seen as a "supply side" model, since its beta coefficients reflect the sensitivity of the underlying asset to economic factors. Thus, factor shocks would cause structural changes in the asset's expected return, or in the case of stocks, in the firm's profitability.

On the other side, the capital asset pricing model is considered a "demand side" model. Its results, although similar to those in the APT, arise from a maximization problem of each investor's utility function, and from the resulting market equilibrium (investors are considered to be the "consumers" of the assets).

USING THE APT

Identifying the Factors

As with the CAPM, the factor-specific Betas are found via a linear regression of historical security returns on the factor in question. Unlike the CAPM, the APT, however, does not itself reveal the identity of its priced factors-the number and nature of these factors is likely to change over time and between economies. As a result, this issue is essentially empirical in nature. Several a priori guidelines as to the characteristics required of potential factors are, however, suggested:

1. their impact on asset prices manifests in their unexpected movements
2. they should represent undiversifiable influences (these are, clearly, more likely to be macroeconomic rather than firm-specific in nature)
3. timely and accurate information on these variables is required
4. the relationship should be theoretically justifiable on economic grounds

Chen, Roll and Ross identified the following macro-economic factors as significant in explaining security returns:

- surprises in inflation;
- surprises in GNP as indicted by an industrial production index;

- surprises in investor confidence due to changes in default premium in corporate bonds;
- surprise shifts in the yield curve.

As a practical matter, indices or spot or futures market prices may be used in place of macro-economic factors, which are reported at low frequency (e.g. monthly) and often with significant estimation errors. Market indices are sometimes derived by means of factor analysis. More direct "indices" that might be used are:

- short term interest rates;
- the difference in long-term and short term interest rates;
- a diversified stock index such as the S&P 500 or NYSE Composite Index;
- oil prices
- gold or other precious metal prices
- Currency exchange rates

RATIONAL PRICING

Rational pricing is the assumption in financial economics that asset prices (and hence asset pricing models) will reflect the arbitrage-free price of the asset as any deviation from this price will be "arbitraged away".

This assumption is useful in pricing fixed income securities, particularly bonds, and is fundamental to the pricing of derivative instruments.

Arbitrage Mechanics

Arbitrage is the practice of taking advantage of a state of imbalance between two (or possibly more) markets. Where this mismatch can be exploited (i.e. after transaction costs, storage costs, transport costs, dividends etc.) the arbitrageur "locks in" a risk free profit without investing any of his own money.

In general, arbitrage ensures that "the law of one price" will hold; arbitrage also equalises the prices of assets with identical cash flows, and sets the price of assets with known future cash flows.

The Law of one Price

The same asset must trade at the same price on all markets ("the law of one price"). Where this is not true, the arbitrageur will:

1. buy the asset on the market where it has the lower price, and simultaneously sell it (short) on the second market at the higher price
2. deliver the asset to the buyer and receive that higher price
3. pay the seller on the cheaper market with the proceeds and pocket the difference.

Assets with Identical Cash Flows

Two assets with identical cash flows must trade at the same price. Where this is not true, the arbitrageur will:

1. sell the asset with the higher price (short sell) and simultaneously buy the asset with the lower price
2. fund his purchase of the cheaper asset with the proceeds from the sale of the expensive asset and pocket the difference
3. deliver on his obligations to the buyer of the expensive asset, using the cash flows from the cheaper asset.

An Asset with a known Future-price

An asset with a known price in the future, must today trade at that price discounted at the risk free rate.

Note that this condition can be viewed as an application of the above, where the two assets in question are the asset to be delivered and the risk free asset.

(a) where the discounted future price is higher than today's price:

   1. The arbitrageur agrees to deliver the asset on the future date (i.e. sells forward) and simultaneously buys it today with borrowed money.
   2. On the delivery date, the arbitrageur hands over the underlying, and receives the agreed price.

3. He then repays the lender the borrowed amount plus interest.
4. The difference between the agreed price and the amount owed is the arbitrage profit.

(b) where the discounted future price is lower than today's price:

1. The arbitrageur agrees to pay for the asset on the future date (i.e. buys forward) and simultaneously sells (short) the underlying today; he invests the proceeds.
2. On the delivery date, he cashes in the matured investment, which has appreciated at the risk free rate.
3. He then takes delivery of the underlying and pays the agreed price using the matured investment.
4. The difference between the maturity value and the agreed price is the arbitrage profit.

It will be noted that (b) is only possible for those holding the asset but not needing it until the future date. There may be few such parties if short-term demand exceeds supply, leading to backwardation.

Fixed Income Securities

Rational pricing is one approach used in pricing fixed rate bonds. Here, each cash flow can be matched by trading in some multiple of a "risk free" government issue zero coupon bond with the corresponding maturity, or in a corresponding strip and ZCB.

Given that the cash flows can be replicated, the price of the bond, must today equal the sum of each of its cash flows discounted at the same rate as the corresponding government securities-i.e. the corresponding risk free rate (here, assuming similar credit worthiness).

Were this not the case, arbitrage would be possible and would bring the price back into line with the price based on the government issued securities.

The pricing formula is as below, where each cash flow C_t is discounted at the rate which matches that of the correspon-ding government zero coupon instrument:

$$\text{Price} = P_0 = \sum_{t=1}^{T} \frac{C_t}{(1+r_t)^t}$$

Often, the formula is expressed as $P_0 = \sum_{t=1}^{T} C(t) \times P(t)$, using prices instead of rates, as prices are more readily available.

Pricing Derivatives

A derivative is an instrument which allows for buying and selling of the same asset on two markets-the spot market and the derivatives market. Mathematical finance assumes that any imbalance between the two markets will be arbitraged away. Thus, in a correctly priced derivative contract, the derivative price, the strike price (or reference rate), and the spot price will be related such that arbitrage is not possible.

Futures

In a futures contract, for no arbitrage to be possible, the price paid on delivery (the forward price) must be the same as the cost (including interest) of buying and storing the asset. In other words, the rational forward price represents the expected future value of the underlying discounted at the risk free rate. Thus, for a simple, non-dividend paying asset, the value of the future/forward, F(t), will be found by discounting the present value S(t) at time t to maturity T by the rate of risk-free return r.

$$F(t) = S(t) \times (1+r)^{(T-t)}$$

This relationship may be modified for storage costs, dividends, dividend yields, and convenience yields; see futures contract pricing.

Any deviation from this equality allows for arbitrage as follows.

- In the case where the forward price is higher:
  1. The arbitrageur sells the futures contract and buys the underlying today (on the spot market) with borrowed money.
  2. On the delivery date, the arbitrageur hands over the underlying, and receives the agreed forward price.
  3. He then repays the lender the borrowed amount plus interest.
  4. The difference between the two amounts is the arbitrage profit.
- In the case where the forward price is lower:
  1. The arbitrageur buys the futures contract and sells the underlying today (on the spot market); he invests the proceeds.
  2. On the delivery date, he cashes in the matured investment, which has appreciated at the risk free rate.
  3. He then receives the underlying and pays the agreed forward price using the matured investment. [If he was short the underlying, he returns it now.]
  4. The difference between the two amounts is the arbitrage profit.

Options

As above, where the value of an asset in the future is known (or expected), this value can be used to determine the asset's rational price today. In an option contract, however, exercise is dependent on the price of the underlying, and hence payment is uncertain. Option pricing models therefore include logic which either "locks in" or "infers" this value; both approaches deliver identical results. Methods which lock-in future cash flows assume arbitrage free pricing, and those which infer expected value assume risk neutral valuation.

Both approaches assume a "Binomial model" for the behavior of the underlying instrument, which allows for only two states-up or down. If S is the current price, then in the next period the price will either be S up or S down. Here, the value of the share in the up-state is S × u, and in the down-state is S × d (where u and d are multipliers with d < 1 < u and assuming d < 1+r < u; see the binomial options model).

Given these two states, the "arbitrage free" approach creates a position which will have an identical value in either state- the cash flow in one period is therefore known, and arbitrage pricing is applicable. The risk neutral approach infers expected option value from the intrinsic values at the later two nodes.

Although this logic appears far removed from the Black-Scholes formula and the lattice approach in the Binomial options model, it in fact underlies both models. The assumption of binomial behaviour in the underlying price is defensible as the number of time steps between today (valuation) and exercise increases, and the period per time-step is increasingly short. The Binomial options model allows for a high number of very short time-steps (if coded correctly), while Black-Scholes, in fact, models a continuous process.

The examples below have shares as the underlying, but may be generalised to other instruments. The value of a put option can be derived as below, or may be found from the value of the call using put-call parity.

Arbitrage Free Pricing

Here, the future payoff is "locked in" using either "delta hedging" or the "replicating portfolio" approach. As above, this payoff is then discounted, and the result is used in the valuation of the option today.

Delta Hedging

It is possible to create a position consisting of Δ calls sold and 1 share, such that the position's value will be identical in the S up and S down states, and hence known with certainty. This value corresponds to the forward price above, and as above, for no arbitrage to be possible, the present value of the position must be its expected future value discounted at the risk free rate, r. The value of a call is then found by equating the two.

(1) Solve for Δ such that:

value of position in one period = S up - $\Delta \times$ (S up - strike price) = S down - $\Delta \times$ (S down - strike price)

(2) solve for the value of the call, using Δ, where:

value of position today = value of position in one period $\div$ (1 + r) = S current - $\Delta \times$ value of call

The Replicating Portfolio

It is possible to create a position consisting of Δ shares and \$B borrowed at the risk free rate, which will produce identical cash flows to one option on the underlying share. The position created is known as a "replicating portfolio" since its cash flows replicate those of the option. As shown, in the absence of arbitrage opportunities, since the cash flows produced are identical, the price of the option today must be the same as the value of the position today.

(1) Solve simultaneously for Δ and B such that:

(i) $\Delta \times$ S up - B $\times$ (1 + r) = MAX (0, S up - strike price)

(ii) $\Delta \times$ S down - B $\times$ (1 + r) = MAX (0, S down- strike price)

(2) solve for the value of the call, using Δ and B, where:

call = $\Delta \times$ S current - B

Risk Neutral Valuation

Here the value of the option is calculated using the risk neutrality assumption. Under this assumption, the "expected value" (as opposed to "locked in" value) is discounted. The expected value is calculated using the intrinsic values from the later two nodes: "Option up" and "Option down", with u and d as price multipliers as above. These are then weighted by their respective probabilities: "probability" p of an up move in the underlying, and "probability" (1-p) of a down move. The expected value is then discounted at r, the risk free rate.

(1) solve for p for no arbitrage to be possible in the share, today's price must represent its expected value discounted at the risk free rate:

S = [p × (up value) + (1-p) ×(down value)] ÷ (1+r) = [p × S × u + (1-p) × S × d] ÷ (1+r)

then, p = [(1+r) - d] ÷ [u - d]

(2) solve for call value, using p

for no arbitrage to be possible in the call, today's price must represent its expected value discounted at the risk free rate:

Option value = [p × Option up + (1-p)× Option down] ÷ (1+r)

= [p × (S up - strike) + (1-p)× (S down - strike)] ÷ (1+r)

The Risk Neutrality Assumption

Note that above, the risk neutral formula does not refer to the volatility of the underlying - p as solved, relates to the risk-neutral measure as opposed to the actual probability distribution of prices. Nevertheless, both Arbitrage free pricing and Risk neutral valuation deliver identical results. In fact, it can be shown that "Delta hedging" and "Risk neutral valuation" use identical formulae expressed differently. Given this equivalence, it is valid to assume "risk neutrality" when pricing derivatives.

Swaps

Rational pricing underpins the logic of swap valuation. Here, two counterparties "swap" obligations, effectively exchanging cash flow streams calculated against a notional principal amount, and the value of the swap is the present value (PV) of both sets of future cash flows "netted off" against each other.

VALUATION AT INITIATION

To be arbitrage free, the terms of a swap contract are such that, initially, the Net present value of these future cash flows is equal to zero; see swap valuation. For example, consider a fixed-to-floating Interest rate swap where Party A pays a fixed rate, and Party B pays a floating rate. Here, the fixed rate would be such that the present value of future fixed rate payments by Party A is equal to the present value of the expected future floating rate payments (i.e. the NPV is zero). Were this not the case, an Arbitrageur, C, could:

1. assume the position with the lower present value of payments, and borrow funds equal to this present value
2. meet the cash flow obligations on the position by using the borrowed funds, and receive the corresponding payments-which have a higher present value
3. use the received payments to repay the debt on the borrowed funds
4. pocket the difference-where the difference between the present value of the loan and the present value of the inflows is the arbitrage profit.

Subsequent Valuation

Once traded, swaps can also be priced using rational pricing. For example, the Floating leg of an interest rate swap can be "decomposed" into a series of Forward rate agreements. Here, since the swap has identical payments to the FRA, arbitrage free pricing must apply as above-*i.e.* the value of this leg is equal to the value of the corresponding FRAs. Similarly, the "receive-fixed" leg of a swap, can be valued by comparison to a Bond with the same schedule of payments.

PRICING SHARES

The Arbitrage pricing theory (APT), a general theory of asset pricing, has become influential in the pricing of shares. APT holds that the expected return of a financial asset, can be modelled as a linear function of various macro-economic factors, where sensitivity to changes in each factor is represented by a factor specific beta coefficient:

$$E\left(r_j\right) = r_f + b_{j1}F_1 + b_{j2}F_2 + \ldots + b_{jn}F_n + \varepsilon_j$$

where

- $E(r_j)$ is the risky asset's expected return,
- r_f is the risk free rate,
- F_k is the macroeconomic factor,

- b_{jk} is the sensitivity of the asset to factor k,
- and ε_j is the risky asset's idiosyncratic random shock with mean zero.

The model derived rate of return will then be used to price the asset correctly-the asset price should equal the expected end of period price discounted at the rate implied by model. If the price diverges, arbitrage should bring it back into line. Here, to perform the arbitrage, the investor "creates" a correctly priced asset (a synthetic asset) being a portfolio which has the same net-exposure to each of the macroeconomic factors as the mispriced asset but a different expected return; see the APT article for detail on the construction of the portfolio. The arbitrageur is then in a position to make a risk free profit as follows:

- Where the asset price is too low, the portfolio should have appreciated at the rate implied by the APT, whereas the mispriced asset would have appreciated at more than this rate. The arbitrageur could therefore:
  1. Today: short sell the portfolio and buy the mispriced-asset with the proceeds.
  2. At the end of the period: sell the mispriced asset, use the proceeds to buy back the portfolio, and pocket the difference.
- Where the asset price is too high, the portfolio should have appreciated at the rate implied by the APT, whereas the mispriced asset would have appreciated at less than this rate. The arbitrageur could therefore:
  1. Today: short sell the mispriced-asset and buy the portfolio with the proceeds.
  2. At the end of the period: sell the portfolio, use the proceeds to buy back the mispriced-asset, and pocket the difference.

Note that under "true arbitrage", the investor locks-in a guaranteed payoff, whereas under APT arbitrage, the investor locks-in a positive expected payoff. The APT thus assumes "arbitrage in expectations"-*i.e* that arbitrage by investors will bring asset prices back into line with the returns expected by the model. The Capital asset pricing model (CAPM) is an earlier, (more) influential theory on asset pricing. Although based on different assumptions, the CAPM can, in some ways, be considered a "special case" of the APT; specifically, the CAPM's Securities market line represents a single-factor model of the asset price, where Beta is exposure to changes in value of the Market.

EFFICIENT MARKET HYPOTHESIS

In finance, the efficient market hypothesis (EMH) asserts that financial markets are "informationally efficient", or that prices on traded assets, e.g., stocks, bonds, or property, already reflect all known information and therefore are unbiased in the sense that they reflect the collective beliefs of all investors about future prospects. The efficient market hypothesis states that it is not possible to consistently outperform the market by using any information that the market already knows, except through luck. Information or news in the EMH is defined as anything that may affect prices that is unknowable in the present and thus appears randomly in the future.

Assumptions

Beyond the normal utility maximizing agents, the efficient market hypothesis requires that agents have rational expectations; that on average the population is correct (even if no one person is) and whenever new relevant information appears, the agents update their expectations appropriately.

Note that it is not required that the agents be rational (which is different from rational expectations; rational agents act coldly and achieve what they set out to do). EMH allows that when faced with new information, some investors may overreact and some may underreact. All that is required by the EMH is that investors' reactions be random and follow a normal distribution pattern so that the net effect on market prices cannot be reliably exploited to make an abnormal profit, especially when considering transaction costs (including commissions and spreads). Thus, any one person can be wrong about the market-indeed, everyone can be-but the market as a whole is always right.

There are three common forms in which the efficient market hypothesis is commonly stated-weak form efficiency, semi-strong form efficiency and strong form efficiency, each of which have different implications for how markets work.

Weak-form Efficiency

- No excess returns can be earned by using investment strategies based on historical share prices or other financial data.
- Weak-form efficiency implies that Technical analysis techniques will not be able to consistently produce excess returns, though some forms of fundamental analysis may still provide excess returns.
- In a weak-form efficient market current share prices are the best, unbiased, estimate of the value of the security. Theoretical in nature, weak form efficiency advocates assert that fundamental analysis can be used to identify stocks that are undervalued and overvalued. Therefore, keen investors looking for profitable companies can earn profits by researching financial statements.

Semi-strong form Efficiency

- Share prices adjust within an arbitrarily small but finite amount of time and in an unbiased fashion to publicly available new information, so that no excess returns can be earned by trading on that information.
- Semi-strong form efficiency implies that Fundamental analysis techniques will not be able to reliably produce excess returns.
- To test for semi-strong form efficiency, the adjustments to previously unknown news must be of a reasonable size and must be instantaneous. To test for this, consistent upward or downward adjustments after the initial change must be looked for. If there are any such adjustments it would suggest that investors had interpreted the information in a biased fashion and hence in an inefficient manner.

Strong-form Efficiency

- Share prices reflect all information and no one can earn excess returns.
- If there are legal barriers to private information becoming public, as with insider trading laws, strong-form efficiency is impossible, except in the case where the laws are universally ignored. Studies on the U.S. stock market have shown that people do trade on inside information.
- To test for strong form efficiency, a market needs to exist where investors cannot consistently earn excess returns over a long period of time. Even if some money managers are consistently observed to beat the market, no refutation even of strong-form efficiency follows: with tens of thousands of fund managers worldwide, even a normal distribution of returns (as efficiency predicts) should be expected to produce a few dozen "star" performers.

Arguments Concerning the Validity of the Hypothesis

Some observers dispute the notion that markets behave consistently with the efficient market hypothesis, especially in its stronger forms. Some economists, mathematicians and market practitioners cannot believe that man-made markets are strong-form efficient when there are prima facie reasons for inefficiency including the slow diffusion of information, the relatively great power of some market participants (e.g. financial institutions), and the existence of apparently sophisticated professional investors. The way that markets react to surprising news is perhaps the most visible flaw in the efficient market hypothesis. For example, news events such as surprise interest rate changes from central banks are not instantaneously taken account of in stock prices, but rather cause sustained movement of prices over periods from hours to months.

Another observed discrepancy between the theory and real markets is that at market extremes what fundamentalists might consider irrational behaviour is the norm: in the late stages of a bull market, the market is driven by buyers who take little notice of underlying value. Towards the end of a crash, markets go into free fall as participants extricate themselves from positions regardless of the unusually good value that their positions represent. This is indicated by the large differences in the valuation of stocks compared to fundamentals (such as forward price to earnings ratios) in bull markets compared to bear markets. A theorist might say that rational (and hence, presumably, powerful) participants should always immediately take advantage of the artificially high or artificially low prices caused by the irrational participants by taking opposing positions, but this is observably not, in general, enough to prevent bubbles and crashes developing. It may be inferred that many rational participants are aware of the irrationality of the market at extremes and are willing to allow irrational participants to drive the market as far as they will, and only take advantage of the prices when they have more than merely fundamental reasons that the market will return towards fair value. Behavioural finance explains that when entering positions market participants are not driven primarily by whether prices are cheap or expensive, but by whether they expect them to rise or fall. To ignore this can be hazardous: Alan Greenspan warned of "irrational exuberance" in the markets in 1996, but some traders who sold short new economy stocks that seemed to be greatly overpriced around this time had to accept serious losses as prices reached even more extraordinary levels. As John Maynard Keynes succinctly commented, "Markets can remain irrational longer than you can remain solvent."

The efficient market hypothesis was introduced in the late 1960s. Prior to that, the prevailing view was that markets were inefficient. Inefficiency was commonly believed to exist e.g. in the United States and United Kingdom stock markets. However, earlier work by Kendall (1953) suggested that changes in UK stock market prices were random. Later work by Brealey and Dryden, and also by Cunningham found that there were no significant dependences in price changes suggesting that the UK stock market was weak-form efficient.

Further to this evidence that the UK stock market is weak form efficient, other studies of capital markets have pointed toward them being semi strong-form efficient. Studies by Firth

(1976, 1979 and 1980) in the United Kingdom have compared the share prices existing after a takeover announcement with the bid offer. Firth found that the share prices were fully and instantaneously adjusted to their correct levels, thus concluding that the UK stock market was semi strong-form efficient. The market's ability to efficiently respond to a short term and widely publicized event such as a takeover announcement cannot necessarily be taken as indicative of a market efficient at pricing regarding more long term and amorphous factors however.

Other empirical evidence in support of the EMH comes from studies showing that the return of market averages exceeds the return of actively managed mutual funds. Thus, to the extent that markets are inefficient, the benefits realized by seizing upon the inefficiencies are outweighed by the internal fund costs involved in finding them, acting upon them, advertising etc. These findings gave inspiration to the formation of passively managed index funds.

It may be that professional and other market participants who have discovered reliable trading rules or stratagems see no reason to divulge them to academic researchers. It might be that there is an information gap between the academics who study the markets and the professionals who work in them. Some observers point to seemingly inefficient features of the markets that can be exploited *e.g* seasonal tendencies and divergent returns to assets with various characteristics. E.g. factor analysis and studies of returns to different types of investment strategies suggest that some types of stocks may outperform the market long-term (e.g in the UK, the USA and Japan).

Skeptics of EMH argue that there exists a small number of investors who have outperformed the market over long periods of time, in a way which is difficult to attribute luck, including Peter Lynch, Warren Buffett, George Soros, and Bill Miller. These investors' strategies are to a large extent based on identifying markets where prices do not accurately reflect the available information, in direct contradiction to the efficient market hypothesis which explicitly implies that no such opportunities exist. Among the skeptics is Warren Buffett who has argued that the EMH is not correct, on one occasion wryly saying "I'd be a bum on the street with a tin cup if the markets were always efficient" and on another saying "The professors who taught Efficient Market Theory said that someone throwing darts at the stock tables could select stock portfolio having prospects just as good as one selected by the brightest, most hard-working securities analyst. Observing correctly that the market was frequently efficient, they went on to conclude incorrectly that it was always efficient." Adherents to a stronger form of the EMH argue that the hypothesis does not preclude-indeed it predicts-the existence of unusually successful investors or funds occurring through chance. They also argue that presentation of anecdotal evidence of star-performers to cast doubt on the hypothesis is rife with survivorship bias.

However, importantly, in 1962 Warren Buffett wrote: "I present this data to indicate the Dow as an investment competitor is no pushover, and the great bulk of investment funds in the country are going to have difficulty in bettering, or... even matching, its performance. Our portfolio is very different from that of the Dow. Our method of operation is substantially different from that of mutual funds."

The EMH and Popular Culture

EMH is commonly rejected by the general public due to a misconception concerning its meaning. Many believe that EMH says that a security's price is a correct representation of the value of that business, as calculated by what the business's future returns will actually be. In other words, they believe that EMH says a stock's price correctly predicts the underlying company's future results. Since stock prices clearly do not reflect company future results in many cases, many people reject EMH as clearly wrong.

However, EMH makes no such statement. Rather, it says that a stock's price represents an aggregation of the probabilities of all future outcomes for the company, based on the best information available at the time. Whether that information turns out to have been correct is not something required by EMH. Put another way, EMH does not require a stock's price to reflect a company's future performance, just the best possible estimate of that performance that can be made with publicly available information. That estimate may still be grossly wrong without violating EMH.

An Alternative Theory: Behavioral Finance

Opponents of the EMH sometimes cite examples of market movements that seem inexplicable in terms of conventional theories of stock price determination, for example the stock market crash of October 1987 where most stock exchanges crashed at the same time. It is virtually impossible to explain the scale of those market falls by reference to any news event at the time. The explanation may lie either in the mechanics of the exchanges (e.g. no safety nets to discontinue trading initiated by program sellers) or the peculiarities of human nature.

Behavioural psychology approaches to stock market trading are among some of the more promising alternatives to EMH (and some investment strategies seek to exploit exactly such inefficiencies). A growing field of research called behavioral finance studies how cognitive or emotional biases, which are individual or collective, create anomalies in market prices and returns that may be inexplicable via EMH alone. Ironically, the behaviourial finance programme can also be used to tangentially support the EMH-or rather it can explain the skepticism drawn by EMH-in that it helps to explain the human tendency to find and exploit patterns in data even where none exist. Some relevant examples of the Cognitive biases highlighted by the programme are: the Hindsight Bias; the Clustering illusion; the Overconfidence effect; the Observer-expectancy effect; the Gambler's fallacy; and the Illusion of control.

FAIR VALUE

Fair value, also called fair price, is a concept used in finance and economics, defined as a rational and unbiased estimate of the potential market price of a good, service, or asset, taking into account such factors as:

- relative scarcity
- perceived utility (economist's term for subjective value based on personal needs)

- potential risk/return characteristics (i.e., for a tradable asset)
- replacement costs, or costs of close substitutes
- production/distribution costs, including a cost of capital

Fair Value vs Market Price

There are two schools of thought about the relation between the market price and fair value in any kind of market, but especially with regards to tradable assets:

- The efficient market hypothesis asserts that, in a well organized, reasonably transparent market, the market price is generally equal to or close to the fair value, as investors react quickly to incorporate new information about relative scarcity, utility, or potential returns in their bids; see also Rational pricing.
- Behavioral finance asserts that the market price often diverges from fair value because of various, common cognitive biases among buyers or sellers. However, even proponents of behavioral finance generally acknowledge that behavioral anomalies that may cause such a divergence often do so in ways that are unpredictable, chaotic, or otherwise difficult to capture in a sustainably profitable trading strategy, especially when accounting for transaction costs.

Fair Value Measurements (US markets): Exposure Draft

The Financial Accounting Standards Board (FASB) issued Exposure Draft 1201-100 on June 23, 2004, to provide proposed guidance about how entities should determine fair value estimations for financial reporting purposes. The draft would apply broadly to financial and nonfinancial assets and liabilities measured at fair value under other authoritative accounting pronouncements. Absence of one single consistent framework for applying fair value measurements and developing a reliable estimate of a fair value in the absence of quoted prices has created inconsistencies and incomparability. The purpose of this exposure draft is to eliminate the inconsistencies by developing a solid framework to be used in any fair value measurements. The draft suggests the following definition for fair value: the price at which an asset or liability could be exchanged in a current transaction between knowledgeable, unrelated willing parties. It notes that the price is an estimate in the absence of an actual exchange. The exposure draft emphasizes the use of market inputs in valuing an asset or liability. The specific market inputs mentioned include: quoted prices, interest rates, yield curve, credit data, etc. Fair value is, by definition, derived from a current transaction which happens in an active market with knowledgeable and unrelated parties. When fair value is not available due to the lack of an actual transaction, it is logical to use information from an active market. However, sometimes quoted prices might not represent the best estimate of fair value.

The basis of the framework in the exposure draft centers on a fair value hierarchy. The hierarchy is suggested as a guide to determining what inputs to include in valuing an asset or liability at fair value. The hierarchy is broken down into three levels. Level One requires the use of quoted prices from an active market for identical assets or liabilities. To use this level, the entity must have immediate access to the market (could exchange in current condition). If more than one market is available, the exposure draft requires the use of the "most advantageous market." Both the price and costs to do the transaction must be considered.

Level Two requires the use of quoted prices for similar assets or liabilities in active markets. While in Level One an entity is not permitted to make any change to the quoted price, an entity may make price adjustments, as necessary, in Level Two since the assets or liabilities are only similar, not identical. It is stated, however, that any adjustment must be objective. If the adjustment is not objective or there are no similar goods in the active market, an entity must measure the fair value based on Level Three. This level requires the use of valuation techniques. The draft suggests the use of the market, income, and cost approach, unless the use of all three produces undue costs and effort. If that is the case, an entity is to use the approach that produces the best approximation of the fair value. Inputs used to determine the value should be external to the entity. The entity may only rely on internal information if the cost and effort to obtain external information is too high.

A working draft has been established for the fair value exposure draft. The working draft was released for comment on October 21, 2005. One of the noticeable changes in the working draft compared to the exposure draft is the addition of two more levels in the fair value hierarchy. Level three has been adjusted to only include assets or liabilities that have observable inputs other than quoted prices. It is also explained that financial instruments must have an input that is observable over the entire term of the instrument. The addition of the additional levels helps to eliminate the ambiguity associated with the first exposure draft. Instruments that have inputs that are not directly observable, but have corroboration through other data, are considered level four. Level Five encompasses any remaining valuation that requires all entity inputs and no market inputs.

Fundamental Theorem of Arbitrage-free Pricing

In a general sense, the fundamental theorem of arbitrage finance is a way to relate arbitrage opportunities with risk neutral measures that are equivalent to the original probability measure.

The Fundamental Theorem in a Finite State Market

In a finite state market, the fundamental theorem of arbitrage has two parts. The first part relates to existence of a risk neutral measure, while the second relates to the uniqueness of the measure:

1. The first part states that there is no arbitrage if and only if there exists a risk neutral measure that is equivalent to the original probability measure.
2. The second part states that a market is complete if and only if there is a unique risk neutral measure that is equivalent to the original probability measure.

The fundamental theorem of pricing is a way for the concept of arbitrage to be converted to a question about whether or not a risk neutral measure exists.

The fundamental theorem in more general markets. When stock price returns follow a single Brownian motion, there is a unique risk neutral measure. When the stock price process is assumed to follow a more general semi-martingale, then the concept of arbitrage is too strong, and a weaker concept such as no free lunch with vanishing risk must be used to describe these opportunities in an infinite dimensional setting.

HOMO ECONOMICUS

Homo economicus, or Economic man, is the concept in some economic theories of man (that is, a human) as a rational and self-interested actor who desires wealth, avoids unnecessary labor, and has the ability to make judgments towards those ends.

History of the Term

The term Economic Man was used for the first time in the late nineteenth century by critics of John Stuart Mill's work on political economy. Below is a passage from Mill's work that those 19th-century critics were referring to:

> *"[Political economy] does not treat the whole of man's nature as modified by the social state, nor of the whole conduct of man in society. It is concerned with him solely as a being who desires to possess wealth, and who is capable of judging the comparative efficacy of means for obtaining that end."*

Later in the same work, Mill goes on to write that he is proposing "an arbitrary definition of man, as a being who inevitably does that by which he may obtain the greatest amount of necessaries, conveniences, and luxuries, with the smallest quantity of labour and physical self-denial with which they can be obtained." Although the term did not come into use until the 19th century, it is often associated with the ideas of 18th century thinkers like Adam Smith and David Ricardo. In The Wealth of Nations, Smith wrote:

> *"It is not from the benevolence of the butcher, the brewer, or the baker that we expect our dinner, but from their regard to their own interest."*

This suggests the same sort of rational, self-interested, labor-averse individual that Mill proposes.

A wave of economists in the late 19th century-Francis Edgeworth, William Stanley Jevons, Leon Walras, and Vilfredo Pareto-built mathematical models on these assumptions. In the 20th century, Lionel Robbins' rational choice theory came to dominate mainstream economics and the term Economic Man took on a more specific meaning of a person who acted rationally on complete knowledge out of self-interest and the desire for wealth.

The Model

Homo economicus is a term used for an approximation or model of Homo sapiens that acts to obtain the highest possible well-being for himself given available information about opportunities and other constraints, both natural and institutional, on his ability to achieve his predetermined goals. This approach has been formalized in certain social science models, particularly in economics.

Homo economicus is seen as "rational" in the sense that well-being as defined by the utility function is optimized given perceived opportunities. That is, the individual seeks to attain very specific and predetermined goals to the greatest extent with the least possible cost. Note that this kind of "rationality" does not say that the individual's actual goals are "rational" in some larger ethical, social, or human sense, only that he tries to attain them at minimal cost. Only naive applications of the Homo economicus model assume that this hypothetical individual knows what is best for his long-term physical and mental health and can be relied upon to always make the right decision for himself. See rational choice theory and rational expectations for further discussion; the article on rationality widens the discussion.

As in social science in general, these assumptions are at best approximations. The term is often used derogatorily in academic literature, perhaps most commonly by sociologists, many of whom tend to prefer structural explanations to ones based on rational action by individuals.

The use of the Latin form Homo economicus is certainly long established; Persky (1995) traces it back to Pareto (1906) but notes that it may be older. The English term economic man can be found even earlier, in John Kells Ingram's A History of Political Economy (1888). The Oxford English Dictionary (O.E.D.) does not mention Homo economicus, but it is one of a number of phrases that imitate the scientific name for the human species. According to the O.E.D., the human genus name Homo is:

> *Used with L. or mock-L. adjs. in names imitating Homo sapiens, etc., and intended to personify some aspect of human life or behaviour (indicated by the adj.). Homo faber ("feIb@(r)) [H. Bergson L'Evolution Créatrice (1907) ii. 151], a term used to designate man as a maker of tools.) Variants are often comic: Homo insipiens; Homo turisticus.*

Note that such forms should logically keep the capital for the "genus" name-i.e., Homo economicus rather than homo economicus. Actual usage is inconsistent.

Criticisms

Homo economicus bases his choices on a consideration of his own personal "utility function". Economic man is also amoral, ignoring all social values unless adhering to them gives him utility. Some believe such assumptions about humans are not only empirically inaccurate but unethical.

Economists Thorstein Veblen, John Maynard Keynes, Herbert Simon, and many of the Austrian School criticise Homo economicus as an actor with too great of an understanding of macroeconomics and economic forecasting in his decision making. They stress uncertainty and bounded rationality in the making of economic decisions, rather than relying on the rational man who is fully informed of all circumstances impinging on his decisions. They argue that perfect knowledge never exists, which means that all economic activity implies risk.

Empirical studies by Amos Tversky questioned the assumption that investors are rational. In 1995, Tversky demonstrated the tendency of investors to make risk-averse choices in gains, and risk-seeking choices in losses. The investors appeared as very risk-averse for small losses but indifferent for a small chance of a very large loss. This violates economic rationality as usually understood. Further research on this subject, showing other deviations from conventionally-defined economic rationality, is being done in the growing field of experimental or behavioral economics. Some of the broader issues involved in this criticism are studied in Decision Theory of which Rational Choice Theory is only a subset.

Other critics of the Homo economicus model of humanity, such as Bruno Frey, point to the excessive emphasis on extrinsic motivation (rewards and punishments from the social environment) as opposed to intrinsic motivation. For example, it is difficult if not impossible to understand how Homo economicus would be a hero in war or would get inherent pleasure from craftsmanship. Frey and others argue that too much emphasis on rewards and punishments can "crowd out" (discourage) intrinsic motivation: paying a boy for doing household tasks may push him from doing those tasks "to help the family" to doing them simply for the reward.

Altruistic economics rejects the model as unrealistically selfish, arguing that real people have friends to whom they are to a greater or lesser degree altruistic, so it relaxes the restriction that people's utility functions must be independent.

Other critics argue that the purely self-interested behavior of the Homo economicus reflects the behavior of the psycopath and not that of the average participant in the economy. As such the Homo economicus can be considered to be a purely theoretical construct.

Another weakness is highlighted by sociologists, who argue that Homo economicus ignores an extremely important question, i.e., the origins of tastes and the parameters of the utility function by social influences, training, education, and the like. The exogeneity of tastes (preferences) in this model is the major distinction from Homo sociologicus, in which tastes are taken as partially or even totally determined by the societal environment.

Further critics, learning from the broadly-defined psychoanalytic tradition, criticize the Homo economicus model as ignoring the inner conflicts that real-world individuals suffer, as between short-term and long-term goals (e.g., eating chocolate cake and losing weight) or between individual goals and societal values. Such conflicts may lead to "irrational" behavior involving inconsistency, psychological paralysis, neurosis, and/or psychic pain.

One criticism contends that the Homo economicus model works as a self-fulfilling prophecy if a group of people (a company, a society) accepts its premises, particularly the idea that individuals only ever consider their personal utility function and that-as is often claimed-the "Invisible Hand" works to make these purely self-interested decisions promote the interest of society. Governance structures and social norms of such a group will effectively reward selfishness and discourage or ridicule deviant behavior like altruism, fairness, or teamwork; its idols will be those who most ruthlessly maximize their own utility function. This aspect has risen to wider attention in disciplines like organization science where extrinsic motivation has been found to be not nearly as effective with knowledge workers as it had been for traditional industries, creating a renewed interest in forms of motivation that do not fit into the Homo economicus model. This view however does not account for the fact that acting selfishly is not necessarily the same as acting in a self-interested manner, especially in social units in which altruistic and unselfish behavior is expected.

The clearest case of a self-fulfilling prophecy concerning Homo economicus has been in the teaching of economics. Several research studies have indicated that those students who take economics courses end up being more self-centered than before they took the courses. For example, they are less willing to co-operate with the other player in a "prisoner's-dilemma"-type game.

Responses

Economists tend to disagree with these critiques, arguing that it may be relevant to analyze the consequences of enlightened egoism just as it may be worthwhile to consider altruistic or social behavior. Others argue that we need to understand the consequences of such narrow-minded greed even if only a small percentage of the population embraces such motives. Free riders, for example, would have a major negative impact on the provision of public goods. However, economists' supply and demand predictions might obtain even if only a significant minority of market participants act like Homo economicus. In this view, the assumption of Homo economicus can and should be simply a preliminary step on the road to a more sophisticated model.

Yet others argue that Homo economicus is a reasonable approximation for behavior within market institutions, since the individualized nature of human action in such social settings encourages individualistic behavior. Not only do market settings encourage the application of a simple cost/benefit calculus by individuals, but they reward and thus attract the more individualistic people. It can be difficult to apply social values (as opposed to following self-interest) in an extremely competitive market; a company that refuses to pollute (for example) may find itself bankrupt.

Defenders of the Homo economicus model see many critics of the dominant school as using a straw-man technique. For example, it is common for critics to argue that real people do not have cost-less access to infinite information and an innate ability to instantly process it. However, in advanced-level theoretical economics, scholars have found ways of addressing these problems, modifying models enough to more realistically depict real-life decision-making. For example, models of individual behavior under bounded rationality and of people suffering from envy can be found in the literature. It is primarily when targeting the limiting assumptions made in constructing undergraduate models that the criticisms listed above are valid. These criticisms are especially valid to the extent that the professor asserts that the simplifying assumptions are true and/or uses them in a propagandistic way.

The more sophisticated economists are quite conscious of the empirical limitations of the Homo economicus model. In theory, the views of the critics can be combined with the Homo economicus model to attain a more accurate model.

One problem with making the Homo economicus model more sophisticated is that sometimes the model becomes tautologically true, i.e., true by definition. If someone has a "taste" for variety, for example, it becomes difficult if not impossible to distinguish economic rationality from irrationality. In this case, the Homo economicus model may not add any new information at all to our economic understanding.

Homo Sociologicus

Comparisons between economics and sociology have resulted in a corresponding term Homo sociologicus (introduced by German Sociologist Ralf Dahrendorf in 1958), to parody the image of human nature given in some sociological models that attempt to limit the social forces that determine individual tastes and social values. (The alternative or additional source of these would be biology.) Hirsch, Michaels, and Friedman (1990, p. 44) say that Homo sociologicus is largely a tabula rasa upon which societies and cultures write values and goals; unlike economicus, sociologicus acts not to pursue selfish interests but to fulfill social roles. This "individual" may appear to be all society and no individual. This suggests the need to combine the insights of Homo economicus models with those of Homo sociologicus models in order to create a synthesis, rather than rejecting one or the other.

RATIONAL CHOICE THEORY

Rational choice theory, also known as rational action theory, is a framework for understanding and often formally modeling social and economic behavior. It is the dominant theoretical paradigm in microeconomics. It is also central to modern political science and is used by scholars in other disciplines such as sociology. The 'rationality' described by rational choice theory is different from colloquial and most philosophical uses of rationality. Models of rational choice are very diverse but they share one thing in common. They all assume that individuals choose the best action according to stable preference functions and constraints facing them. Most models have additional assumptions. Proponents of rational choice models do not claim that a model's assumptions are a full description of reality, only that good models can aid reasoning and provide help in formulating falsifiable hypotheses, whether intuitive or not. Successful hypotheses are those that survive empirical tests.

Rational choice theory is a successor of much older descriptions of rational behavior. It is widely used as an assumption of the behavior of individuals in microeconomic models and analysis. Although rationality cannot be directly empirically tested, empirical tests can be conducted on some of the results derived from the models. Over the last decades it has also become increasingly employed in social sciences other than economics, such as sociology and political science.

Models that rely on rational choice theory often adopt methodological individualism, the assumption that social situations or collective behaviors are the result of individual actions.

Actions, Assumptions, and Individual Preferences

Rational decision making entails choosing an action given one's preferences, the actions one could take, and expectations about the outcomes of those actions. Actions are often expressed as a set, for example a set of j exhaustive and exclusive actions:

$A = \{a_1, ..., a_i, ..., a_j\}$

For example, if a person is to vote for either Roger, Sara, or abstain, her set of possible voting actions is:

A = {Roger, Sara, abstain}

Individuals can also have similar sets of possible outcomes.

Rational choice theory makes two assumptions about individuals' preferences for actions. First, is the assumption of completeness, that is that all actions can be ranked in an order of preference (indifference between two or more is possible). Second, is the transitivity, the assumption that if action a_1 is preferred to a_2, and action a_2 is preferred to a_3, then a_1 is preferred to a_3.

Together these assumptions form the result that given a set of exhaustive and exclusive actions to chose from, an individual can rank them in terms of her preferences, and that her preferences are consistent.

An individual's preferences can also take forms:

- Strict Preference occurs when an individual prefers a_1 to a_2, but not a_2 to a_1. In some models, a weak preference can be held in which an individual has a preference for at least a_j, similar to the mathematical operator $\leq$.
- Indifference occurs when an individual does not prefer a_1 to a_2, or a_2 to a_1.

In more complex models, other assumptions are often incorporated, such as the assumption of independence axiom. Also, with dynamic models that include decision-making over time, time inconsistency may affect an individual's preferences.

Other Assumptions

Often, to simplify calculation and facilitate testing, some possibly unrealistic assumptions are made about the world. These can include:

- An individual has full or perfect information about exactly what will occur under any choice made. More complex models rely on probability to describe outcomes.
- An individual has the cognitive ability, or time to weigh every choice against every other choice. Studies in to the limitations of this assumption are included in theories of bounded rationality.

Utility Maximization

Often preferences are described by their utility function or payoff function. This is an ordinal number an individual assigns over the available actions, such as:

$$u(a_i) > u(a_j)\ u(a_i) > u(a_j)$$

The individual's preferences are then expressed as the relation between these ordinal assignments. For example, if an individual prefers the candidate Sara over Roger over abstaining, their preferences would have the relation:

$$u(\text{sara}) > u(\text{roger}) > u(\text{abstain})$$

Criticism

Both the assumptions and the behavioral predictions of rational choice theory have sparked criticism from various camps. Some people have developed models of bounded rationality, which hope to be more psychologically plausible without completely abandoning the idea that reason underlies decision-making processes. For a long time, a popular strain of critique was a lack of empirical basis, but experimental economics and experimental game theory have largely changed that critique (although they have added other critiques, mainly by demonstrating some human behavior that consistently deviates from rational choice theory).

Rational choice has had far-reaching impacts on the study of political science, especially in fields like the study of interest groups, elections, behaviour in legislatures, coalitions, and bureaucracy.

Benefits of Rational Choice Theory

Describing the decisions made by individuals as rational and utility maximizing may seem to be a tautological explanation of their behavior that provided very little new information. While there may be many reasons for a rational choice theory approach, two are important for the social sciences. First, assuming humans make decisions in a rational, rather than stochastic manner implies that their behavior can be modeled and thus predictions can be made about future actions. Second, the mathematical formality of rational choice theory models allows social scientists to derive results from their models that may have otherwise not been seen.

Rationality

Rationality as a term is related to the idea of reason, a word which following Webster's may be derived as much from older terms referring to thinking itself as from giving an account or an explanation. This lends the term a dual aspect. One aspect associates it with comprehension, intelligence, or inference, particularly when an inference is drawn in ordered ways (thus a syllogism is a rational argument in this sense). The other part associates rationality with explanation, understanding or justification, particularly if it provides a ground or a motive. What is irrational, therefore, is defined as that which is not endowed with reason or understanding.

Rationality Contra Logic

A logical argument is sometimes described as "rational" if it is logically valid. However, rationality is a much broader term than logic, as it includes "uncertain but sensible" arguments based on probability, expectation, personal experience and the like, whereas logic deals principally with provable facts and demonstrably valid relations between them.

For example, ad hominem arguments are logically unsound, but in many cases they may be rational. A simple philosophical definition of rationality refers to one's use of a "practical syllogism". For example,

I am cold

If I close the window I will not be cold

Therefore, I closed the window

We should note that standard form practical syllogisms follow a very specific format and are always valid if constructed correctly though they are not necessarily sound. There are several notable implications of such a definition.

First, rationality is objective-it exists only when a valid practical syllogism is used.

Second, a choice is either rational or it is not-there is no gradation since there is no gradation between valid and invalid arguments.

Third, rationality only applies to actions-i.e., shutting the window is a rational thing to do if you are cold (assuming it is cold outside). Evidence bears on belief but not on rationality. All that is required for an action to be rational is that you believe that X and that if X then Y so you do Y. Arguments about belief are couched in the terms valid and sound-logically you must believe something if the argument supporting it is sound. In some cases, such as religious belief, the argument may be valid but its soundness cannot be known for the truth of its premises cannot be known.

Rationality in the Humanities and Social Sciences

In philosophy, rationality and reason are the key methods used to analyse the data gathered through systematically gathered observations. In economics, sociology, and political science, a decision or situation is often called rational if it is in some sense optimal, and individuals or organizations are often called rational if they tend to act somehow optimally in pursuit of their goals. Thus one speaks, for example, of a rational allocation of resources, or of a rational corporate strategy. In this concept of "rationality", the individual's goals or motives are taken for granted and not made subject to criticism, ethical or otherwise. Thus rationality simply refers to the success of goal attainment, whatever those goals may be. Sometimes, in this context, rationality is equated with behavior that is self-interested to the point of being selfish. Sometimes rationality implies having complete knowledge about all the details of a given situation. It might be said that because the goals are not important in definition of rationality, it really only demands logical consistency in choice making.

Debates arise in these three fields about whether or not people or organizations are "really" rational, as well as whether it make sense to model them as such in formal models. Some have argued that a kind of bounded rationality makes more sense for such models. Others think that any kind of rationality along the lines of rational choice theory is a useless concept for understanding human behavior; the term homo economicus (economic man: the imaginary logically consistent but amoral being assumed in economic models) was coined largely in honor of this view.

Rationality is a central principle in artificial intelligence, where a rational agent is specifically defined as an agent which always chooses the action which maximises its expected performance, given all of the knowledge it currently possesses.

Theories on Rationality

The German sociologist Max Weber proposed an interpretation of social action that distinguished between four different types of rationality. The first, which he called Zweckrational or purposive/instrumental rationality, is related to the expectations about the behavior of other human beings or objects in the environment. These expectations serve as means for a particular actor to attain ends, ends which Weber noted were "rationally pursued and calculated." The second type, Weber called Wertrational or value/belief-oriented. Here the action is undertaken for what one might call reasons intrinsic to the actor: some ethical, aesthetic, religious or other motive, independent of whether it will lead to success. The third type was effectual, determined by an actor's specific affect, feeling, or emotion-to which Weber himself said that this was a kind of rationality that was on the borderline of what he considered "meaningfully oriented." The fourth was traditional, determined by ingrained habituation. Weber emphasized that it was very unusual to find only one of these orientations: combinations were the norm. His usage also makes clear that he considered the first two as more significant than the others, and it is arguable that the third and fourth are subtypes of the first two. These kinds of rationality were ideal types.

The advantage in this interpretation is that it avoids a value-laden assessment, say, that certain kinds of beliefs are irrational. Instead, Weber suggests that a ground or motive can be given-for religious or affect reasons, for example-that may meet the criterion of explanation or justification even if it is not an explanation that fits the Zweckrational orientation of means and ends. The opposite is therefore also true: some means-ends explanations will not satisfy those whose grounds for action are 'Wertrational'.

Based on the premise that 'feelings of worthlessness' are a maladaptive by-product of the evolution of rationality, Phil Roberts, Jr. has proposed a theory in which the rationality of an end is presumed to correlate with the comprehensiveness of its underlying considerations, and in which no concrete objective is presumed to be rational in any but a relative sense of the term. In addition to its ability to explain what morality is (a shared subconscious theory of rationality), Roberts has also demonstrated how his theory can be employed to address a number of rationality paradoxes, including the paradox of rational irrationality, cognitive versus practical rationality conflict, the "rationality debate" (Cohen vs. Kahneman and Tversky) and the paradox of the Prisoner's Dilemma.

Use of the Term Rational

In a number of kinds of speech, "rational" may also denote a hodge-podge of generally positive attributes, including:

- reasonable: "having sound judgement and practical implementation" (Webster's)
- reasonable: "not extreme or excessive" (Webster's)
- justifiable on the basis of reason. (logical)
- economical, not wasteful ("rational management," "to rationalise" something)
- not foolish
- coherent

VOLATILITY ARBITRAGE

Volatility arbitrage, a.k.a. Vol Arb, is a type of statistical arbitrage that is implemented by trading a delta neutral portfolio of an option and its underlier. The objective is to take advantage of differences between the implied volatility of the option, and a forecast of future realized volatility of the option's underlier. In volatility arbitrage, volatility is used as the unit of relative measure rather than price-that is, traders attempt to buy "volatility" when it's low and sell "volatility" when it's high.

Overview

To an option trader engaging in volatility arbitrage, an option contract is a way to speculate in the volatility of the underlying rather than a directional bet on the underlier's price. If a trader buys options as part of a delta-neutral portfolio, he is said to be long volatility. If he sells options, he is said to be short volatility. So long as the trading is done delta-neutral, buying an option is a bet that the underlier's future realized volatility will be high, while selling an option is a bet that future realized volatility will be low. Because of put call parity, it doesn't matter if the options traded are calls or puts. This is true because put-call parity posits a risk neutral equivalence relationship between a call, a put and some amount of the underlier. Therefore, being long a delta neutral call results in the same returns as being long a delta neutral put.

Forecast Volatility

To engage in volatility arbitrage, a trader must first forecast the underlier's future realized volatility. This is typically done by computing the historic daily returns for the underlier for a given past sample such as 252 days, the number of trading days in a year. The trader may also use other factors, such as whether the period was unusually volatile, or if there are going to be unusual events in the near future, to adjust his forecast. For instance, if the current 252-day volatility for the returns on a stock is computed to be 15%, but it's known that an important patent dispute will likely be settled in the next year, the trader may decide that the appropriate forecast volatility for the stock is 18%. That is, based on past movements and upcoming events, the stock is most likely to be 18% higher or lower from its current price one year from today.

Market (Implied) Volatility

As described in option valuation techniques, there are a number of factors that are used to determine the theoretical value of an option. However, in practice, the only two inputs to the model that change during the day are the price of the underlier and the volatility. Therefore, the theoretical price of an option can be expressed as:

$$C = f(S, \sigma, .)$$

where is the price of the underlier, and is the estimate of future volatility. Because the theoretical price function f(.) is a monotonically increasing function of g(), there must be a corresponding monotonically increasing function that expresses the volatility implied by the option's market price $\bar{C}$, or

$$\sigma_{\bar{C}} = g(\bar{C}, .)$$

Or, in other words, when all other inputs including the stock price C are held constant, there exists no more than one implied volatility $\sigma_{\bar{C}}$ for each market price $\bar{C}$ for the option.

Because implied volatility of an option can remain constant even as the underlier's value changes, traders use it as a measure of relative value rather than the option's market price. For instance, if a trader can buy an option whose implied volatility $\sigma_{\bar{C}}$ is 10%, it's common to say that the trader can "buy the option for 10%". Conversely, if the trader can sell an option whose implied volatility is 20%, it is said the trader can "sell the option at 20%". For example, assume a call option is trading at $1.90 with the underlier's price at $45.50, yielding an implied volatility of 17.5%. A short time later, the same option might trade at $2.50 with the underlier's price at $46.36, yielding an implied volatility of 16.8%. Even though the option's price is higher at the second measurement, the option is still considered cheaper because the implied volatility is lower. The reason this is true is because the trader can sell stock needed to hedge the long call at a higher price.

Mechanism

Armed with a forecast volatility, and capable of measuring an option's market price in terms of implied volatility, the trader is ready to begin a volatility arbitrage trade. A trader looks for options where the implied volatility, $\sigma_{\bar{C}}$ is either significantly lower than or higher than the forecast realized volatility σ, for the underlier. In the first case, the trader buys the option and hedges with the underlier to make a delta neutral portfolio. In the second case, the trader sells the option and then hedges them. Over the holding period, the trader will realize a profit on the trade if the underlier's realized volatility is closer to his forecast than it is to the market's forecast (i.e. the implied volatility). The profit is extracted from the trade through the continual re-hedging required to keep the portfolio delta neutral.

CAPITAL ASSET PRICING MODEL

The Capital Asset Pricing Model (CAPM) is used in finance to determine a theoretically appropriate required rate of return (and thus the price if expected cash flows can be estimated) of an asset, if that asset is to be added to an already well-diversified portfolio, given that asset's non-diversifiable risk. The CAPM formula takes into account the asset's sensitivity to non-diversifiable risk (also known as systematic risk or market risk), in a number often referred to as beta (β) in the financial industry, as well as the expected return of the market and the expected return of a theoretical risk-free asset.

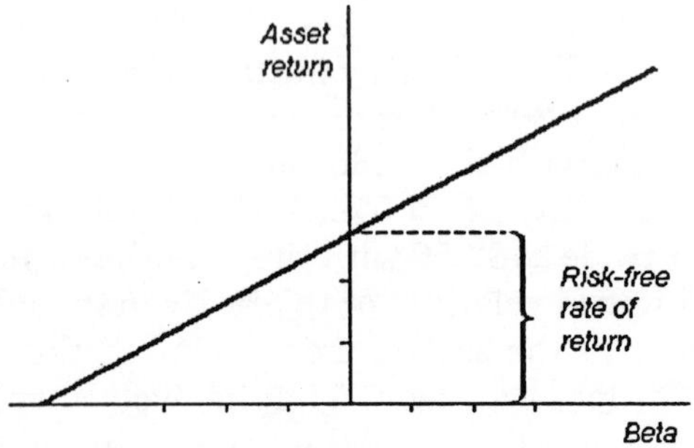

The Security Market Line, seen here in a graph, describes a relation between the beta and the asset's expected rate of return.

The model was introduced by Jack Treynor, William Sharpe, John Lintner and Jan Mossin independently, building on the earlier work of Harry Markowitz on diversification and modern portfolio theory. Sharpe received the Nobel Memorial Prize in Economics (jointly with Harry Markowitz and Merton Miller) for this contribution to the field of financial economics.

The Formula

The CAPM is a model for pricing an individual security (asset) or a portfolio. For individual security perspective, we made use of the security market line (SML) and its relation to expected return and systematic risk (beta) to show how the market must price individual securities in relation to their security risk class. The SML enables us to calculate the reward-to-risk ratio for any security in relation to that of the overall market. Therefore, when the expected rate of return for any security is deflated by its beta coefficient, the reward-to-risk ratio for any individual security in the market is equal to the market reward-to-risk ratio, thus:

Individual security's / beta = Market's securities (portfolio)
Reward-to-risk ratio Reward-to-risk ratio

$$\frac{E(R_i) - R_f}{\beta_{im}} = E(R_m) - R_f,$$

The market reward-to-risk ratio is effectively the market risk premium and by rearranging the above equation and solving for E(Ri), we obtain the Capital Asset Pricing Model (CAPM).

$$E(R_i) = R_f + \beta_{im}\left(E(R_m) - R_f\right).$$

Where:

- $E(R_i)$ is the expected return on the capital asset
- R_f is the risk-free rate of interest
- β_{im} (the beta coefficient) the sensitivity of the asset returns to market returns, or also $\beta_{im} = \frac{Cov(R_i, R_m)}{Var(R_m)}$,
- $E(R_m)$ is the expected return of the market
- $E(R_m)-R_f$ is sometimes known as the market premium or risk premium (the difference between the expected market rate of return and the risk-free rate of return). Note 1: the expected market rate of return is usually measured by looking at the arithmetic average of the historical returns on a market portfolio (i.e. S&P 500). Note 2: the risk free rate of return used for determining the risk premium is usually the arithmetic average of historical risk free rates of return and not the current risk free rate of return.

Asset Pricing

Once the expected return, $E(R_i)$, is calculated using CAPM, the future cash flows of the asset can be discounted to their present value using this rate ($E(R_i)$), to establish the correct price for the asset. In theory, therefore, an asset is correctly priced when its observed price is the same as its value calculated using the CAPM derived discount rate. If the observed price is higher than the valuation, then the asset is overvalued (and undervalued when the observed price is below the CAPM valuation).

Alternatively, one can "solve for the discount rate" for the observed price given a particular valuation model and compare that discount rate with the CAPM rate. If the discount rate in the model is lower than the CAPM rate then the asset is overvalued (and undervalued for a too high discount rate).

Asset-specific Required Return

The CAPM returns the asset-appropriate required return or discount rate-i.e. the rate at which future cash flows produced by the asset should be discounted given that asset's relative riskiness. Betas exceeding one signify more than average "riskiness"; betas below one indicate lower than average. Thus a more risky stock will have a higher beta and will be discounted at a higher rate; less sensitive stocks will have lower betas and be discounted at a lower rate. The CAPM is consistent with intuition-investors (should) require a higher return for holding a more risky asset.

Since beta reflects asset-specific sensitivity to non-diversifiable, i.e. market risk, the market as a whole, by definition, has a beta of one. Stock market indices are frequently used as local proxies for the market-and in that case (by definition) have a beta of one. An investor in a large, diversified portfolio (such as a mutual fund) therefore expects performance in line with the market.

Risk and Diversification

The risk of a portfolio comprises systematic risk and unsystematic risk which is also known as idiosyncratic risk. Systematic risk refers to the risk common to all securities-i.e. market risk. Unsystematic risk is the risk associated with individual assets. Unsystematic risk can be diversified away to smaller levels by including a greater number of assets in the portfolio. (specific risks "average out"); systematic risk (within one market) cannot. Depending on the market, a portfolio of approximately 30-40 securities in developed markets such as UK or US (more in case of developing markets because of higher asset volatilities) will render the portfolio sufficiently diversified to limit exposure to systemic risk only.

A rational investor should not take on any diversifiable risk, as only non-diversifiable risks are rewarded within the scope of this model. Therefore, the required return on an asset, that is, the return that compensates for risk taken, must be linked to its riskiness in a portfolio context-i.e. its contribution to overall portfolio riskiness-as opposed to its "stand alone riskiness." In the CAPM context, portfolio risk is represented by higher variance i.e. less predictability. In other words the beta of the portfolio is the defining factor in rewarding the systematic exposure taken by an investor.

The Efficient Frontier

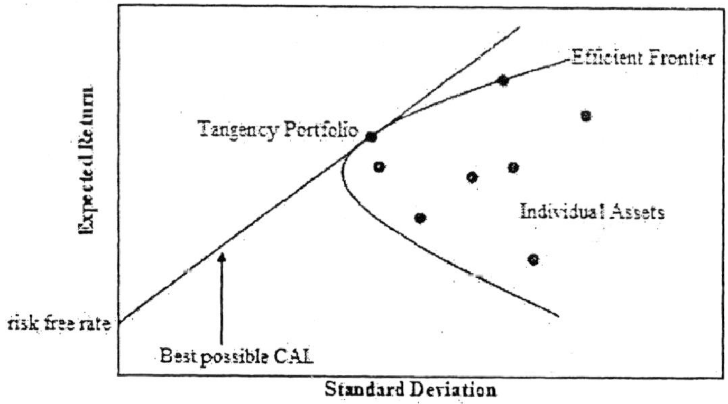

The (Markowitz) Efficient Frontier

The CAPM assumes that the risk-return profile of a portfolio can be optimized-an optimal portfolio displays the lowest possible level of risk for its level of return. Additionally, since each additional asset introduced into a portfolio further diversifies the portfolio, the optimal portfolio must comprise every asset, (assuming no trading costs) with each asset value-weighted to achieve the above (assuming that any asset is infinitely divisible). All such optimal portfolios, i.e., one for each level of return, comprise the efficient frontier.

Because the unsystematic risk is diversifiable, the total risk of a portfolio can be viewed as beta.

The Market Portfolio

An investor might choose to invest a proportion of his or her wealth in a portfolio of risky assets with the remainder in cash-earning interest at the risk free rate (or indeed may borrow money to fund his or her purchase of risky assets in which case there is a negative cash weighting). Here, the ratio of risky assets to risk free asset does not determine overall return-this relationship is clearly linear. It is thus possible to achieve a particular return in one of two ways:

1. By investing all of one's wealth in a risky portfolio,
2. or by investing a proportion in a risky portfolio and the remainder in cash (either borrowed or invested).

For a given level of return, however, only one of these portfolios will be optimal (in the sense of lowest risk). Since the risk free asset is, by definition, uncorrelated with any other asset, option 2 will generally have the lower variance and hence be the more efficient of the two.

This relationship also holds for portfolios along the efficient frontier: a higher return portfolio plus cash is more efficient than a lower return portfolio alone for that lower level of return. For a given risk free rate, there is only one optimal portfolio which can be combined with cash to achieve the lowest level of risk for any possible return. This is the market portfolio.

Assumptions of CAPM

- All investors have rational expectations.
- There are no arbitrage opportunities.
- Returns are distributed normally.
- Fixed quantity of assets.
- Perfectly efficient capital markets.
- Investors are solely concerned with level and uncertainty of future wealth
- Separation of financial and production sectors.
- Thus, production plans are fixed.
- Risk-free rates exist with limitless borrowing capacity and universal access.
- The Risk-free borrowing and lending rates are equal.
- No inflation and no change in the level of interest rate exists.

- Perfect information, hence all investors have the same expectations about security returns for any given time period.

Shortcomings of CAPM

- The model assumes that asset returns are (jointly) normally distributed random variables. It is however frequently observed that returns in equity and other markets are not normally distributed. As a result, large swings (3 to 6 standard deviations from the mean) occur in the market more frequently than the normal distribution assumption would expect.
- The model assumes that the variance of returns is an adequate measurement of risk. This might be justified under the assumption of normally distributed returns, but for general return distributions other risk measures (like coherent risk measures) will likely reflect the investors' preferences more adequately.
- The model does not appear to adequately explain the variation in stock returns. Empirical studies show that low beta stocks may offer higher returns than the model would predict. Some data to this effect was presented as early as a 1969 conference in Buffalo, New York in a paper by Fischer Black, Michael Jensen, and Myron Scholes. Either that fact is itself rational (which saves the efficient markets hypothesis but makes CAPM wrong), or it is irrational (which saves CAPM, but makes EMH wrong-indeed, this possibility makes volatility arbitrage a strategy for reliably beating the market).
- The model assumes that given a certain expected return investors will prefer lower risk (lower variance) to higher risk and conversely given a certain level of risk will prefer higher returns to lower ones. It does not allow for investors who will accept lower returns for higher risk. Casino gamblers clearly pay for risk, and it is possible that some stock traders will pay for risk as well.
- The model assumes that all investors have access to the same information and agree about the risk and expected

return of all assets. (Homogeneous expectations assumption)

- The model assumes that there are no taxes or transaction costs, although this assumption may be relaxed with more complicated versions of the model.
- The market portfolio consists of all assets in all markets, where each asset is weighted by its market capitalization. This assumes no preference between markets and assets for individual investors, and that investors choose assets solely as a function of their risk-return profile. It also assumes that all assets are infinitely divisible as to the amount which may be held or transacted.
- The market portfolio should in theory include all types of assets that are held by anyone as an investment (including works of art, real estate, human capital...) In practice, such a market portfolio is unobservable and people usually substitute a stock index as a proxy for the true market portfolio. Unfortunately, it has been shown that this substitution is not innocuous and can lead to false inferences as to the validity of the CAPM, and it has been said that due to the inobservability of the true market portfolio, the CAPM might not be empirically testable. This was presented in greater depth in a paper by Richard Roll in 1977, and is generally referred to as Roll's Critique. Theories such as the Arbitrage Pricing Theory (APT) have since been formulated to circumvent this problem.
- Because CAPM prices a stock in terms of all stocks and bonds, it is really an arbitrage pricing model which throws no light on how a firm's beta gets determined.

3

Modern Portfolio Theory

CAPITAL MARKET LINE

Modern portfolio theory (MPT) proposes how rational investors will use diversification to optimize their portfolios, and how a risky asset should be priced. The basic concepts of the theory are Markowitz diversification, the efficient frontier, capital asset pricing model, the alpha and beta coefficients, the Capital Market Line and the Securities Market Line.

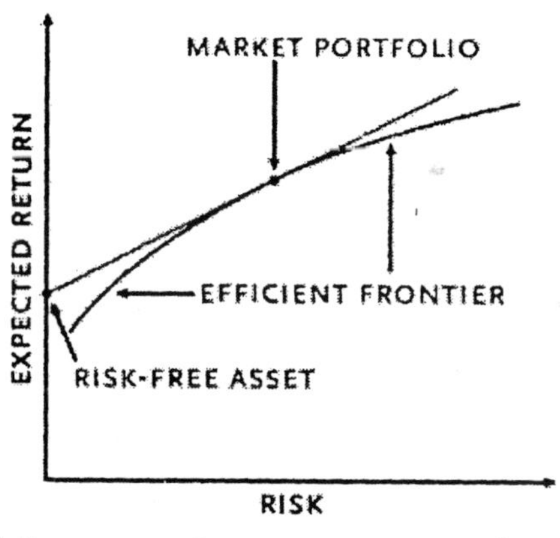

MPT models an asset's return as a random variable, and models a portfolio as a weighted combination of assets; the return of a portfolio is thus the weighted combination of the assets' returns. Moreover, a portfolio's return is a random variable, and consequently has an expected value and a variance. Risk, in this model, is the standard deviation of the portfolio's return.

RISK AND REWARD

The model assumes that investors are risk averse. This means that given two assets that offer the same expected return, investors will prefer the less risky one. Thus, an investor will take on increased risk only if compensated by higher expected returns. Conversely, an investor who wants higher returns must accept more risk. The exact trade-off will differ by investor based on individual risk aversion characteristics. The implication is that a rational investor will not invest in a portfolio if a second portfolio exists with a more favourable risk-return profile-i.e. if for that level of risk an alternative portfolio exists which has better expected returns.

MEAN AND VARIANCE

It is further assumed that investor's risk / reward preference can be described via a quadratic utility function. The effect of this assumption is that only the expected return and the volatility (i.e. mean return and standard deviation) matter to the investor. The investor is indifferent to other characteristics of the distribution of returns, such as its skew. Note that the theory uses a historical parameter, volatility, as a proxy for risk, while return is an expectation on the future.

Recent innovations in portfolio theory, particularly under the rubric of Post-Modern Portfolio Theory (PMPT), have exposed many flaws in this total reliance on standard deviation as the investor's risk proxy. Under the model:

- Portfolio return is the proportion-weighted combination of the constituent assets' returns.
- Portfolio volatility is a function of the correlation of the component assets. The change in volatility is non-linear as the weighting of the component assets changes.

Mathematically

In general:

- Expected return:

$$E(R_p) = \sum_i w_i E(R_i)$$

Where R is return.

- Portfolio variance:

$$\sigma_P^2 = \sum_i \sum_j w_i w_j \sigma_{ij} = \sum_i \sum_j w_i w_j \sigma_i \sigma_j \rho_{ij}$$

- Portfolio volatility:

$$\sigma_P = \sqrt{\sigma_P^2}$$

For a two asset portfolio:

- Portfolio return:

$$E(R_P) = w_A E(R_A) + (1 - w_A) E(R_B)$$

$$= w_A E(R_A) + w_B E(R_B)$$

- Portfolio variance:

$$\sigma_P^2 = w_A^2 \sigma_A^2 + w_B^2 \sigma_B^2 + 2 w_A w_B \rho_{AB} \sigma_A \sigma_B$$

For a three asset portfolio, the variance is:

$$w_A^2 \sigma_A^2 + w_B^2 \sigma_B^2 + w_C^2 \sigma_C^2$$

$$+2 w_A w_B \rho_{AB} \sigma_A \sigma_B + 2 w_A w_C \rho_{AC} \sigma_A \sigma_C + 2 w_B w_C \rho_{BC} \sigma_B \sigma_C$$

As can be seen, as the number of assets (n) in the portfolio increases, the calculation becomes "computationally intensive"- the number of covariance terms = n (n-1) /2. For this reason, portfolio computations usually require specialized software. These values can also be modeled using matrices; for a manageable number of assets, these statistics can be calculated using a spreadsheet.

DIVERSIFICATION

An investor can reduce portfolio risk simply by holding instruments which are not perfectly correlated. In other words, investors can reduce their exposure to individual asset risk by holding a diversified portfolio of assets. Diversification will allow for the same portfolio return with reduced risk. For diversification to work the component assets must not be perfectly correlated, i.e. correlation coefficient not equal to 1. As the formula above shows, if all assets of a portfolio have a correlation of 0, the portfolio variance and hence volatility will be the weighted average of the individual instruments' volatilities. If correlation is less than zero, that is, the assets are inversely correlated, the portfolio's volatility is less than the weighted average of the volatilities, and vice-versa.

CAPITAL ALLOCATION LINE

The Capital Allocation Line (CAL) is the line of expected return plotted against risk (standard deviation) that connects all portfolios that can be formed using a risky asset and a riskless asset. It can be proven that it is a straight line and that it has the following equation.

$$\text{CAL}: E(r_C) = r_F + \sigma_C \frac{E(r_P) - r_F}{\sigma_P}$$

In this formula P is the risky portfolio, F is the riskless portfolio and C is a combination of portfolios P and F.

The efficient frontier

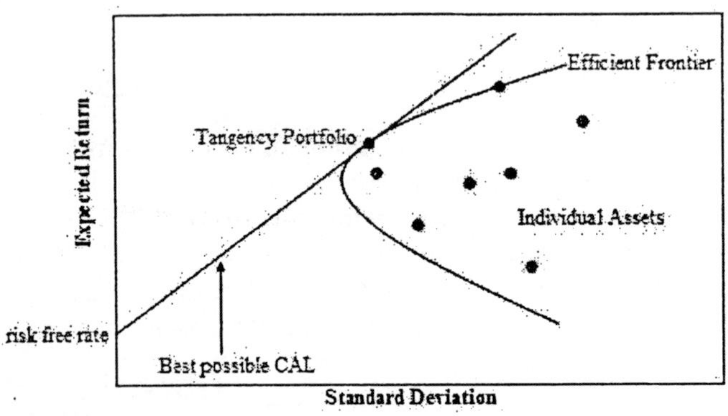

EFFICIENT FRONTIER

Every possible asset combination can be plotted in risk-return space, and the collection of all such possible portfolios defines a region in this space. The line along the upper edge of this region is known as the efficient frontier (sometimes "the

Markowitz frontier"). Combinations along this line represent portfolios for which there is lowest risk for a given level of return. Conversely, for a given amount of risk, the portfolio lying on the efficient frontier represents the combination offering the best possible return. Mathematically the Efficient Frontier is the intersection of the Set of Portfolios with Minimum Variance and the Set of Portfolios with Maximum Return.

The efficient frontier is illustrated above, with return μ_p on the y axis, and risk σ_p on the x axis; an alternative illustration from the diagram in the CAPM article is at right.

The efficient frontier will be convex-this is because the risk-return characteristics of a portfolio change in a non-linear fashion as its component weightings are changed. (As described above, portfolio risk is a function of the correlation of the component assets, and thus changes in a non-linear fashion as the weighting of component assets changes.) The efficient frontier is a parabola (hyperbola) when expected return is plotted against variance (standard deviation).

The region above the frontier is unachievable by holding risky assets alone. No portfolios can be constructed corresponding to the points in this region. Points below the frontier are suboptimal. A rational investor will hold a portfolio only on the frontier.

THE RISK-FREE ASSET

The risk-free asset is the (hypothetical) asset which pays a risk-free rate-it is usually proxied by an investment in short-dated Government securities. The risk-free asset has zero variance in returns (hence is risk-free); it is also uncorrelated with any other asset (by definition: since its variance is zero). As a result, when it is combined with any other asset, or portfolio of assets, the change in return and also in risk is linear.

Because both risk and return change linearly as the risk-free asset is introduced into a portfolio, this combination will plot a straight line in risk-return space. The line starts at 100% in cash and weight of the risky portfolio = 0 (i.e. intercepting the return axis at the risk-free rate) and goes through the portfolio in question where cash holding = 0 and portfolio weight = 1.

Mathematically:

Using the formulae for a two asset portfolio as above:

- Return is the weighted average of the risk free asset, f, and the risky portfolio, p, and is therefore linear:

$$\text{Return} = w_f E(R_f) + w_P E(R_P)$$

- Since the asset is risk free, portfolio standard deviation is simply a function of the weight of the risky portfolio in the position. This relationship is linear.

$$\text{Standard deviation} = w_f^2\sigma_f^2 + w_P^2\sigma_P^2 + 2w_f w_P \sigma_{fP}$$

$$= \sqrt{w_f^2.0 + w_P^2\sigma_P^2 + 2w_f w_P.0}$$

$$= \sqrt{w_P^2\sigma_P^2}$$

$$= w_P\sigma_P$$

PORTFOLIO LEVERAGE

An investor can add leverage to the portfolio by borrowing the risk-free asset. The addition of the risk-free asset allows for a position in the region above the efficient frontier. Thus, by combining a risk-free asset with risky assets, it is possible to construct portfolios whose risk-return profiles are superior to those on the efficient frontier.

- An investor holding a portfolio of risky assets, with a holding in cash, has a positive risk-free weighting (a de-leveraged portfolio). The return and standard deviation will be lower than the portfolio alone, but since the efficient frontier is convex, this combination will sit above the efficient frontier-i.e. offering a higher return for the same risk as the point below it on the frontier.
- The investor who borrows money to fund his/her purchase of the risky assets has a negative risk-free weighting-i.e a leveraged portfolio. Here the return is geared to the risky portfolio. This combination will again offer a return superior to those on the frontier.

THE MARKET PORTFOLIO

The efficient frontier is a collection of portfolios, each one optimal for a given amount of risk. A quantity known as the Sharpe ratio represents a measure of the amount of additional return (above the risk-free rate) a portfolio provides compared to the risk it carries. The portfolio on the efficient frontier with the highest Sharpe Ratio is known as the market portfolio, or sometimes the super-efficient portfolio; it is the tangency-portfolio in the above diagram.

This portfolio has the property that any combination of it and the risk-free asset will produce a return that is above the efficient frontier-offering a larger return for a given amount of risk than a portfolio of risky assets on the frontier would.

CAPITAL MARKET LINE

When the market portfolio is combined with the risk-free asset, the result is the Capital Market Line. All points along the CML have superior risk-return profiles to any portfolio on the efficient frontier. (The market portfolio with zero cash weighting is on the efficient frontier; additions of cash or leverage with the risk-free asset in combination with the market portfolio are on the Capital Market Line. All of these portfolio represent the highest Sharpe ratios possible.)

The CML is illustrated above, with return μ_p on the y axis, and risk σ_p on the x axis.

One can prove that the CML is the optimal CAL and that its equation is:

$$\text{CAL} : E(r_C) = r_F + \sigma_C \frac{E(r_P) - r_F}{\sigma_M}$$

ASSET PRICING

A rational investor would not invest in an asset which does not improve the risk-return characteristics of his existing portfolio. Since a rational investor would hold the market portfolio, the asset in question will be added to the market portfolio. MPT derives the required return for a correctly priced asset in this context.

Systematic Risk and Specific Risk

Specific risk is the risk associated with individual assets-within a portfolio these risks can be reduced through diversification (specific risks "cancel out").

Systematic risk, or market risk, refers to the risk common to all securities-except for selling short as noted below, systematic risk cannot be diversified away (within one market). Within the market portfolio, asset specific risk will be diversified away to the extent possible. Systematic risk is therefore equated with the risk (standard deviation) of the market portfolio.

Since a security will be purchased only if it improves the risk / return characteristics of the market portfolio, the risk of a security will be the risk it adds to the market portfolio. In this context, the volatility of the asset, and its correlation with the market portfolio, is historically observed and is therefore a given (there are several approaches to asset pricing that attempt to price assets by modelling the stochastic properties of the moments of assets' returns-these are broadly referred to as conditional asset pricing models).

The (maximum) price paid for any particular asset (and hence the return it will generate) should also be determined based on its relationship with the market portfolio.

Systematic risks within one market can be managed through a strategy of using both long and short positions within one portfolio, creating a "market neutral" portfolio.

Security Characteristic Line

The Security Characteristic Line (SCL) represents the relationship between the market return (r_M) and the return of a given asset i (r_i) at a given time t.

In general, it is reasonable to assume that the SCL is a straight line and can be illustrated as a statistical equation:

$$SCL = r_{it} = \alpha_i + \beta_i r_{Mt} + \varepsilon_{it}$$

where ai is called the asset's alpha coefficient and βi the asset's beta coefficient.

CAPITAL ASSET PRICING MODEL

The asset return depends on the amount for the asset today. The price paid must ensure that the market portfolio's risk / return characteristics improve when the asset is added to it. The CAPM is a model which derives the theoretical required return (i.e. discount rate) for an asset in a market, given the risk-free rate available to investors and the risk of the market as a whole.

The CAPM is usually expressed:

$$E(R_i) = R_f + \beta_i \left(E(R_m) - R_f\right)$$

- β, Beta, is the measure of asset sensitivity to a movement in the overall market; Beta is usually found via regression on historical data. Betas exceeding one signify more than average "riskiness"; betas below one indicate lower than average.
- $(E(R_M)-R_f)$ is the market premium, the historically observed excess return of the market over the risk-free rate.

Once the expected return, $E(r_i)$, is calculated using CAPM, the future cash flows of the asset can be discounted to their present value using this rate to establish the correct price for the asset. (Here again, the theory accepts in its assumptions that a parameter based on past data can be combined with a future expectation.)

A more risky stock will have a higher beta and will be discounted at a higher rate; less sensitive stocks will have lower betas and be discounted at a lower rate. In theory, an asset is correctly priced when its observed price is the same as its value calculated using the CAPM derived discount rate. If the observed price is higher than the valuation, then the asset is overvalued; it is undervalued for a too low price.

Mathematically:

(1) The incremental impact on risk and return when an additional risky asset, a, is added to the market portfolio, m, follows from the formulae for a two asset portfolio.

These results are used to derive the asset appropriate discount rate.

$$\text{Risk} = w_m^2\sigma_m^2 + \left[w_a^2\sigma_a^2 + 2w_m w_a \rho_{am}\sigma_a\sigma_m\right]$$

Hence, risk added to portfolio = $\left[w_a^2\sigma_a^2 + 2w_m w_a \rho_{am}\sigma_a\sigma_m\right]$

but since the weight of the asset will be relatively low, $w_a^2 \approx 0$

i.e. additional risk = $[2w_m w_a \rho_{am}\sigma_a\sigma_m]$

$$\text{Return} = \left(w_m E(R_m) + \left[w_a E(R_a)\right]\right)$$

Hence additional return = $\left[w_a E(R_a)\right]$

(2) If an asset, a, is correctly priced, the improvement in risk to return achieved by adding it to the market portfolio, m, will at least match the gains of spending that money on an increased stake in the market portfolio. The assumption is that the investor will purchase the asset with funds borrowed at the risk-free rate, R_f; this is rational if $E(R_a) > R_f$.

$$\text{Thus: } \left[w_a\left(E(R_a) - R_f\right)\right] / \left[2w_m w_a \rho_{am}\sigma_a\sigma_m\right]$$

$$= \left[w_a\left(E(R_m) - R_f\right) 2w_m w_a \sigma_m\sigma_m\right]$$

$$\text{i.e.: } \left[E(R_a)\right] = R_f + \left[E(R_m) - R_f\right] * \left[\rho_{am}\sigma_a\sigma_m\right] / \left[\sigma_m\sigma_m\right]$$

$$\text{i.e.: } \left[E(R_a)\right] = R_f + \left[E(R_m) - R_f\right] * \left[\sigma_{am}\right] / \left[\sigma_{mm}\right]$$

$[\sigma_{am}]/[\sigma_{mm}]$ is the "beta", β-- the covariance between the asset and the market compared to the variance of the market, i.e. the sensitivity of the asset price to movement in the market portfolio.

Securities Market Line

The SML essentially graphs the results from the capital asset pricing model (CAPM) formula. The X-axis represents the risk (beta), and the Y-axis represents the expected return. The market risk premium is determined from the slope of the SML.

The relationship between Beta & required return is plotted on the securities market line (SML) which shows expected return as a function of β. The intercept is the risk-free rate available for the market, while the slope is $\left(E\left(R_m\right)-R_f\right)$.. The Securities market line can be regarded as representing a single-factor model of the asset price, where Beta is exposure to changes in value of the Market. The equation of the SML is thus:

$$SML: E\left(R_i\right)-R_f=\beta_i\left(E\left(R_M\right)-R_f\right)$$

It is a useful tool in determining if an asset being considered for a portfolio offers a reasonable expected return for risk. Individual securities are plotted on the SML graph. If the security's risk versus expected return is plotted above the SML, it is undervalued since the investor can expect a greater return for the inherent risk. And a security plotted below the SML is overvalued since the investor would be accepting less return for the amount of risk assumed.

Comparison with Arbitrage Pricing Theory

The SML and CAPM are often contrasted with the Arbitrage pricing theory (APT), which holds that the expected return of a financial asset can be modeled as a linear function of various macro-economic factors, where sensitivity to changes in each factor is represented by a factor specific beta coefficient.

The APT is less restrictive in its assumptions: it allows for an explanatory (as opposed to statistical) model of asset returns, and assumes that each investor will hold a unique portfolio with its own particular array of betas, as opposed to the identical "market portfolio". Unlike the CAPM, the APT, however, does not itself reveal the identity of its priced factors-the number and nature of these factors is likely to change over time and between economies.

Super-diversification

The highest degree of diversification occurs when institutional asset class funds are used to construct a financial portfolio. The term was first introduced in Wealth Without Worry by Jim Whiddon and Lance Alston (Brown Books, 2005) who apply the fundamental academic research of Eugene Fama and Professor Kenneth French.

A super-diversified, asset class portfolio holds somewhere between 10,000 and 12,000 securities through a smaller number of institutional asset class funds.

EARNINGS RESPONSE COEFFICIENT

In arbitrage pricing theory, the earnings response coefficient (ERC) expresses the relationship between equity returns and unexpected earnings announcements.

The efficient market hypothesis posits that equity prices reflect all relevant information at a given time. Consequently, any change in equity value results from a change in relevant information. To this end, the earnings response coefficient measures equity returns related to unexpected earnings information.

The ERC is expressed mathematically as follows:

$$R = a + b(ern - u) + e$$

R = the expected return

a = benchmark rate

b = earning response coefficient

(ern-u) = unexpected earnings

e = random movement

There is some debate concerning the nature and strength of this relationship. As demonstrated in the above model, the ERC is generally considered to be the slope coefficient of a linear relationship between unexpected earnings and equity return. However, certain research results suggest that the relationship is nonlinear.

Post Earnings Announcement Drift

The post earnings announcement drift anomaly means the tendency for stocks to earn abnormally high returns in the three quarters following a positive earnings announcement, and to earn abnormally low returns in the three quarters following a negative earnings announcement.

The phenomenon can be explained with a number of hypotheses. The most widely accepted explanation for the effect is investor under-reaction to earnings announcements.

This was initially proposed by the information content study of R. Ball & P. Brown, 'An empirical evaluation of accounting income numbers', Journal of Accounting Research, Autumn 1968, pp. 159-178.

4

VALUE INVESTING

Value investing is a style of investment strategy from the so-called "Graham & Dodd" School. Followers of this style, known as value investors, generally buy companies whose shares appear underpriced by some forms of fundamental analysis; these may include shares that are trading at, for example, high dividend yields or low price-to-earning or price-to-book ratios.

The main proponents of value investing, such as Benjamin Graham and Warren Buffett, have argued that the essence of value investing is buying stocks at less than their intrinsic value. The discount of the market price to the intrinsic value is what Benjamin Graham called the "margin of safety". The intrinsic value is the discounted value of all future distributions.

However, the future distributions and the appropriate discount rate can only be assumptions. Warren Buffett has taken the value investing concept even further as his thinking has evolved to where for the last 25 years or so his focus has been on "finding an outstanding company at a sensible price" rather than generic companies at a bargain price.

HISTORY

Benjamin Graham

Value investing was established by Benjamin Graham and David Dodd, both professors at Columbia University and teachers of many famous investors. In Graham's book The Intelligent Investor, he advocated the important concept of margin of safety-first introduced in Security Analysis, a 1934 book he coauthored with David Dodd-which calls for a cautionary approach to investing. In terms of picking stocks, he recommended defensive investment in stocks trading not far from their tangible book value as a safeguard to adverse future developments often encountered in the stock market.

FURTHER EVOLUTION

However, the concept of value (as well as "book value") has evolved significantly since the 1970s. Book value is meaningful only in some traditional stable industries where the value of an asset is well defined. When an industry is going through fast technological advancements, the value of its assets is not easily estimated. Sometimes, the production power of an asset can be significantly reduced due to competitive disruptive innovation and therefore its value can suffer permanent impairment. One good example of decreasing asset value is a personal computer. An example of where book value does not mean much is the service and retail sectors. One modern model of calculating value is the discounted cash flow model (DCF). The value of an asset is the sum of its future cash flows, discounted back to the present.

VALUE INVESTING PERFORMANCE

Performance, Value Strategies

Value investing has proved to be a successful investment strategy. There are several ways to evaluate its success. One way is to examine the performance of simple value strategies, such as buying low PE ratio stocks, low price-to-cash-flow ratio stocks, or low price-to-book ratio stocks. Numerous academics have published studies investigating the effects of buying value stocks. These studies have consistently found that value stocks outperform growth stocks and the market as a whole.

Performance, Value Investors

Another way to examine the performance of value investing strategies is to examine the investing performance of well-known value investors. Simply examining the performance of the best known value investors would not be instructive, because investors do not become well known unless they are successful. This introduces a selection bias. A better way to investigate the performance of a group of value investors was suggested by Warren Buffett, in his May 17, 1984 speech that was published as The Superinvestors of Graham-and-Doddsville. In this speech, Buffett examined the performance of those investors who worked at Graham-Newman Corporation and were thus most influenced by Benjamin Graham. Buffett's conclusion is identical to that of the academic research on simple value investing strategies--value investing is, on average, successful in the long run.

During about a 25-year period (1965-90), published research and articles in leading journals of the value ilk were few. Warren Buffett once commented, "You couldn't advance in a finance department in this country unless you taught that the world was flat."

Well known Value Investors

Benjamin Graham is regarded by many to be the father of value investing. Along with David Dodd, he wrote Security Analysis, first published in 1934. The most lasting contribution of this book to the field of security analysis was to emphasize the quantifiable aspects of security analysis (such as the evaluations of earnings and book value) while minimizing the importance of more qualitative factors such as the quality of a company's management. Graham later wrote The Intelligent Investor, a book that brought value investing to individual investors. Aside from Buffett, many of Graham's other students, such as William J. Ruane, Irving Kahn, and Charles Brandes have gone on to become successful investors in their own right.

Graham's most famous student, however, was Warren Buffett, who ran successful investing partnerships before closing them in 1969 to focus on running Berkshire Hathaway. Charlie Munger joined Buffett at Berkshire Hathaway in the 1970s and has since worked as Vice Chairman of the company. Buffett has credited Munger with encouraging him to focus on long-term sustainable growth rather than on simply the valuation of current cash flows or assets.

Another famous value investor is John Templeton. He first achieved investing success by buying shares of a number of companies in the aftermath of the stock market crash of 1929.

Martin J. Whitman is another well-regarded value investor. His approach is called safe-and-cheap, which was hitherto referred to as financial-integrity approach. Martin Whitman focuses on acquiring common shares of companies with extremely strong financial position at a price reflecting meaningful discount to the estimated NAV of the company concerned.

Martin Whitman believes it is ill-advised for investors to pay much attention to the trend of macro-factors (like employment, movement of interest rate, GDP, etc.) not so much because they are not important as because attempts to predict their movement are almost always futile. Martin Whitman's letters to shareholders of his Third Avenue Value Fund (TAVF) are considered a valuable resources "for investors to pirate good ideas" by another famous investor Joel Greenblatt in his book on special-situation investment."

Joel Greenblatt achieved annual returns at the hedge fund Gotham Capital of over 50% per year for 10 years from 1985 to 1995 before closing the fund and returning his investors' money. He is known for investing in special situations such as spin-offs, mergers, and divestitures. Edward Lampert is the chief of ESL Investments. He is best known for buying large stakes in Sears and Kmart and then merging the two companies.

INDEX FUND

An index fund or index tracker is a collective investment scheme that aims to replicate the movements of an index of a specific financial market, or a set of rules of ownership that are held constant, regardless of market conditions.

Tracking can be achieved by trying to hold all of the securities in the index, in the same proportions as the index. Other methods include statistically sampling the market and holding "representative" securities. Many index funds rely on a computer model with little or no human input in the decision as to which securities to purchase and is therefore a form of passive management.

The lack of active management (stock picking and market timing) gives the advantage of lower fees and lower taxes in taxable accounts. However, the fees will always reduce the return to the investor relative to the index. In addition it is impossible to precisely mirror the index as the models for sampling and mirroring, by their nature, cannot be 100% accurate. The difference between the index performance and the fund performance is known as the 'tracking error'.

Index funds are available from many investment managers. Some common indices include the S&P 500, the Wilshire 5000, the FTSE 100 and the FTSE All-Share Index. Less common indexes come from academics like Eugene Fama and Kenneth French, who created "research indexes" in order to develop asset pricing models, such as their Three Factor Model.

The Fama French Three Factor model is used by Dimensional Fund Advisors to design their index funds. Robert Arnott and Professor Jeremy Siegel have also created new competing fundamentally based indexes based on such criteria as dividends, earnings, book value, and sales that are being deployed in ETF products.

Origins of the Index Fund

In 1973, Burton Malkiel published his book A Random Walk Down Wall Street, which presented academic findings for the lay public. It was becoming well-known in the lay financial press that most mutual funds were not beating the market indices, to which the standard reply was made "of course, you can't buy an index." Malkiel said, "It's time the public can."

John Bogle graduated from Princeton University in 1951, where his senior thesis was titled: "Mutual Funds can make no claims to superiority over the Market Averages." Bogle wrote that his inspiration came from three sources, all of which confirmed his 1951 research: Paul Samuelson's 1974 paper, "Challenge to Judgment", Charles Ellis' 1975 study, "The Loser's Game," and Al Ehrbar's 1975 Fortune magazine article on indexing. Bogle founded The Vanguard Group in 1974; it is now the second-largest mutual fund company in the United States as of 2005.

When Bogle started the First Index Investment Trust on December 31, 1975, it was labeled Bogle's follies and regarded as un-American, because it sought to achieve the averages rather than insisting that Americans had to play to win. This first Index mutual fund offered to individual investors was later renamed the Vanguard 500 Index Fund, which tracks the Standard and Poor's 500 Index.

It started with comparatively meager assets of $11 million but crossed the $100 billion milestone in November 1999; this astonishing increase was funded by the market's increasing willingness to invest in such a product. Bogle predicted in January 1992 that it would very likely surpass the Magellan Fund before 2001, which it did in 2000. "But in the financial markets it is always wise to expect the unexpected"

John McQuown and David Booth at Wells Fargo and Rex Sinquefield at American National Bank in Chicago both established the first Standard and Poor's Composite Index Funds in 1973. Both of these funds were established for institutional clients; individual investors were excluded. Wells Fargo started with $5 million from their own pension fund, while Illinois Bell put in $5 million of their pension funds at American National Bank.

In 1981, David Booth and Rex Sinquefield started Dimensional Fund Advisors (DFA), many years later McQuown joined its Board of Directors. DFA further developed indexed based investment strategies and currently has $120 billion under management (as of Dec. 2006).

Wells Fargo sold its indexing operation to Barclay's Bank of London, and it now operates as Barclays Global Investors; it is one of the world's largest money managers with over $1.5 trillion under management as of 2005.

Economic Theory

Eugene Fama said, "I take the market efficiency hypothesis to be the simple statement that security prices fully reflect all available information." A precondition for this strong version of the hypothesis is that information and trading costs, the costs of getting prices to reflect information, are always 0 (Grossman and Stiglitz (1980))." A weaker and economically more sensible version of the efficiency hypothesis says that prices reflect information to the point where the marginal benefits of acting on information (the profits to be made) do not exceed marginal costs (Jensen (1978)). Economists cite the efficient market hypothesis as the fundamental premise that justifies the creation of the index funds.

The hypothesis implies that fund managers and stock analysts are constantly looking for securities that may out-perform the market; and that this competition is so effective that any new information about the fortune of a company will rapidly be incorporated into stock prices. It is postulated therefore that it is very difficult to tell ahead of time which stocks will out-perform the market. By creating an index fund that mirrors the whole market the inefficiencies of stock selection are avoided.

5

METHODS OF INDEXING

Synthetic Indexing

Synthetic indexing is a modern technique of using a combination of equity index futures contracts and investments in low risk bonds to replicate the performance of a similar overall investment in the equities making up the index. Although maintaining the future position has a slightly higher cost structure than traditional passive sampling, synthetic indexing can result in more favourable tax treatment, particularly for international investors who are subject to U.S. dividend withholding taxes. The bond portion can also hold higher yielding instruments, with a trade-off of corresponding higher risk, a technique referred to as enhanced indexing.

Enhanced Indexing

Enhanced indexing is an approach to index fund management that uses a variety of techniques to create index funds that seek to emphasize performance, possibly using active management. Enhanced index funds employ a variety of enhancement techniques, including customized indexes (instead of relying on commercial indexes), trading strategies, exclusion rules, and timing strategies. Cost advantage of indexing could be reduced by employing active management. The processes are constantly evolving and new techniques and methodologies are constantly coming up.

ADVANTAGES

Low Costs: Because the composition of a target index is a known quantity, it costs less to run an index fund. No highly paid stock pickers or analysts are needed. Typically expense ratios of an index fund ranges from 0.15 for U.S. Large Company Indexes to 0.97% for Emerging Market Indexes. The expense ratio of the average large cap actively managed mutual fund as of 2005 is 1.36%. If a mutual fund produces 10% return before expenses, taking account of the expense ratio difference would result in an after expense return of 9.85% for the large cap index fund versus 8.64% for the actively managed large cap fund.

Simplicity

The investment objectives of index funds are easy to understand. Once an investor knows the target index of an index fund, what securities the index fund will hold can be determined directly. Managing one's index fund holdings may be as easy as rebalancing every six months or every year.

Lower Turnovers

Turnover refers to the selling and buying of securities by the fund manager. Selling securities in some jurisdictions may result in capital gains tax charges, which are sometimes passed on to fund investors. Because index funds are passive investments, the turnovers are lower than actively managed funds.

According to a study conducted by John Bogle over a sixteen-year period, investors only get to keep 47% of the cumulative return of the average actively managed mutual fund, but they keep 87% in a market index fund. This means $10,000 invested in the index fund grew to $90,000 vs. $49,000 in the average actively managed stock mutual fund. That is a 40% gain from the reduction of silent partners.

DISADVANTAGES

Possible Tracking Error from Index

Since index funds aim to match market returns, both under and over-performance compared to the market is considered a "tracking error". For example, an inefficient index fund may generate a positive tracking error in a falling market by holding too much cash, which holds its value compared to the market.

According to The Vanguard Group, a well run S&P 500 index fund should have a tracking error of 5 basis points or less, but a Morningstar survey found an average of 38 basis points across all index funds.

Investors should remember after all expenses and fees are subtracted their rate of return will not exactly be the market return of the index; however, it should be very close.

Owning a diversified stock index fund does not make an investor immune to systematic risk (e.g., a stock market bubble). When the U.S. technology sector bubble burst in 2000, the S&P 500 dropped significantly, recovering sufficiently to produce a 8.7% total return from January 1, 2000 to January 31, 2007.

The Objective to Minimize Tracking Errors can be Expensive

The stated objective of index funds (in their prospectus) is to minimize the tracking error as they follow the designated index. Whenever an index changes, the fund is then faced with the prospect of selling all the stock that has been removed from the index, and purchasing the stock that was added to the index. The S&P 500 index has a typical turnover of between 1% and 9% per year.

As a result, the price of the stock that has been removed from the index tends to be driven down. The price of stock that has been added to the index tends to be driven up. The index fund, however, has suffered market impact costs because they had to sell stock whose price was depressed, and buy stock whose price was inflated. All in all, however, these losses are small relative to an index fund's over-all advantage gained by its overall total low costs.

Diversification

Diversification refers to the number of different securities in a fund. A fund with more securities is said to be better diversified than a fund with smaller number of securities. Owning many securities reduces the impact of a single security performing very below average. A Wilshire 5000 index would be considered diversified, but a bio-tech ETF would not.

Since some indices like the S&P 500, and FTSE 100 are dominated by large company stocks, an index fund may have a high percentage of the fund concentrated in a few large companies. This position represents a reduction of diversity and can lead to increased volatility and investment risk for an investor who seeks a diversified fund.

Asset Allocation and Achieving Balance

Asset allocation is the process of determining the mix of stocks, bonds and other classes of investable assets to match the investor's risk capacity, which includes attitude towards risk, net income, net worth, knowledge about investing concepts, and time horizon. Index funds capture asset classes in a low cost and tax efficient manner and are used to design balanced portfolios.

A combination of various index mutual funds or ETF's could be used to implement a full range of investment policies from low risk to high risk.

Comparison of Index Funds with Index ETFs

Some index ETFs have lower expense ratio as compared to regular index funds. However, brokerage expenses of index ETFs should not be over-looked. Nevertheless, some online brokers do not charge commissions on ETF transactions, and consequently, the above sentence may no longer be valid .

6

Growth Investing

Growth investing is a style of investment strategy. Those who follow this style, known as growth investors, invest in companies that exhibit signs of above-average growth, even if the share price appears expensive in terms of metrics such as price-to-earning or price-to-book ratios. In typical usage, the term "growth investing" contrasts with the strategy known as value investing.

However, some notable investors such as Warren Buffett have stated that there is no theoretical difference between the concepts of value and growth ("Growth and Value Investing are joined at the hip"), in consideration of the concept of an asset's intrinsic value. In addition, when just investing in one style of stocks, diversification could be negatively impacted.

GROWTH AT REASONABLE PRICE

After the busting of the dotcom bubble, "growth at any price" has fallen from favour. Attaching a high price to a security in the hope of high growth may be risky, since if the growth rate fails to live up to expectations, the price of the security can plummet. It is often more fashionable now to seek out stocks with high growth rates that are trading at reasonable valuations.

GROWTH INVESTMENT VEHICLES

There are many ways to execute a growth investment strategy. Some of these include:

- Emerging markets

- Recovery shares
- Blue chips
- Internet and technology stock
- Smaller companies
- Special situations
- Second-hand life policies

SOCIALLY RESPONSIBLE INVESTING

Socially responsible investing describes an investment strategy which combines the intentions to maximize both financial return and social good. In general, socially responsible investors favor corporate practices which are environmentally responsible, support workplace diversity, and increase product safety and quality.

History

The beginning of socially responsible investing could be attributed to many people and many places. Many believe social investing began with the Religious Society of Friends (Quakers). In 1758, the Quaker Philadelphia Yearly Meeting prohibited members from participating in the business of buying or selling humans. Religious institutions have been at the forefront of social investing ever since. One of the most articulate early adopters of SRI was John Wesley (1703-1791), one of the founders of the Methodist Church. A sermon of his, entitled "The Use of Money," outlined his basic tenets of social investing- i.e. not to harm your neighbor through your business practices and to avoid industries like tanning and chemical production that pollute rivers and streams.

Modern SRI movement began during the Vietnam War. Many people living during the era remember a picture in June of 1972 of a naked nine year-old girl, Phan Thi Kim Phúc, running towards a photographer screaming, her back burning from the napalm dropped on her village. That photograph channelled outrage against Dow Chemical, the manufacturer of napalm, and prompted protests across the country against Dow Chemical and other companies profiting from the Vietnam

War. In the late 1970s, SRI activism turned its attention to nuclear power and automobile emissions control.

From the 70's to the early 90's, large institutions avoided investment in companies that were related to the government and apartheid policies of South Africa. After the Sharpeville Massacre in 1960, international opposition to apartheid strengthened. In 1976 the United Nations imposed a mandatory arms embargo against South Africa. In 1971, Reverend Leon Sullivan (at the time a board member for General Motors) drafted a code of conduct for practicing business in South Africa which became known as the "Sullivan Principles." These principles sought to document the practices of American companies within South Africa . Reports documenting the application of the Sullivan Principles discovered that US companies were not attempting to lessen discrimination within South Africa. Because of these reports and mounting political pressure; cities, states, colleges, faith-based groups and pension funds throughout the United States began divesting (or removing their investments) from companies operating in South Africa. The subsequent negative flow of investment dollars eventually forced a group of businesses, representing 75% of South African employers, to draft a charter calling for an end to apartheid. While the SRI efforts alone didn't bring an end to apartheid, it did focus persuasive international pressure on the South African business community.

Modern Applications

Socially responsible investing (SRI) in the United States remained robust during 2001 and 2002, even as the rest of the investment world was stagnant. Assets in socially screened portfolios climbed to $2.15 trillion in 2003, an increase over the $2.01 trillion counted in 2001. Screened portfolios grew 7 percent from 2001, while the broader universe of all professionally managed portfolios fell 4 percent during the same period, according to the Social Investment Forum's 2003 Report on Socially Responsible Investing Trends in the United States.

Screened portfolios, with $2.15 trillion in assets, represent the largest amount of assets in SRI. Community investing and shareholder advocacy contribute additional assets, resulting in a total of $2.18 trillion in professionally managed assets for all SRI.

MUTUAL FUNDS

Socially responsible mutual funds counted by the 2003 Trends Report increased in number to 200 in 2003, up from 181 in 2001, 168 in 1999, and 139 in 1997. Assets in socially screened mutual funds identified by the Trends Report grew by 19 percent, to $162 billion, up from $136 billion in 2001. More than half (51 percent) of this growth is attributed to both newly identified and newly created funds, and 49 percent represents growth in existing assets. In terms of attracting investor assets, socially screened mutual funds grew on a net basis in 2002 while the rest of the mutual fund industry contracted. According to Lipper, socially responsible mutual funds saw net inflows of $1.5 billion during 2002. Over the same time, U.S. diversified equity funds posted outflows of nearly $10.5 billion.

SEPARATELY MANAGED ACCOUNTS

Of the $2.15 trillion in socially screened portfolios, $1.99 trillion are found in separate accounts (portfolios privately managed for individuals and institutions) with the remaining $162 billion residing in mutual funds. Assets in socially screened separate accounts grew by seven percent since the "2001 Report." Screened private portfolios climbed to $1.99 trillion in 2003, as compared with $1.87 trillion in 2001, $1.34 trillion in 1999, and just $433 billion in 1997.

Shareholder Advocacy

Between 2001 and 2003, shareholder advocacy activity increased by 15 percent, growing from 269 social and crossover resolutions (which combined aspects of both "social" and traditional corporate governance issues) filed in 2001 to 310 in 2003. Likewise, the average percentage of votes received on these resolutions increased from 8.7 percent in 2001 to 11.4 percent in 2003. Of the total $2.15 trillion in all socially screened portfolios, $441 billion are in portfolios controlled by investors who are also involved in shareholder advocacy on various social issues.

Shareholder resolutions are filed by a wide variety of institutional investors, including public pension funds, faith-based investors, socially responsible mutual funds, and labor unions. In 2004, faith-based organizations filed 129 resolutions, while socially responsible funds filed 56 resolutions]

Regulations governing shareholder resolutions vary from country to country. In the United States they are determined by the Securities and Exchange Commission, which also requires mutual funds to disclose how they voted on behalf of their investors. U.S. shareholders have organized various groups to facilitate jointly filing resolutions. These include the Council of Institutional Investors, the Interfaith Center on Corporate Responsibility, and the Social Investment Forum.

Community Investing

Community investing climbed 84 percent between 2001 and 2003. Assets held and invested locally by community development financial institutions (CDFIs) based in the United States totaled $14 billion in 2003, up from $7.6 billion in 2001.

INVESTING STRATEGIES

Social investors use four basic strategies to maximize financial return and attempt to maximize social good. Screening excludes certain securities from investment consideration based on social and/or environmental criteria. For example, many socially responsible investors screen out tobacco company investments. This is an example of a social screen at work.

Divesting is the act of removing stocks from a portfolio based on mainly ethical, non-financial reasons. An investor divests upon realizing that, at some point, "the cup of endurance runs over, and (is)..no longer willing to be plunged into an abyss of despair" over certain business activities of a corporation. Recently, CalSTRS (California State Teachers' Retirement System) announced the removal of more than $237 million in tobacco holdings from its investment, portfolio after 6 months of financial analysis and deliberations.

Shareholder activism efforts attempt to positively influence corporate behavior. These efforts include initiating conversations with corporate management on issues of concern, and submitting and voting proxy resolutions.

These activities are undertaken with the belief that social investors, working cooperatively, can steer management on a course that will improve financial performance over time and enhance the well being of the stockholders, customers, employees, vendors, and communities.

Positive investing involves making investments in activities and companies believed to have a high and positive social impact. Positive investing activities tend to target underserved communities. These efforts may support activities designed to provide mortgage and small business credit to minority and low-income communities.

Satire and Market Response

At least one mutual fund, the Vice Fund (VICEX), was created specifically to contrast with the trend in socially responsible investing. VICEX specializes in investing in the defense, alcohol, tobacco, and gambling industries, and has greatly outperformed both the S&P 500 and most socially responsible mutual funds.

In addition, the Free Enterprise Action Fund files shareholder resolutions which oppose the general trend of socially responsible investing, for example by asking GE to "justify lobbying for global warming regulation."

CORPORATE SOCIAL RESPONSIBILITY

Corporate Social Responsibility (CSR) is a concept that organizations, especially (but not only) corporations, have an obligation to consider the interests of customers, employees, shareholders, communities, and ecological considerations in all aspects of their operations.

This obligation is seen to extend beyond their statutory obligation to comply with legislation.

CSR is closely linked with the principles of Sustainable Development, which argues that enterprises should make decisions based not only on financial factors such as profits or dividends, but also based on the immediate and long-term social and environmental consequences of their activities.

Development and Analysis

Today's heightened interest in the role of businesses in society has been promoted by increased sensitivity to and awareness of environmental and ethical issues. Issues like environmental damage, improper treatment of workers, and faulty production that inconveniences or endangers customers are highlighted in the media.

In some countries government regulation regarding environmental and social issues has increased. Also, standards and laws are often set at a supranational level (e.g., by the European Union). Some investors and investment fund managers have begun to take account of a corporation's CSR policy in making investment decisions, a practice known as socially responsible investment.

Many advocates would distinguish CSR from charitable donations and "good works" (i.e., philanthropy, e.g., Habitat for Humanity or Ronald McDonald House).

Corporations have often, in the past, spent money on community projects, the endowment of scholarships, and the establishment of foundations. They have also often encouraged their employees to volunteer to take part in community work and thereby create goodwill in the community, which will directly enhance the reputation of the company and strengthen its brand.

CSR goes beyond charity and requires that a responsible company take into full account its impact on all stakeholders and on the environment when making decisions. This requires the company to balance the needs of all stakeholders with its need to make a profit and reward shareholders adequately.

A widely quoted definition by the World Business Council for Sustainable Development states that "Corporate social responsibility is the continuing commitment by business to behave ethically and contribute to economic development while improving the quality of life of the work-force and their families as well as of the local community and society at large.".

Auditing and Reporting

To demonstrate good business citizenship, firms can report compliance with a number of CSR standards, including:

- Accountability's AA1000 standard, based on John Elkington's triple bottom line (3BL) reporting
- Global Reporting Initiative's Sustainability Reporting Guidelines
- Verite's Monitoring Guidelines
- Social Accountability International's SA8000 standard
- The ISO 14000 environmental management standard

Some nations require CSR reporting, though agreement on meaningful measurements of social and environmental performance is difficult. Many companies now produce externally audited annual reports that cover Sustainable Development and CSR issues, but the reports vary widely in format, style, and evaluation methodology (even within the same industry). Critics dismiss these reports as lip service, citing examples such as Enron's yearly "Corporate Responsibility Annual Report" and tobacco corporations' social reports.

The Business Case for CSR

The scale and nature of the benefits of CSR for an organisation can vary depending on the nature of the enterprise, and are difficult to quantify, though there is a large body of literature exhorting business to adopt measures beyond financial ones (e.g., Deming's Fourteen Points, balanced scorecards).

Orlizty, Schmidt, and Rynes found a correlation between social/environmental performance and financial performance. However, businesses may not be looking at short-run financial returns when developing their CSR strategy.

The definition of CSR used within an organisation can vary from the strict "stakeholder impacts" definition used by many CSR advocates and will often include charitable efforts and volunteering. CSR may be based within the human resources, business development or PR departments of an organisation, or may be given a separate unit reporting to the CEO or in some cases directly to the board. Some companies may implement CSR-type values without a clearly defined team or programme.

The business case for CSR within a company will likely rest on one or more of these arguments:

Human Resources

A CSR programme can be seen as an aid to recruitment and retention, particularly within the competitive graduate student market. Potential recruits are increasingly likely to ask about a firm's CSR policy during an interview and having a comprehensive policy can give an advantage. CSR can also help to build a "feel good" atmosphere among existing staff, particularly when they can become involved through payroll giving, fundraising activities or community volunteering.

Risk Management

Managing risk is a central part of many corporate strategies. Reputations that take decades to build up can be ruined in hours through incidents such as corruption scandals or environmental accidents. These events can also draw unwanted attention from regulators, courts, governments and media. Building a genuine culture of 'doing the right thing' within a corporation can offset these risks.

Brand Differentiation

In crowded marketplaces companies strive for a unique selling proposition which can separate them from the competition in the minds of consumers. CSR can play a role in building customer loyalty based on distinctive ethical values. Several major brands, such as The Co-operative Group and The Body Shop are built on ethical values. Business service organisations can benefit too from building a reputation for integrity and best practice.

LICENSE TO OPERATE

Corporations are keen to avoid interference in their business through taxation or regulations. By taking substantive voluntary steps they can persuade governments and the wider public that they are taking current issues like health and safety, diversity or the environment seriously and so avoid intervention. This also applies to firms seeking to justify eye-catching profits and high levels of boardroom pay.

Those operating away from their home country can make sure they stay welcome by being good corporate citizens with respect to labour standards and impacts on the environment.

DISPUTED BUSINESS MOTIVES

Critics of CSR will attribute other business motives, which the companies would dispute. For example, some believe that CSR programmes are often undertaken in an effort to distract the public from the ethical questions posed by their core operations.

Some that have been accused of this motivation include British American Tobacco (BAT) which produces major CSR reports and the petroleum giant BP which is well known for its high profile advertising campaigns on environmental aspects of their operations.

Criticism

The critics of CSR break down into two broad categories:

- Those who argue that CSR hinders the operation of the free market;
- Those who believe that CSR is essentially cynical and utilitarian.

Criticism from a free market perspective.

This group are generally supporters of Milton Friedman who argued that a corporation's principal purpose is to maximize returns to its shareholders, while obeying the laws of the countries within which it works.

Because of this, moderate critics would suggest that CSR activity is most effective in achieving social or environmental outcomes when there is a direct link to profits. This approach to CSR requires that the resources applied to CSR activities must have at least as good a return as that that these resources could generate if applied anywhere else. This analysis drastically narrows the possible scope of CSR activities.

Critics who believe that CSR runs against capitalism would go further and say that improvements in health, longevity or infant mortality have been created by economic growth attributed to free enterprise.

Investment in less developed countries contributes to the welfare of those societies, notwithstanding that these countries have fewer protections in place for workers. Failure to invest in these countries decreases the opportunity to increase social welfare.

This group may also point to:

- The rule of corporate law that a corporation's directors are prohibited from any activity that would reduce profits
- The burden of the existing social and environmental regulation that companies must comply with
- Other mechanisms established to manage the principal-agent problem, such as accounting oversight, stock options, performance evaluations, deferred compensation and other mechanisms to increase accountability to shareholders

Critics who Believe that CSR is Essentially Cynical

This group argue that the only reason corporations put in place social projects is utilitarian; that they see a commercial benefit in raising their reputation with the public or with government. They suggest a number of reasons why self-interested corporations, solely seeking to maximise profits are unable to advance the interests of society as a whole.

A conflict can arise when a corporation espouses CSR and its commitment to Sustainable Development on the one hand, whilst damaging revelations about its business practices emerge on the other.

For example the McDonald's Corporation has been criticised by CSR campaigners for unethical business practices, and was the subject of a decision by Justice Roger Bell in the McLibel case (which upheld some of these claims, regarding mistreatment of workers, misleading advertising, and unnecessary cruelty to animals). Similarly Shell has a much publicised CSR policy and was a pioneer in triple bottom line reporting, but was involved in 2004 in a scandal over the misreporting of its oil reserves which seriously damaged its reputation and led to charges of hypocrisy.

Other views from this perspective include:

- Corporations really care little for the welfare of workers or the environment, and given the opportunity will move production to sweatshops in less well regulated countries.
- Companies do not pay the full costs of their impact. For example the costs of cleaning pollution often fall on society in general. As a result profits of corporations are enhanced at the expense of social or ecological welfare.
- Stronger regulation rather than voluntary measures is the best way to ensure that companies remain socially responsible.

7

MUTUAL FUND

A mutual fund is a form of collective investment that pools money from many investors and invests their money in stocks, bonds, short-term money market instruments, and/or other securities. In a mutual fund, the fund manager trades the fund's underlying securities, realizing capital gains or losses, and collects the dividend or interest income. The investment proceeds are then passed along to the individual investors. The value of a share of the mutual fund, known as the net asset value per share (NAV), is calculated daily based on the total value of the fund divided by the number of shares currently issued and outstanding.

Legally known as an "open-end company" under the Investment Company Act of 1940 (the primary regulatory statute governing investment companies), a mutual fund is one of three basic types of investment companies available in the United States. Outside of the United States (with the exception of Canada, which follows the U.S. model), mutual fund is a generic term for various types of collective investment vehicle. In the United Kingdom and western Europe (including offshore jurisdictions), other forms of collective investment vehicle are prevalent, including unit trusts, open-ended investment companies (OEICs), SICAVs and unitized insurance funds.

In Australia the term "mutual fund" is generally not used; the name "managed fund" is used instead. However, "managed fund" is somewhat generic as the definition of a managed fund in Australia is any vehicle in which investors' money is managed by a third party (NB: usually an investment professional or organization). Most managed funds are open-ended (i.e., there is no established maximum number of shares that can be issued); however, this need not be the case. Additionally the Australian government introduced a compulsory superannuation/pension scheme which, although strictly speaking a managed fund, is rarely identified by this term and is instead called a "superannuation fund" because of its special tax concessions and restrictions on when money invested in it can be accessed.

HISTORY

Massachusetts Investors Trust was founded on March 21, 1924, and, after one year, had 200 shareholders and $392,000 in assets. The entire industry, which included a few closed-end funds, represented less than $10 million in 1924.

The stock market crash of 1929 slowed the growth of mutual funds. In response to the stock market crash, Congress passed the Securities Act of 1933 and the Securities Exchange Act of 1934. These laws require that a fund be registered with the Securities and Exchange Commission (SEC) and provide prospective investors with a prospectus that contains required disclosures about the fund, the securities themselves, and fund manager. The SEC helped draft the Investment Company Act of 1940, which sets forth the guidelines with which all SEC-registered funds today must comply.

With renewed confidence in the stock market, mutual funds began to blossom. By the end of the 1960s, there were approximately 270 funds with $48 billion in assets. The first retail index fund, the First Index Investment Trust, was formed in 1976 and headed by John Bogle, who conceptualized many of the key tenets of the industry in his 1951 senior thesis at Princeton University. It is now called the Vanguard 500 Index Fund and is one of the largest mutual funds ever with in excess of $100 billion in assets.

One of the largest contributors of mutual fund growth was individual retirement account (IRA) provisions added to the Internal Revenue Code in 1975, allowing individuals (including those already in corporate pension plans) to contribute $2,000 a year. Mutual funds are now popular in employer-sponsored defined contribution retirement plans (401(k)s), IRAs and Roth IRAs. As of April 2006, there are 8,606 mutual funds that belong to the Investment Company Institute (ICI), the national association of investment companies in the United States, with combined assets of $9.207 trillion.

USAGE

Mutual funds can invest in many different kinds of securities. The most common are cash, stock, and bonds, but there are hundreds of sub-categories. Stock funds, for instance, can invest primarily in the shares of a particular industry, such as technology or utilities. These are known as sector funds. Bond funds can vary according to risk (e.g., high-yield or junk bonds, investment-grade corporate bonds), type of issuers (e.g., government agencies, corporations, or municipalities), or maturity of the bonds (short-or long-term). Both stock and bond funds can invest in primarily U.S. securities (domestic funds), both U.S. and foreign securities (global funds), or primarily foreign securities (international funds).

Most mutual funds' investment portfolios are continually adjusted under the supervision of a professional manager, who forecasts the future performance of investments appropriate for the fund and chooses those which he or she believes will most closely match the fund's stated investment objective. A mutual fund is administered through a parent management company, which may hire or fire fund managers.

Mutual funds are liable to a special set of regulatory, accounting, and tax rules. Unlike most other types of business entities, they are not taxed on their income as long as they distribute substantially all of it to their shareholders. Also, the type of income they earn is often unchanged as it passes through to the shareholders. Mutual fund distributions of tax-free municipal bond income are also tax-free to the shareholder. Taxable distributions can be either ordinary income or capital gains, depending on how the fund earned those distributions.

NET ASSET VALUE

The net asset value, or NAV, is the current market value of a fund's holdings, usually expressed as a per-share amount.

For most funds, the NAV is determined daily, after the close of trading on some specified financial exchange, but some funds update their NAV multiple times during the trading day. Open-end funds sell and redeem their shares at the NAV, and so process orders only after the NAV is determined. Closed-end funds (the shares of which are traded by investors) may trade at a higher or lower price than their NAV; this is known as a premium or discount, respectively. If a fund is divided into multiple classes of shares, each class will typically have its own NAV, reflecting differences in fees and expenses paid by the different classes.

Some mutual funds own securities which are not regularly traded on any formal exchange. These may be shares in very small or bankrupt companies; they may be derivatives; or they may be private investments in unregistered financial instruments (such as stock in a non-public company). In the absence of a public market for these securities, it is the responsibility of the fund manager to form an estimate of their value when computing the NAV. How much of a fund's assets may be invested in such securities is stated in the fund's prospectus.

TURNOVER

Turnover is a measure of the fund's securities transactions, usually calculated over a year's time, and usually expressed as a percentage of net asset value.

This value is usually calculated as the value of all transactions (buying, selling) divided by 2 divided by the fund's total holdings; i.e., the fund counts one security sold and another one bought as one "turnover". Thus turnover measures the replacement of holdings.

In Canada, under NI 81-106 (required disclosure for investment funds) turnover ratio is calculated based on the lesser of purchases or sales divided by the average size of the portfolio (including cash).

Turnover generally has tax consequences for a fund, which are passed through to investors. In particular, when selling an investment from its portfolio, a fund may realize a capital gain, which will ultimately be distributed to investors as taxable income. The process of buying and selling securities also has its own costs, such as brokerage commissions, which are borne by the fund's shareholders.

EXPENSES AND TER'S

Mutual funds bear expenses similar to other companies. The fee structure of a mutual fund can be divided into two or three main components: management fee, nonmanagement expense, and 12b-1/non-12b-1 fees. All expenses are expressed as a percentage of the average daily net assets of the fund.

MANAGEMENT FEES

The management fee for the fund is usually synonymous with the contractual investment advisory fee charged for the management of a fund's investments. However, as many fund companies include administrative fees in the advisory fee component, when attempting to compare the total management expenses of different funds, it is helpful to define management fee as equal to the contractual advisory fee + the contractual administrator fee. This "levels the playing field" when comparing management fee components across multiple funds.

Contractual advisory fees may be structured as "flat-rate" fees, i.e., a single fee charged to the fund, regardless of the asset size of the fund. However, many funds have contractual fees which include breakpoints, so that as the value of a fund's assets increases, the advisory fee paid decreases. Another way in which the advisory fees remain competitive is by structuring the fee so that it is based on the value of all of the assets of a group or a complex of funds rather than those of a single fund.

NON-MANAGEMENT EXPENSES

Apart from the management fee, there are certain non-management expenses which most funds must pay. Some of the more significant (in terms of amount) non-management expenses are: transfer agent expenses (this is usually the person you get on the other end of the phone line when you want to purchase/ sell shares of a fund), custodian expense (the fund's assets are kept in custody by a bank which charges a custody fee), legal/ audit expense, fund accounting expense, registration expense (the SEC charges a registration fee when funds file registration statements with it), board of directors/trustees expense (the disinterested members of the board who oversee the fund are usually paid a fee for their time spent at board meetings), and printing and postage expense (incurred when printing and delivering shareholder reports).

12b-1/Non-12b-1 Service Fees

12b-1 service fees/shareholder servicing fees are contractual fees which a fund may charge to cover the marketing expenses of the fund. Non-12b-1 service fees are marketing/shareholder servicing fees which do not fall under SEC rule 12b-1. While funds do not have to charge the full contractual 12b-1 fee, they often do.

When investing in a front-end load or no-load fund, the 12b-1 fees for the fund are usually .250% (or 25 basis points). The 12b-1 fees for back-end and level-load share classes are usually between 50 and 75 basis points but may be as much as 100 basis points. While funds are often marketed as "no-load" funds, this does not mean they do not charge a distribution expense through a different mechanism. It is expected that a fund listed on an online brokerage site will be paying for the "shelf-space" in a different manner even if not directly through a 12b-1 fee.

Fees and Expenses Borne by the Investor (not the Fund)

Fees and expenses borne by the investor vary based on the arrangement made with the investor's broker. Sales loads (or contingent deferred sales loads (CDSL)) are not included in the fund's total expense ratio (TER) because they do not pass through the statement of operations for the fund. Additionally, funds may charge early redemption fees to discourage investors from swapping money into and out of the fund quickly, which may force the fund to make bad trades to obtain the necessary liquidity. For example, Fidelity Diversified International Fund (FDIVX) charges a 1 percent fee on money removed from the fund in less than 30 days.

Brokerage Commissions

An additional expense which does not pass through the statement of operations and cannot be controlled by the investor is brokerage commissions. Brokerage commissions are incorporated into the price of the fund and are reported usually 3 months after the fund's annual report in the statement of additional information. Brokerage commissions are directly related to portfolio turnover (portfolio turnover refers to the number of times the fund's assets are bought and sold over the course of a year). Usually the higher the rate of the portfolio turnover, the higher the brokerage commissions. The advisors of mutual fund companies are required to achieve "best execution" through brokerage arrangements so that the commissions charged to the fund will not be excessive.

TYPES OF MUTUAL FUNDS

Open-end Fund

The term mutual fund is the common name for an open-end investment company. Being open-ended means that, at the end of every day, the fund issues new shares to investors and buys back shares from investors wishing to leave the fund.

Mutual funds may be legally structured as corporations or business trusts but in either instance are classed as open-end investment companies by the SEC.

Other funds have a limited number of shares; these are either closed-end funds or unit investment trusts, neither of which is a mutual fund.

Exchange-Traded Funds

A relatively new innovation, the exchange traded fund (ETF), is often formulated as an open-end investment company. ETFs combine characteristics of both mutual funds and closed-end funds. An ETF usually tracks a stock index. Shares are issued or redeemed by institutional investors in large blocks (typically of 50,000). Investors typically purchase shares in small quantities through brokers at a small premium or discount to the net asset value; this is how the institutional investor makes its profit. Because the institutional investors handle the majority of trades, ETFs are more efficient than traditional mutual funds (which are continuously issuing new securities and redeeming old ones, keeping detailed records of such issuance and redemption transactions, and, to effect such transactions, continually buying and selling securities and maintaining liquidity position) and therefore tend to have lower expenses. ETFs are traded throughout the day on a stock exchange, just like closed-end funds.

Exchange traded funds are also valuable for foreign investors who are often able to buy and sell securities traded on a stock market, but who, for regulatory reasons, are unable to participate in traditional US mutual funds.

EQUITY FUNDS

Equity funds, which consist mainly of stock investments, are the most common type of mutual fund. Equity funds hold 50 percent of all amounts invested in mutual funds in the United States. Often equity funds focus investments on particular strategies and certain types of issuers.

Capitalization

Fund managers and other investment professionals have varying definitions of mid-cap, and large-cap ranges. The following ranges are used by Russell Indexes:

- Russell Microcap Index - micro-cap ($54.8 - 539.5 million)
- Russell 2000 Index - small-cap ($182.6 million - 1.8 billion)
- Russell Midcap Index - mid-cap ($1.8 - 13.7 billion)
- Russell 1000 Index - large-cap ($1.8 - 386.9 billion)

Growth vs. Value

Another distinction made between growth funds, which invest in stocks of companies that have the potential for large capital gains, and value funds, which concentrate on stocks that are undervalued. Growth stocks typically have the potential for a greater return; however, such investments also bear larger risks. Growth funds tend not to pay regular dividends. Sector funds focus on specific industry sectors, such as biotechnology or energy. Income funds tend to be more conservative investments, with a focus on stocks that pay dividends. A balanced fund may use a combination of strategies, typically including some level of investment in bonds, to stay more conservative when it comes to risk, yet aim for some growth.

INDEX FUNDS VERSUS ACTIVE MANAGEMENT

An index fund maintains investments in companies that are part of major stock (or bond) indices, such as the S&P 500, while an actively managed fund attempts to outperform a relevant index through superior stock-picking techniques. The assets of an index fund are managed to closely approximate the performance of a particular published index. Since the composition of an index changes infrequently, an index fund manager makes fewer trades, on average, than does an active fund manager. For this reason, index funds generally have lower trading expenses than actively managed funds, and typically incur fewer short-term capital gains which must be passed on to shareholders. Additionally, index funds do not incur expenses to pay for selection of individual stocks (proprietary selection techniques, research, etc.) and deciding when to buy, hold or sell individual holdings. Instead, a fairly simple computer model can identify whatever changes are needed to bring the fund back into agreement with its target index.

The performance of an actively managed fund largely depends on the investment decisions of its manager. Statistically, for every investor who outperforms the market, there is one who underperforms. Among those who outperform their index before expenses, though, many end up underperforming after expenses. Before expenses, a well-run index fund should have average performance. By minimizing the impact of expenses, index funds should be able to perform better than average.

Certain empirical evidence seems to illustrate that mutual funds do not beat the market and actively managed mutual funds under-perform other broad-based portfolios with similar characteristics. One study found that nearly 1,500 U.S. mutual funds under-performed the market in approximately half of the years between 1962 and 1992. Moreover, funds that performed well in the past are not able to beat the market again in the future (shown by Jensen, 1968; Grimblatt and Titman, 1989.

BOND FUNDS

Bond funds account for 18% of mutual fund assets. Types of bond funds include term funds, which have a fixed set of time (short-, medium-, or long-term) before they mature. Municipal bond funds generally have lower returns, but have tax advantages and lower risk. High-yield bond funds invest in corporate bonds, including high-yield or junk bonds. With the potential for high yield, these bonds also come with greater risk.

MONEY MARKET FUNDS

Money market funds hold 26% of mutual fund assets in the United States. Money market funds entail the least risk, as well as lower rates of return. Unlike certificates of deposit (CDs), money market shares are liquid and redeemable at any time. The interest rate quoted by money market funds is known as the 7 Day SEC Yield.

Funds of Funds

Funds of funds (FoF) are mutual funds which invest in other underlying mutual funds (i.e., they are funds comprised of other funds). The funds at the underlying level are typically funds which an investor can invest in individually. A fund of funds will typically charge a management fee which is smaller than that of a normal fund because it is considered a fee charged for asset allocation services. The fees charged at the underlying fund level do not pass through the statement of operations, but are usually disclosed in the fund's annual report, prospectus, or statement of additional information. The fund should be evaluated on the combination of the fund-level expenses and underlying fund expenses, as these both reduce the return to the investor.

Most FoFs invest in affiliated funds (i.e., mutual funds managed by the same advisor), although some invest in funds managed by other (unaffiliated) advisors. The cost associated with investing in an unaffiliated underlying fund is most often higher than investing in an affiliated underlying because of the investment management research involved in investing in fund advised by a different advisor. Recently, FoFs have been classified into those that are actively managed (in which the investment advisor reallocates frequently among the underlying funds in order to adjust to changing market conditions) and those that are passively managed (the investment advisor allocates assets on the basis of on an allocation model which is rebalanced on a regular basis).

The design of FoFs is structured in such a way as to provide a ready mix of mutual funds for investors who are unable to or unwilling to determine their own asset allocation model. Fund companies such as TIAA-CREF, Vanguard, and Fidelity have also entered this market to provide investors with these options and take the "guess work" out of selecting funds. The allocation mixes usually vary by the time the investor would like to retire: 2020, 2030, 2050, etc. The more distant the target retirement date, the more aggressive the asset mix.

HEDGE FUNDS

Hedge funds in the United States are pooled investment funds with loose SEC regulation and should not be confused with mutual funds. Certain hedge funds are required to register with SEC as investment advisers under the Investment Advisers Act. The Act does not require an adviser to follow or avoid any particular investment strategies, nor does it require or prohibit specific investments. Hedge funds typically charge a management fee of 1% or more, plus a "performance fee" of 20% of the hedge fund's profits. There may be a "lock-up" period, during which an investor cannot cash in shares.

MUTUAL FUNDS VS. OTHER INVESTMENTS

Mutual funds offer several advantages over investing in individual stocks. For example, the transaction costs are divided among all the mutual fund shareholders, who also benefit by having a third party (professional fund managers) apply their expertise, dedicate their time to manage and research investment options. However, despite the professional management, mutual funds are not immune to risks. They share the same risks associated with the investments made. If the fund invests primarily in stocks, it is usually subject to the same ups and downs and risks as the stock market.

SHARE CLASSES

Many mutual funds offer more than one class of shares. For example, you may have seen a fund that offers "Class A" and "Class B" shares. Each class will invest in the same pool (or investment portfolio) of securities and will have the same investment objectives and policies. But each class will have different shareholder services and/or distribution arrangements with different fees and expenses. These differences are supposed to reflect different costs involved in servicing investors in various classes; for example, one class may be sold through brokers with a front-end load, and another class may be sold direct to the public with no load but a "12b-1 fee" included in the class's expenses (sometimes referred to as "Class C" shares). Still a third class might have a minimum investment of $10,000,000 and be available only to financial institutions (a so-called "institutional" share class). In some cases, by aggregating regular investments made by many individuals, a retirement plan (such as a 401(k) plan) may qualify to purchase "institutional" shares (and gain the benefit of their typically lower expense ratios) even though no members of the plan would qualify individually. As a result, each class will likely have different performance results.

A multi-class structure offers investors the ability to select a fee and expense structure that is most appropriate for their investment goals (including the length of time that they expect to remain invested in the fund).

Load and Expenses

A front-end load or sales charge is a commission paid to a broker by a mutual fund when shares are purchased, taken as a percentage of funds invested. The value of the investment is reduced by the amount of the load. Some funds have a deferred sales charge or back-end load. In this type of fund an investor pays no sales charge when purchasing shares, but will pay a commission out of the proceeds when shares are redeemed depending on how long they are held. Another derivative structure is a level-load fund, in which no sales charge is paid when buying the fund, but a back-end load may be charged if the shares purchased are sold within a year.

Load funds are sold through financial intermediaries such as brokers, financial planners, and other types of registered representatives who charge a commission for their services. Shares of front-end load funds are frequently eligible for breakpoints (i.e., a reduction in the commission paid) based on a number of variables. These include other accounts in the same fund family held by the investor or various family members, or committing to buy more of the fund within a set period of time in return for a lower commission "today".

It is possible to buy many mutual funds without paying a sales charge. These are called no-load funds. In addition to being available from the fund company itself, no-load funds may be sold by some discount brokers for a flat transaction fee or even no fee at all. (This does not necessarily mean that the broker is not compensated for the transaction; in such cases, the fund may pay brokers' commissions out of "distribution and marketing" expenses rather than a specific sales charge. The purchaser is therefore paying the fee indirectly through the fund's expenses deducted from profits.)

No-load funds include both index funds and actively managed funds. The largest mutual fund families selling no-load index funds are Vanguard and Fidelity, though there are a number of smaller mutual fund families with no-load funds as well. Expense ratios in some no-load index funds are less than 0.2% per year versus the typical actively managed fund's expense ratio of about 1.5% per year.

Load funds usually have even higher expense ratios when the load is considered. The expense ratio is the anticipated annual cost to the investor of holding shares of the fund. For example, on a $100,000 investment, an expense ratio of 0.2% means $200 of annual expense, while a 1.5% expense ratio would result in $1,500 of annual expense. These expenses are before any sales commissions paid to purchase the mutual fund.

Many fee-only financial advisors strongly suggest no-load funds such as index funds. If the advisor is not of the fee-only type but is instead compensated by commissions, the advisor may have a conflict of interest in selling high-commission load funds.

CRITICISM OF MANAGED MUTUAL FUNDS

Historically, only a small percentage of actively managed mutual funds, over long periods of time, have returned as much, or more than comparable index mutual funds. This, of course, is a criticism of one type of mutual fund over another.

Another criticism concerns sales commissions on load funds, an upfront or deferred fee as high as 8.5 percent of the amount invested in a fund (although the average up-front load is no more than 5% normally). *(Mutual Funds have to qualify to charge the maximum allowed by law, which is 8.5% and most of them DO NOT qualify for this.)

In addition, no-load funds typically charge a 12b-1 fee in order to pay for shelf space on the exchange the investor uses for purchase of the fund, but they do not pay a load directly to a mutual fund broker, who sells it. Critics point out that high sales commissions can sometimes represent a conflict of interest, as high commissions benefit the sales people but hurt the investors. Although in reality, "A shares", which appear to have the highest up front load, (around 5%) are the "cheapest" for the investor, if the investor is planning on 1) keeping the fund for more than 5 years, 2) investing more than 100,000 in one fund family, which likely will qualify them for "breakpoints",which is a form of discount, or 3) staying with that "fund family" for more than 5 years, but switching "funds" within the same fund company.

In this case, the up front load is best for the client, and at times "outperforms" the "no load" or "B or C shares". High commissions can sometimes cause sales people to recommend funds that maximize their income. This can be easily solved, buy working with a "registered investment advisor" instead of a "broker", where the investment advisor can charge strictly for advise, and not charge a "load, or commission" for their work, at all.

This is a discussion of criticism, and solutions regarding one mutual fund over another.

12b-1 fees, which are found on most "no load funds" can motivate the fund company to focus on advertising to attract more and more new investors, as new investors would also cause the fund assets to increase, thus increasing the amount of money that the mutual fund managers make.

Mutual fund managers, and companies need to disclose by law, if they have a conflict of interest due to the way they are paid. In particular fund managers may be encouraged to take more risks with investors' money than they ought to: Fund flows (and therefore compensation) towards successful, market beating funds are much larger than outflows from funds that lose to the market. Fund managers may therefore have an incentive to purchase high risk investments in the hopes of increasing their odds of beating the market and receiving the high inflows, with relatively less fear of the consequences of losing to the market (1).

Many analysts, however, believe that the larger the pool of money one works with, the harder it is to manage actively, and the harder it is to squeeze good performance out of it. This is true, due to the fact that there are only so many companies that one can identify to put the money into (buy shares of) that fit with the "style" of the mutual fund, due to what is disclosed in the propectus.

Thus some fund companies can be focused on attracting new customers, and forget to "close" their mutual funds to new customers, when they get too big, to invest the assets properly, thereby hurting its existing investors' performance. A great deal of a fund's costs are flat and fixed costs, such as the salary for the manager. Thus it can be more profitable for the fund to try to allow it to grow as large as possible, instead of limiting its assets. Most fund companies, have closed some funds to new investors to maintain the integrity of the funds for existing investors. If the funds reach more than 1 billion dollars, many times, these funds, have gotten too large, before they are closed, and when this happens, the funds tend to not have a place to put the money and can and tend to lose value.

Other critisicms of mutual funds are that some funds illegally are guilty of market timing (although many fund companies tightly control this) and that some fund managers accept extravagant gifts in exchange for trading stocks through certain investment banks, which presumably charge the fund more for transactions than would non-gifting investment bank.

This practice, although done, is completely illegal. As a result, all fund companies strictly limit--or completely bar--such gifts.

SOCIAL RESPONSIBILITY

Social responsibility is a doctrine that claims that an entity whether it is state, government, corporation, organization or individual has a responsibility to society. Among these entities, activist groups and local communities can also be associated with social responsibility, not only business or governmental entities. This responsibility can be "negative," in that it is a responsibility to refrain from acting (resistance stance) or it can be "positive," meaning there is a responsibility to act (proactive stance).

There is a large inequality in the means and roles of different entities to fulfill their claimed responsibility. This would imply the different entities have different responsibilities, insomuch as states should ensure the civil rights of their citizens, that corporations should respect and encourage the human rights of their employees and that citizens should abide with written laws. But social responsibility can mean more than these examples.

Many NGOs accept that their role and the responsibility of their members as citizens is to help improve society by taking a proactive stance in their societal roles. It can also imply that corporations have an implicit obligation to give back to society (such as is claimed as part of corporate social responsibility and/or stakeholder theory). Social responsibility is voluntary; it is about going above and beyond what is called for by the law (legal responsibility).

It involves an idea that it is better to be proactive toward a problem rather than reactive to a problem. Social responsibility means eliminating corrupt, irresponsible or unethical behavior that might bring harm to the community, its people, or the environment before the behavior happens.

Human Responsibility

One half of social responsibility is being responsible to people, for the actions of people, and for actions that affect people. Social responsibility is about holding a group, organization or company accountable for its effect on the people around it. People within the company, people working with the company, the community the company is in and those who buy from the company.

The idea of being responsible to customers has actually long been imbedded in the ethics of business. The idea of treating a customer with respect and attention is not new particularly in sales and commission based work. What is new is the idea that it's not to profit from the customer, but to genuinely care about what the customer wants and needs.

Accountability for people inside a company is something new. Many times when a scandal or irresponsible behavior comes to light in the corporate world the company and those involved often try to distance themselves as much as possible. Cover ups, buy offs and "golden parachutes" all fall under this behavior. Social responsibility would nearly be the opposite of what goes on in the business world today-a company taking the blame and doing what is needed to fix the problem rather than committing more crimes to cover up the first one.

In many countries, by law, a corporation's only responsibility is to make as much money as possible for shareholders (economic responsibility) and to obey the law (legal responsibility). Social responsibility holds companies and organizations responsible for the people they affect, even indirectly.

It also holds a company responsible for inaction, or indecision. Basing on the idea that a company or organization has the power to help people or, at the least, not harm them, it has the moral responsibility to do so. Social Responsibility is a doctrine that says that every being whether it is a village, town, state, corporation, organization, government or individual has responsibility to society.

Environmental Responsibility

The second half of social responsibility is the idea that a company has even more responsibility to the environment and the world around it then an individual. Companies by nature act on a far larger scale then an individual could. Thus, their environmental impacts are often far greater and have much farther reaching impacts then an individual consumer could.

Choices made by the company often have far reaching affects and even unknown consequences. Business have proven this time and time again. They also have actions and have products that are not readily available to consumers. There are very few people in the world with access to toxic or nuclear waste and even fewer have been convicted of illegally dumping or producing those products.

Also choices companies make effect the environmental impacts of their consumers. Many products use far more packaging then is required. This environmental impact and cost is handed over directly to the consumer who is responsible for disposing of the packaging in an environmentally friendly manner. It is also not the responsibility of the company to provide the environmentally friendly option for disposing of the packaging, or even the product in some cases.

A socially responsible business would take these considerations into account when making a decision. It often falls to management and share holders to push for a company to be run responsibly and take initiative for its actions. This has often proven profitable for a company in the long right to spite short term costs.

Criticism of the Doctrine of Positive Responsibility

Many, particularly libertarians, assert there is no "social responsibility" to do anything, but to refrain from doing. They argue that social responsibility only exists to the extent that an individual or business should not initiate physical force, threat of force, or fraud against another. In his famous article The Social Responsibility of Business is to Increase Profits, Nobel economist Milton Friedman (Classical View/theory of

Social Responsibility) asserts that businesses have no social responsibility other than to increase profits and refrain from engaging in deception and fraud. He maintains that when businesses seek to maximize profits, they almost always incidentally do what is good for society.

Friedman does not argue that business should not help the community but that it may indeed be in the long-run self-interest of a business to "devote resources to providing amenities to [the] community..." in order to "generate goodwill" and thereby increase profits.

Another famous economist highly critical of this doctrine is R. Edward Freeman, author of a number of papers on stakeholder theory from an explicitly libertarian perspective.

8

Capital Accumulation

INTRODUCTION

Most generally, the accumulation of capital refers simply to the gathering or amassment of objects of value; the increase in wealth; or the creation of wealth. Capital can be generally defined as assets invested for profit.

In economics, accounting and Marxian economics, capital accumulation is often equated with investment, especially in real capital goods.

But capital accumulation can refer variously to

- real investment in tangible means of production.
- financial investment in paper assets.
- investment in non-productive physical assets such as residential real estate that appreciate in value.
- "human capital accumulation," i.e., new education and training increasing the skills of the (potential) labour force.

Non-financial capital accumulation is an essential factor for economic growth, since additional investment is essential to enlarge the scale of production and increase employment opportunities. Without this, the total amount of tangible wealth that can be traded would not increase.

In modern macroeconomics and econometrics the term capital formation is often used in preference to "accumulation", though UNCTAD refers nowadays to "accumulation".

HARROD-DOMAR MODEL

In macroeconomics, following the Harrod-Domar model, the savings ratio (s) and the capital coefficient (k) are regarded as critical factors for accumulation and growth, assuming that all saving is used to finance fixed investment. The rate of growth of the real stock of fixed capital (K) is:

$$\frac{\Delta K}{K} = \frac{\frac{\Delta K}{Y}}{\frac{K}{Y}} = \frac{s}{K}$$

where Y is the real national income. If the capital-output ratio or capital coefficient $\left(k = \frac{K}{Y}\right)$ is constant, the rate of growth of Y is equal to the rate of growth of K. This is determined by s (the ratio of net fixed investment or saving to Y) and k.

A country might for example save and invest 12% of its national income, and then if the capital coefficient is 4:1 (i.e. \$4 billion must be invested to increase the national income by 1 billion) the rate of growth of the national income might be 3% annually. However, as Keynesian economics points out, savings do not automatically mean investment (as liquid funds may be hoarded for example). Investment may also not be investment in fixed capital.

Assuming that the turnover of total production capital invested remains constant, the proportion of total investment which just maintains the stock of total capital, rather than enlarging it, will typically increase as the total stock increases. The growth rate of incomes and net new investments must then also increase, in order to accelerate the growth of the capital stock. Simply put, the bigger capital grows, the more capital it takes to keep it growing and the more markets must expand.

THE MEASUREMENT OF ACCUMULATION

Accumulation can be measured as the monetary value of investments, or as the change in the value of assets owned. Using company balance sheets, tax data and direct surveys as a basis, government statisticians estimate total investments and assets for the purpose of national accounts, Input-output tables national balance of payments and Flow of funds statistics. Usually the Reserve Banks and the Treasury provide interpretations and analysis of this data. Standard indicators include Capital formation, Gross fixed capital formation, fixed capital, household asset wealth, and foreign direct investment.

Organisations such as the International Monetary Fund, UNCTAD, the World Bank Group, the OECD, and the Bank for International Settlements used national investment data to estimate world trends. The Bureau of Economic Analysis, Eurostat and the Japan Statistical Office provide data on the USA, Europe and Japan respectively.

Other useful sources of investment information are business magazines such as Fortune, Forbes, The Economist, Business Weekly etc. as well as various corporate "watchdog" organisations and NGO publications. A reputable scientific journal is the Review of Income & Wealth. In the case of the USA, the "Analytical Perspectives" document (an annex to the yearly budget) provides useful wealth and capital estimates applying to the whole country.

PSYCHOLOGY, SOCIOLOGY AND ETHICS OF CAPITAL ACCUMULATION

There have been numerous psychological and sociological studies of the motivations of investment behaviour by individuals. Most of these suggest that the propensity to accumulate capital is associated with qualities such as an intelligent understanding of property ownership, a positive attitude towards money, the ability to seize a money-making opportunity, and a desire to acquire more wealth. These are not innate or genetic qualities, but learnt through social experience.

However, even if a strong motivation for enrichment exists, the business climate, local culture or social instability may prevent this motivation from being realised. Hernando de Soto for example argues that the reason why poor countries are poor is mainly because of the absence of a legal-cultural infrastructure of "asset management" and of formalised and enforced private property rights. However the most popular argument in this respect remains the vicious cycle of poverty: the poor are poor because they are poor. Critics of this argument object it is an uninformative tautology.

Greed and desire can play a very important role in capital accumulation, but are not a necessary requirement. Indeed according to Max Weber's study of capitalism and the Protestant ethic, frugality, sobriety and saving were among the key values of the rising bourgeoisie in the age of the Reformation.

Some economic historians (e.g. David Landes) refer to national psychology and argue that some nations or cultures (e.g. Europe) are inherently better equipped for capital accumulation, due to cultural habits, customs and values.

Other economic historians (e.g. Paul A. Baran) have argued that psychological factors explain very little, because a nation which previously had a low level of accumulation can suddenly "take off". In that case, the causes must be sought in the prevailing social relations.

Controversies about the ethics of accumulation have occurred ever since commercial trade began. If informal and formal prostitution is regarded as the oldest profession, the first ethical debate about accumulation must have occurred tens of thousands of years ago at the very least. The problem is that trade or market forces do not create any particular morality of their own, beyond the requirement to meet contractual obligations that settle transactions. Some forms of trade may be accepted, others rejected, but there exists no general moral principle for this which can be derived from the trade itself.

A good contemporary illustration of this problem is the gigantic increase in total reported crime and the grey economy or shadow economy after the deregulation of world markets from the 1980s, and the marketisation of the USSR and China. But ancient philosophers and theologians already knew about the problem, which is why they were intensely preoccupied with the politics of the "rule of law" and its enforcement.

The main ethical questions concern which routes to wealth are morally justifiable, and what entitles individuals and groups to appropriate amounts of wealth, in particular wealth which they have not themselves created. The medieval economists invented theories of a just price and the moral debate surfaces again these days e.g. in the controversies about fair trade, imperialism and Islamic banking. Neo-liberal theory emphasises that a "good" person is one who creates new wealth, while socialist theory says a "good" person shares the wealth. The most popular moral theories are similar to that of John Rawls.

Karl Marx illustrated his analysis with sarcastic comments about "Christian accumulation"; some forms of accumulation were believed to be compatible with Jesus Christ, while other were not; some forms of accumulation were forgiven by God afterwards, others were not. Martin Luther for example raged against usury and extortion. For another example, the famous christian hymn Amazing Grace was written by the captain of a slave ship.

Marxism-Leninism is hostile to private property and market activity. It must be kept in mind that the "private property" that Marx refers to is the ownership of the means of production by a generally small elite of wealthy entrepreneurs, a type of oligarchy also in command of the bourgeois state, and not any aspect of personal property per se such as homes, cars, or other assets of personal use. Ideological enemies of Marxism have made much of this confusion, creating fears in the general population that communism is about sharing everything, down to the last towel, toothbrush, and even wives. In fact the original doctrine of Christ is far more radical in its demand for the sharing of property and wealth redistribution than Marx.

But because capital accumulation does not presuppose any particular or specific "moral system", accumulation can also continue regardless of any particular morality advocated by popes, presidents, queens, journalists, pop stars, business tycoons or anybody else. All that is required is (1) the ability to own assets and trade in them and (2) sufficient income beyond subsistence to be able to afford accumulation.

MARXIAN CONCEPT OF CAPITAL ACCUMULATION

In Karl Marx's critique of political economy, capital accumulation refers to the chrematistic operation whereby a sum of money is transformed into a larger sum of money (capitalism is this money-making activity, although Marx often equates capitalism with the capitalist mode of production). Here, capital is defined essentially as economic or commercial asset value in search of additional value or surplus-value. This requires property relations which enable objects of value to be appropriated and owned. According to Marx, capital accumulation has a double origin, namely in trade and in expropriation, both of a legal or illegal kind. The reason is that a stock of capital can be increased through a process of exchange or "trading up" but also through directly taking an asset or resource from someone else, without compensation. David Harvey calls this accumulation by dispossession. Marx does not discuss gifts and grants as a source of capital accumulation, nor does he analyze taxation in detail. Nowadays the tax take is so large (i.e. 25-40% of GDP) that some authors refer to state capitalism.

The continuation and progress of capital accumulation depends on the removal of obstacles to the expansion of trade, and this has historically often been a violent process. As markets expand, more and more new opportunities develop for accumulating capital, because more and more types of goods and services can be traded in. But capital accumulation may also confront resistance, when people refuse to sell, or refuse to buy (for example a strike by investors or workers, or consumer resistance). What spurs accumulation is competition; in business, if you don't go forward, you go backward, and unless the law prevents it, the strong will exploit the weak.

In general, Marx's critique of capital accumulation is that the human chase after wealth and self-enrichment leads to inhuman consequences. The enrichment of some is at the expense of the immiseration of others, and competition becomes brutal. The basis of it all is the exploitation of the labour effort of others. When the "economic cake" expands, this may be obscured because all can gain from trade. But when the "economic cake" shrinks, then capital accumulation can only occur by taking income or assets from other people, other social classes, or other nations. The point is that to exist, capital must always grow, and to ensure that it will grow, people are prepared to do almost anything.

THE RATE OF ACCUMULATION

In Marxian economics, the rate of accumulation is defined as (1) the value of the real net increase in the stock of capital in an accounting period, (2) the proportion of realised surplus-value or profit-income which is reinvested, rather than consumed. This rate can be expressed by means of various ratios between the original capital outlay, the realised turnover, surplus-value or profit and reinvestments (see e.g. the writings of the economist Michal Kalecki).

Other things being equal, the greater the amount of profit-income that is disbursed as personal earnings and used for consumptive purposes, the lower the savings rate and the lower the rate of accumulation is likely to be. However, earnings spent on consumption can also stimulate market demand and higher investment. This is the cause of endless controversies in economic theory about "how much to spend, and how much to save".

In a boom period of capitalism, the growth of investments is cumulative, i.e. one investment leads to another, leading to a constantly expanding market, an expanding labor force, and an increase in the standard of living for the majority of the people.

In a stagnating, decadent capitalism, the accumulation process is increasingly oriented towards investment on military and security forces, real estate, financial speculation, and luxury consumption. In that case, income from value-adding production will decline in favour of interest, rent and tax income, with as a corollary an increase in the level of permanent unemployment.

As a rule, the larger the total sum of capital invested, the higher the return on investment will be. The more capital one owns, the more capital one can also borrow and reinvest at a higher rate of profit or interest. The inverse is also true, and this is one factor in the widening gap between the rich and the poor.

Ernest Mandel emphasized that the rhythm of capital accumulation and growth depended critically on (1) the division of a society's social product between "necessary product" and "surplus product", and (2) the division of the surplus product between investment and consumption. In turn, this allocation pattern reflected the outcome of competition among capitalists, competition between capitalists and workers, and competition between workers. The pattern of capital accumulation can therefore never be simply explained by commercial factors, it also involved social factors and power relationships.

THE ORIGIN OF CAPITAL ACCUMULATION IN TRADE

In the simplest circuit of commercial trade, a sum of money M is loaned and returned with interest as the larger sum M'. Or, as a variation, M is traded for another currency, which rises in value. In counter-trade (a form of barter in which money may be used only to value goods and services), a commodity C exchanges for another commodity C', which may also result in a larger sum of value. Marx calls the additional value surplus-value.

In a slightly more complex trading circuit, a sum of money M buys a commodity C which upon sale yields a larger sum of money M', which can be reinvested. Alternatively, the circuit C - M - C' could substitute for M - C - M' but in this case the enlarged value consists of commodities rather than of money. These circuits are basic to merchant trade.

In the more developed trading circuit of capitalism, however, M buys inputs C (means of production and labour-power) which through new production creates outputs C' and upon sale yield a larger sum of money M'. In this case, we are no longer dealing with merchant capitalism, but with capitalist industry (the capitalist mode of production: all or most of the inputs and outputs of production are available as marketed commodities, and the costs & benefits of total production are rationally calculated in price terms.

In modern capitalism, the circuits of finance, commerce and production have become exceedingly complex, often lack transparency and may involve multilateral exchanges or a lot of fictitious capital. The daily trading volume in the world's foreign exchange markets was estimated at $1.88 trillion in 2004, as against $590 billion in 1989 (current dollars). By comparison, the New York Stock Exchange daily volume is said to be around $25 billion a day, and the international futures markets are said to trade about $35 billion worth of contracts a day. Speculative trading makes up the bulk of the daily trading volumes. Most rich people do not want to bother with the financial management of most of their wealth, and know little about it. Investment specialists make their money from investing the money of the rich using their superior market knowledge, contacts, networks and commercial skills.

THE CIRCUIT OF CAPITAL ACCUMULATION FROM PRODUCTION

Strictly speaking, capital has accumulated only when realised profit income has been reinvested in capital assets. But the process of capital accumulation in production has, as suggested in the first volume of Marx's Das Kapital, at least 7 distinct but linked moments:

- The initial investment of capital (which could be borrowed capital) in means of production and labor power.
- The command over surplus-labour and its appropriation.
- The valorisation of capital through production.
- The appropriation of the new output produced by employees, containing the added value.
- The realisation of surplus-value through output sales.
- The appropriation of realised surplus-value as (profit) income after deduction of costs.
- The reinvestment of profit income in production.

All of these moments do not refer simply to an "economic" or commercial process. Rather, they assume the existence of legal, social, cultural and economic power conditions, without which creation, distribution and circulation of the new wealth could not occur. This becomes especially clear when the attempt is made to create a market where none exists, or where people refuse to trade.

In fact Marx suggests that the original or primitive accumulation of capital often occurs through violence, plunder, slavery, robbery, extortion and theft. He argues that the capitalist mode of production requires that people must be forced to work in value-adding production for someone else, and for this purpose, they must be cut off from sources of income other than selling their labor power.

SIMPLE AND EXPANDED REPRODUCTION

In volume 2 of Das Kapital, Marx continues the story and shows that, with the aid of bank credit, capital in search of growth can more or less smoothly mutate from one form to another, alternately taking the form of money capital (liquid deposits, securities, etc.), commodity capital (tradeable products, real estate etc.), or production capital (means of production and labor power).

His discussion of the simple and expanded reproduction of the conditions of production offers a more sophisticated model of the parameters of the accumulation process as a whole. At simple reproduction, a sufficient amount is produced to sustain society at the given living standard; the stock of capital stays constant. At expanded reproduction, more product-value is produced than is necessary to sustain society at a given living standard (a surplus product; the additional product-value is available for investments which enlarge the scale and variety of production.

Yet there is no economic law according to which capital is necessarily re-invested in the expansion of production; that depends on anticipated profitability, market expectations and perceptions of investment risk. All that Marx proves is that in capitalism production of output is conditional on capital accumulation, i.e. at least in the longer term, if production is not profitable, it will close down.

Ernest Mandel introduced the additional concept of contracted economic reproduction, i.e. reduced accumulation where business operating at a loss outnumbers growing business, or economic reproduction on a decreasing scale, for example due to wars, natural disasters or devalorisation.

Balanced economic growth requires that different factors in the accumulation process expand in appropriate proportions. But markets themselves cannot spontaneously create that balance, in fact what drives business activity is precisely the imbalances between supply and demand: inequality is the motor of growth. This partly explains why the worldwide pattern of economic growth is very uneven and unequal, even although markets have existed almost everwhere for a very long time. It also explains government regulation of market trade and protectionism.

Capital Accumulation as Social Relation

"Accumulation of capital" sometimes also refers in Marxist writings to the reproduction of capitalist social relations (institutions) on a larger scale over time, i.e., the expansion of the size of the proletariat and of the wealth owned by the bourgeoisie. This interpretation emphasizes that capital ownership, predicated on command over labor, is a social relation: the growth of capital implies the growth of the working class (a "law of accumulation"). In the first volume of Das Kapital Marx had illustrated this idea with reference to Edward Gibbon Wakefield's theory of colonisation:

> *"...Wakefield discovered that in the Colonies, property in money, means of subsistence, machines, and other means of production, does not as yet stamp a man as a capitalist if there be wanting the correlative-the wage-worker, the other man who is compelled to sell himself of his own free-will. He discovered that capital is not a thing, but a social relation between persons, established by the instrumentality of things. Mr. Peel, he moans, took with him from England to Swan River, West Australia, means of subsistence and of production to the amount of £50,000. Mr. Peel had the foresight to bring with him, besides, 3,000 persons of the working-class, men, women, and children. Once arrived at his destination, "Mr. Peel was left without a servant to make his bed or fetch him water from the river." Unhappy Mr. Peel, who provided for everything except the export of English modes of production to Swan River!"-*

In the third volume of Das Kapital, Marx refers to the "fetishism of capital" reaching its highest point with interest-bearing capital, because now capital seems to grow of its own accord without anybody doing anything. In this case,

"The relations of capital assume their most externalised and most fetish-like form in interest-bearing capital. We have here M - M', money creating more money, self-expanding value, without the process that effectuates these two extremes. In merchant's capital, M - C - M', there is at least the general form of the capitalistic movement, although it confines itself solely to the sphere of circulation, so that profit appears merely as profit derived from alienation; but it is at least seen to be the product of a social relation, not the product of a mere thing. (...) This is obliterated in M - M', the form of interest-bearing capital. (...) The thing (money, commodity, value) is now capital even as a mere thing, and capital appears as a mere thing. The result of the entire process of reproduction appears as a property inherent in the thing itself. It depends on the owner of the money, i.e., of the commodity in its continually exchangeable form, whether he wants to spend it as money or loan it out as capital. In interest-bearing capital, therefore, this automatic fetish, self-expanding value, money generating money, are brought out in their pure state and in this form it no longer bears the birth-marks of its origin. The social relation is consummated in the relation of a thing, of money, to itself. -Instead of the actual transformation of money into capital, we see here only form without content."

DIFFERENT FORMS OF CAPITAL ACCUMULATION

Essentially, in capitalism the production of output depends on the accumulation of capital. The propensity to invest in production therefore depends a lot on expectations of profitability and sales volume, and on perceptions of market risk. If production stops being profitable, or if sales drop sharply, or if there is social instability, capital will exit more and more from the sphere of production. Or if it cannot or does not, rationalisation investments will be undertaken, to amalgamate unprofitable enterprises into profitable units.

As a corollary, capital accumulation may be the accumulation of production capital (industrial assets), or the accumulation of money capital (financial assets), or the accumulation of commodity capital (products, real estate etc. which can be traded).

But irrespective of whether the additional capital value (or surplus-value happens to take the form of profit, interest, rent, or some kind of tax impost or royalty income, what drives the accumulation process is the perpetual search for more surplus-value, for added value as such.

This requires a constant supply of a labor force which can conserve and add value to inputs and capital assets, and thus create a higher value. Normally, the socio-economic compulsion to work for a living in capitalist society is legally enforced and regulated by the state, for example through workfare and strict conditions for receiving an unemployment benefit.

Although capital accumulation does not necessarily require production, ultimately the basis for it is value-adding production which makes net additions to the stock of wealth. Capital can accumulate by shifting the ownership of assets from one place to another, but ultimately the total stock of assets must increase. Other things being equal, if production fails to grow sufficiently, the level of debt will increase, ultimately causing a breakdown of the accumulation process when debtors cannot pay creditors.

Capital accumulation does not necessarily require trade either, although capital presupposes trade, and the ability to exchange goods for money. The reason is that wealth can be amassed through illegal or legalised expropriation (robbery, plunder, theft, piracy, slavery, embezzlement, fraud and so on). However, a continuous and cumulative accumulation process always presupposes that capital ownership is secure. Consequently, military and police forces have typically been necessary for capital accumulation on a larger scale, to protect property.

In medieval society, typically the bourgeoisie could not protect its capital assets permanently from attacks, which meant that the accumulation process was interrupted, and remained limited in scope. Today however, capitalists can own billions of dollars worth of assets which are well-protected against crime (see the annual Merrill-Lynch survey of the world's wealthy). With the aid of private banking it is easier to obscure or hide the wealth that one owns.

REGIME OF ACCUMULATION

Both the Regulation School of French Marxist economists, inspired by the original writings of Michel Aglietta and developed by Robert S. Boyer, as well as the American social structure of accumulation school founded by the economists Samuel Bowles and David Gordon have emphasized that the processes of capital accumulation occur within a social regime of accumulation.

In other words, a specific political and socio-economic environment is required that enables sustained investment and economic growth. This environment is created partly by state policy, but partly by also by technological innovations, changes in popular culture, commercial developments, the media, and so on. An example of such a regime often cited here is that of Fordism, named after the enterprise of Henry Ford. As the pattern of accumulation changes, the regime of accumulation also changes.

Similar ideas also surface in institutional economics. The main insight here is that market trade cannot flourish without regulation by a legal system plus the enforcement of basic moral conduct and private property by the state. But the regime of accumulation responds to the total experience of living in capitalist society, not just market trade.

ENVIRONMENTAL CRITICISM OF CAPITAL ACCUMULATION

The environmental criticism of capital accumulation focuses on four main ideas.

Firstly, there is the problem of externalities. This means that privately owned industry incurs costs, including environmental and health costs, which are not charged or priced. This happens for example when effluents are discharged on land, water or in the air, which can cause pollution or despoilation of terrains. In recognition of this, environmental taxes are sometimes imposed.

Secondly, commercial activities which may be rational from the point of view of a private enterprise may not be rational from the point of view of society as a whole, or from the point of view of the biosphere, especially when they involve the destruction of natural habitats of flora and fauna, pollution and entropy.

Because a natural resource happens to be a freely available good (for example fish in the open sea), it may be plundered for profit. Or, a lot of energy may be wasted producing and transporting a good to the consumer, to which business people are indifferent because they do not pay for it. Or, the disturbance of subsistence economics by commerce may cause overpopulation.

Thirdly, goods and services may be produced for profit in ways which are directly or indirectly harmful to human life, either because of the nature of the use-value involved, or because of the techniques used to produce them, or because they encourage consumer habits with harmful effects.

Finally, business ethics may often not be reconcilable with human ethics or environmental ethics. This means for example that the imputation of a price to an environmental cost, or imposing an environment tax may be insufficient as a policy, because some things which have value simply have no price.

Nowadays environmental concerns are an essential part of so-called socially responsible business and corporate governance. However, opinion is divided about whether a capitalist market economy can be ecologically sustainable. Some argue that the experience of environmental destruction in the Soviet Union and China proves that state socialism or command economy is ecologically worse than capitalism. Others argue that the ultimate result of capital accumulation must be the destruction of the biosphere, unless drastic steps are taken to control pollution, population growth, and consumerism, and that the examples of the former Soviet Union and China are not exculpatory of Western capitalism since these nations were, in essence, copying within severe economic and strategic constraints, the production and consumerist models of the West, especially those found in the United States. They had simply bought into a false model of the good life.

In the 1970s, many environmentalists argued for a policy of "zero economic growth" in "affluent" Western societies. However, when a long recession began in that decade, halving economic growth rates, most people became more concerned about mass unemployment. Thus, the proponents of zero growth lost popularity. Nowadays, the popular concept is sustainable economic development or growth. But interpretations of what that means can differ wildly. One difficulty is that predictions of future resource scarcity are usually based on extrapolation from the past, "assuming present trends will continue", but they may not.

Today many serious environmentalists consider capitalism, or the "market system" as it is usually called, incapable of complying with the basic requisites of a sustainable and respectful habitation of planet earth. A major problem, inherent in corporate dynamics, and amply represented in its executive sociology, is the constant compulsion to expand production without limits of any kind, disregarding the irrefutable fact that it is irrational to seek infinite expansion in a finite world. In this particular regard, critics point to the corporate penchant to plan in short-term cycles, and with a purview that is only concerned with the fortunes of a single firm or business entity, thereby ignoring the cumulative effect brought to bear on the biosphere by the entire commercial production system.

CAPITAL ACCUMULATION AND RISK

Most capital accumulation involves risk, because capital is committed to an investment without perfect certainty about future earnings. A capital asset could gain value, but it could also lose value in the future. Owners of capital (investors) therefore typically diversify their investment portfolio, and try to minimise the risks involved in investments by every possible means.

In the course of two centuries of capital accumulation based on industrialisation the intensive economising and exploitation of human labour, and technological innovation,

- the value of the assets that are invested in has become very large

- the markets traded in extend around the globe
- the deregulation of markets has increased the level of market uncertainty
- the volume of speculative capital has grown enormously
- the banking industry dominates the ownership of capital assets.

This has led to an enormous expansion of the insurance industry and of the profession of risk management. As a corollary, this powerfully stimulates the construction of mathematical models which aim to assess how probable it is that particular "risky events" will occur.

Some sociologists such as Frank Furedi claim that an exaggerated and unhealthy preoccupation or anxiety about risks has infiltrated the whole of modern society.

Speculation is justified as follows:

"The roles of speculators in a market economy are to absorb risk and to add liquidity to the marketplace by risking their own capital for the chance of monetary reward."

CAPITAL ACCUMULATION AND MILITARY WARS

Capitalist competition for profits, markets and spheres of influence, pushed to an extreme, culminates in military wars. In that sense, the theatre of war expresses the frontline of the accumulation process. Military wars typically cause the destruction of capital assets.

But at the same time wars have been a powerful stimulus for the accumulation of capital and market expansion outside the theatre of war. Often this has induced laws against war profiteering.

War destruction can be illustrated by looking at World War 2. Industrial war damage was heaviest in Japan, where 1/4 of factory buildings and 1/3 of plant & equipment were destroyed; 1/7 of electric power-generating capacity was destroyed and 6/7 of oil refining capacity. The merchant fleet lost 80% of the ships. In Germany in 1944, when air attacks were heaviest, 6.5% of machine tools were damaged or destroyed, but around 90% were repaired. About 10% of steel production capacity was lost.

Germany's total war damage was estimated at about 17.5% of the pre-war total capital stock by value, i.e. about 1/6. In the Berlin area alone, there were 8 million refugees lacking basic necessities. In 1945, less than 10% of the railways were still operating. 2395 rail bridges were destroyed and a total of 7500 bridges, 10,000 locomotives and more than 100,000 goods wagons were destroyed. Less than 40% of the remaining locomotives were operational.

However, by the first quarter of 1946 European rail traffic regained its prewar operational level. At the end of the year, 90% of Germany's railway lines were operating again. In retrospect, the rapidity of social reconstruction appears astonishing.

Initially, in May 1945, Harry S. Truman's directive had been that no steps would be taken towards economic rehabilitation of Germany. In fact, the industry plan of 1946 prohibited production in excess of half of the 1938 level; the iron and steel industry was allowed to produce only less than a third of pre-war output.

In 1946, 2% of Germany's physical capital stock (plant & equipment) was also dismantled and confiscated, about a quarter of it going to the USSR. By 1947, industrial production in Germany was at 1/3 of the 1938 level, and industrial investment at about 1/2 the 1938 level.

The first big strike wave in the Ruhr occurred in early 1947-it was about food rations and housing, but soon there were demands for nationalisation. The US Governor (Newman) however stated at the time that he had to power to break strikes by withholding food rations.

The clear message was: "either back to work, or you starve". By 1951, German industrial production had overtaken the prewar level. The Marshall Aid dollars were important, but, after the currency reform (which permitted German capitalists to revalue their assets) and the establishment of a new political system, much more important was the commitment of the USA to rebuilding German capitalism, rather than keeping Germany in a weak position. Average real wages remained low, lower even than in 1938, until the early 1950s, while profitability was unusually high. So the total investment fund, aided by credits, was also high, resulting in a high rate of accumulation.

In modern times, it has often been possible to rebuild physical capital assets destroyed in wars completely within the space of about 10 years, except in cases of severe pollution by chemical warfare or other kinds of irreparable devastation.

However, damage to human capital has been much more devastating, in terms of fatalities (in the case of world war 2, about 55 million deaths), permanent physical disability, enduring ethnic hostility and psychological injuries which have effects for at least several generations.

NEW DEVELOPMENTS IN CAPITAL ACCUMULATION

New trends in capital accumulation include:

- Financialisation (the extraordinarily strong growth of the international financial markets. This is trade in financial claims to current and future income. As a corollary, the proportion of national income which consists of interest income and rentier income increases. The International Swaps and Derivatives Association reported in September 2006 that the outstanding nominal value of swaps and derivatives at the end of June 2006 was $283 trillion-nearly ten times the combined GDP of the US, Canada, the EU, Japan, and China; or ten times the value of total US home equity (each being valued at about $34 trillion). According to Standard & Poor's, world stock market capitalization is about $41 trillion. Of total swaps and derivatives, some $26 trillion was in the fastest growing area, credit default swaps.
- Modern information technology makes it possible to engage in very complex investment projects and shift

funds extremely quickly from one placement to another in space and time. This increases the rotation speed of capital and raises the profit rate, but can also increase potential financial risks.

- The growing controversies about intellectual property rights and the protection (or security) of ideas which can make money for the owner. Increasingly, the basic conditions necessary for a good, service or idea to become a tradeable commodity are theoretically defined.
- Ongoing privatisation of assets which were previously under public ownership. The IMF estimates suggest that in two decades since 1985 more than $2 trillion US dollars (in 2005 values) worth of state assets were privatised worldwide. Typically, these assets also rise sharply in value within a few years, because they involve enterprises occupying monopoly positions (e.g. utilities) which thus provide guaranteed profits. If profits dry up in the private sector, capitalists plunder public assets paid for by all citizens, with the argument that if they run them, supply will be more efficient.
- The enormous increase in capital gains from rising property values in the richer countries, especially in the housing market. US tax data for fiscal 2000 showed that realised capital gains in the USA peaked at an estimated $644.3 billion worth of income while US GDP in 2000 was at US$9,817.0 billion, in other words realised capital gains assessed for tax purposes were equal to 6.5% of GDP at that point (total capital gains would be larger). Yet GDP, being a measure of value added in production, does not even include this "hidden" personal and business income.
- A growing proportion of capital assets which is not productively invested (overcapitalisation), together with an increase in the amount of consumer debt and liabilities. Some observers see the cause as being an increase in the gap between rich and poor, which causes only sluggish demand growth. "Debt management" has become a distinct and profitable business.

- The crisis of numerous pension funds providing a large amount of investment capital, which are alleged to be badly managed.
- An international "competition of currency values" strongly influenced by speculative capital, which has a big effect on the pattern of international trade. The magnitudes involved can be gauged e.g. from the currency conversion ratios used to establish purchasing power parity. For example, India's GDP valued at "ppp" becomes five times larger. This tends to stimulate counter-trade.
- The acceleration of the concentration and centralisation of capital internationally in very large corporations. The Fortune Magazine "Global 500" largest corporations in 2004 employed more people than the whole work-force of Germany. The after-tax profit volume of the Fortune Global 500 was said to be $731 billion, the combined asset value was $60.8 trillion, gross income (revenues) $14.8 trillion, and stockholders equity $6.8 trillion. For comparison, world GDP in 2004 was valued at $40.9 trillion (World Bank).
- The Merrill lynch/CapGemini World Wealth Report 2005 covering High Net Worth Individuals (HNWI) claims the fortunes of the world's millionaires and billionaires grew strongly in 2004, increasing by 8.2% to US$30.8 trillion in one year. Driven by North America & Asia-Pacific, this represents "the highest growth of HNWI wealth in more than three years".
- Dollarisation-more US currency now circulates outside the US than inside it, and some countries such as Ecuador and El Salvador have adopted the US dollar as national currency. "Dollar hegemony" is maintained by large Asian, Arab and European investments in the United States.
- The tendency for corporate investment to orient towards activities which secure good short-term returns for shareholders. This is called "value-based management".

Most corporate executive officers (CEO's) cite profitability as their prime concern.

- An increasing preoccupation with the conditions for extending credit, and with all sorts of risk factors. World markets are increasingly sensitive to events and disturbances which might cause social instability or panics.
- The declining overall significance of business start-ups, in the sense of enterprises creating new products and services, rather than being just tax-shelters or secondary employment (whether this is a permanent trend remains to be seen).
- The growth of criminal (or illegal) accumulation as measured by crime reports, including business crime and corruption such as fraud, embezzlement, money laundering, insider trading, smurfing and theft, but also prostitution, forced labour, slavery, war plunder etc. The volume of illegal international transactions is now said to be around $1 trillion a year, equal to the GDP of Spain or Canada. National Geographic has reported there are about 27 million slaves in the world. ILO estimates of forced labor are a little over a dozen million. There are possibly 70 million people involved around the world in prostitution of one form or another. But there are many more, employed or unemployed, in "intermediate" positions. Traditional sociological categories may not describe their situation accurately, but a growing "underclass" (which may not be an accurate label) is a policy concern for many governments.
- The most ignored aspect is the changing structure of the international work-force in its totality, specifically the number employed by specific employment status and by income, in different sectors. But just as Marx's Law of Accumulation predicted, the working class has grown enormously within 2 centuries. Deon Filmer estimated that 2,474 million people participated in the worldwide non-domestic labour force in the mid-1990s. Of these around a fifth, 379 million people, worked in industry,

800 million in services, and 1,074 million in agriculture. The majority of workers in industry and services were wage & salary earners-58 percent of the industrial work-force and 65 percent of the services work-force. But a big portion were self-employed or involved in family labour. Filmer suggests the total of employees worldwide in the 1990s was about 880 million, compared with around a billion working on own account on the land (mainly peasants), and some 480 million working on own account in industry and services.

MAGIC FORMULA INVESTING

Magic Formula Investing is a term that refers to an investment technique outlined by Joel Greenblatt. Magic Formula Investing is firmly rooted in the principles of value investing. For the lay investor, it is claimed that it offers market-beating returns without the complexity associated with a discounted cash flow analysis.

Methodology

Greenblatt suggests purchasing 30 Good Companies: cheap stocks with a high earnings yield and a high return on capital.

He touts the success of his magic formula in his book The Little Book that Beats the Market, citing that it does in fact beat the market 96% of the time, and has averaged a 17-year annual return of 30.8% The comparison index used for "the market" in Greenblatt's research is the S&P 500.

Formula

1. Establish a minimum market capitalization (usually greater than $50 million).
2. Exclude utility and financial stocks
3. Exclude foreign companies (American Depositary Receipts)
4. Determine company's earnings yield = EBIT / Enterprise Value.

5. Determine company's return on capital = EBIT / (Net fixed assets + working capital)
6. Rank all companies above chosen market capitalization by highest earnings yield and highest return on capital (ranked as percentages).
7. Invest in 20-30 highest ranked companies, accumulating 2-3 positions per month over a 12-month period.
8. Re-balance portfolio once per year, selling losers one day before the year-mark and winners one day after the year mark.
9. Continue over long-term (3-5 year) period.

Using Magic Formula

1. Choose preferable market capitalization level.
2. Invest in 30 companies from Magic Formula Investing, accumulating 2-3 positions per month over a 12-month period.
3. Follow steps (8-9) above.

9

Investment Management

INTRODUCTION

Investment management is the professional management of various securities (shares, bonds etc) and other assets (e.g. real estate), to meet specified investment goals for the benefit of the investors. Investors may be institutions (insurance companies, pension funds, corporations etc.) or private investors (both directly via investment contracts and more commonly via collective investment schemes e.g. mutual funds) .

The term asset management is often used to refer to the investment management of collective investments, whilst the more generic fund management may refer to all forms of institutional investment as well as investment management for private investors. Investment managers who specialize in advisory or discretionary management on behalf of (normally wealthy) private investors may often refer to their services as wealth management or portfolio management often within the context of so-called "private banking".

The provision of 'investment management services' includes elements of financial analysis, asset selection, stock selection, plan implementation and ongoing monitoring of investments.

Outside of the financial industry, the term "investement management" is often applied to investments other than financial instruments. Investments are often meant to include projects, brands, patents and many things other than stocks and bonds. Even in this case, the term implies that rigorous financial and economic analysis methods are used. Applied Information Economics is one approach developed to apply statistically and economically sound optimization methods to portfolios of other types of investments.

Investment management is a large and important global industry in its own right responsible for caretaking of trillions of dollars, euro, pounds and yen. Coming under the remit of financial services many of the world's largest companies are at least in part investment managers and employ millions of staff and create billions in revenue.

Fund manager (or investment advisor in the U.S.) refers to both a firm that provides investment management services and an individual(s) who directs 'fund management' decisions.

INDUSTRY SCOPE

The business of investment management has several facets, including the employment of professional fund managers, research (of individual assets and asset classes), dealing, settlement, marketing, internal auditing, and the preparation of reports for clients.

The largest financial fund managers are firms that exhibit all the complexity their size demands. Apart from the people who bring in the money (marketers) and the people who direct investment (the fund managers), there are compliance staff (to ensure accord with legislative and regulatory constraints), internal auditors of various kinds (to examine internal systems and controls), financial controllers (to account for the institutions' own money and costs), computer experts, and "back office" employees (to track and record transactions and fund valuations for up to thousands of clients per institution).

KEY PROBLEMS OF RUNNING SUCH BUSINESSES

Key problems include:

- revenue is directly linked to market valuations, so a major fall in asset prices causes a precipitous decline in revenues relative to costs;
- above-average fund performance is difficult to sustain, and clients may not be patient during times of poor performance;

- successful fund managers are expensive and may be headhunted by competitors;
- above-average fund performance appears to be dependent on the unique skills of the fund manager; however, clients are loath to stake their investments on the ability of a few individuals-they would rather see firm-wide success, attributable to a single philosophy and internal discipline;
- evidence suggests that size of an investment firm correlates inversely with fund performance, i.e., the smaller the firm the better the chance of good performance;
- analysts who generate above-average returns often become sufficiently wealthy that they eschew corporate employment in favor of managing their personal portfolios.

The most successful investment firms in the world have probably been those that have been separated physically and psychologically from banks and insurance companies. That is, the best performance and also the most dynamic business strategies (in this field) have generally come from independent investment management firms.

REPRESENTING THE OWNERS OF SHARES

Institutions often control huge shareholdings. In most cases they are acting as agents (intermediaries between owners of the shares and the companies owned) rather than principals (direct owners). The owners of shares theoretically have great power to alter the companies they own...via the voting rights the shares carry and the consequent ability to pressure managements, and if necessary out-vote them at annual and other meetings.

In practice, the ultimate owners of shares often do not exercise the power they collectively hold (because the owners are many, each with small holdings); financial institutions (as agents) sometimes do. There is a general belief that shareholders-in this case, the institutions acting as agents-could and should exercise more active influence over the companies in which they hold shares (e.g., to hold managers to account, to ensure Boards effective functioning). Such action would add a pressure group to those (the regulators and the Board) overseeing management.

However there is the problem of how the institution should exercise this power. One way is for the institution to decide, the other is for the institution to poll its beneficiaries. Assuming that the institution polls should it then vote the entire holding as directed by the majority of votes cast, split vote (where this is allowed) according to the proportions of the vote or respect the abstainers and only vote the respondents holding.

The price signals generated by large active managers holding or not holding the stock contribute to management change.

Some institutions have been more vocal and active in pursuing such matters; for instance, some firms believe that there are investment advantages to accumulating substantial minority shareholdings (i.e, 10% or more) and putting pressure on management to implement significant changes in the business. In some cases, institutions with minority holdings work together to force management change.

Perhaps more frequent is the sustained pressure that large institutions bring to bear on management teams through persuasive discourse and PR. On the other hand, some of the largest investment managers-such as Barclays Global Investors and Vanguard-advocate simply owning every company, reducing the incentive to influence management teams.

The national context in which shareholder representation considerations are set is variable and important. The USA is a litigious society and shareholders use the law as a lever to pressure management teams. In Japan it is traditional for shareholders to be low in the 'pecking order,' which often allows management and labor to ignore the rights of the ultimate owners.

Whereas US firms generally cater to shareholders, Japanese businesses generally exhibit a stakeholder mentality, in which they seek consensus amongst all interested parties (against a background of strong unions and labour legislation).

SIZE OF THE GLOBAL FUND MANAGEMENT INDUSTRY

Assets of the global fund management industry increased for the third year running in 2006 to reach a record $55.0 trillion. This was up 10% on the previous year and 54% on 2002. Growth during the past three years has been due to an increase in capital inflows and strong performance of equity markets.

Pension assets totalled $20.6 trillion in 2005, with a further $16.6 trillion invested in insurance funds and $17.8 trillion in mutual funds. Merrill Lynch also estimates the value of private wealth at $33.3 trillion of which about a third was incorporated in other forms of conventional investment management.

The US was by far the largest source of funds under management in 2005 with 48% of the world total. It was followed by Japan with 11% and the UK with 7%. The Asia-Pacific region has shown the strongest growth in recent years. Countries such as China and India offer huge potential and many companies are showing an increased focus in this region.

PHILOSOPHY, PROCESS AND PEOPLE

The 3-P's (Philosophy, Process and People) are often used to describe the reasons why the manager is able to produce above average results.

- Philosophy refers to the over-arching beliefs of the investment organisation. For example, does the manager buy growth or value shares (and why), does he believe in market timing (and on what evidence), does he rely on external research or does he employ a team of researchers. It is helpful if any and all of such fundamental beliefs are supported by proof-statements.
- Process refers to the way in which the overall philosophy is implemented. For example, which universe of assets is explored before particular assets are chosen as suitable investments; how does the manager decide what to buy and when; how does the manager decide what to sell and when; who takes the decisions and are they taken by committee; what controls are in place to ensure that a rogue fund (one very different from others and from what is intended) cannot arise;

- People refers to the staff, especially the fund managers. The question is who are they, how are they selected, how old are they, who reports to whom, how deep is the team (and do all the members understand the philosophy and process they are supposed to be using), and most important of all how long has the team been working together. This last question is vital because whatever performance record was presented at the outset of the relationship with the client may or may not relate to (have been produced by) a team that is still in place. If the team has changed greatly (high staff turnover), then arguably the performance record is completely unrelated to the existing team (of fund managers).

Investment Managers and Portfolio Structures

At the heart of the investment management industry are the managers who invest and divest client investments. A certified company investment advisor should conduct an assessment of each client's individual needs and risk profile. The advisor then recommends appropriate investments.

ASSET ALLOCATION

The different asset classes are stocks, bonds, real-estate, derivatives, and commodities. The exercise of allocating funds among these assets (and among individual securities within each asset class) is what investment management firms are paid for. Asset classes exhibit different market dynamics, and different interaction effects; thus, the allocation of monies among asset classes will have a significant effect on the performance of the fund. Some research suggests that allocation among asset classes has more predictive power than the choice of individual holdings in determining portfolio return. Arguably, the skill of a successful investment manager resides in constructing the asset allocation, and separately the individual holdings, so as to outperform certain benchmarks (e.g., the peer group of competing funds, bond and stock indices).

Long-term Returns

It is important to look at the evidence on the long-term returns to different assets, and to holding period returns (the returns that accrue on average over different lengths of investment). For example, over very long holding periods (*eg.* 10+ years) in most countries, equities have generated higher returns than bonds, and bonds have generated higher returns than cash. According to financial theory, this is because equities are riskier (more volatile) than bonds which are themselves more risky than cash.

Diversification

Against the background of the asset allocation, fund managers consider the degree of diversification that makes sense for a given client (given its risk preferences) and construct a list of planned holdings accordingly. The list will indicate what percentage of the fund should be invested in each particular stock or bond. The theory of portfolio diversification was originated by Markowitz and effective diversification requires management of the correlation between the asset returns and the liability returns, issues internal to the portfolio (individual holdings volatility), and cross-correlations between the returns.

Investment Styles

There are a range of different styles of fund management that the institution can implement. For example, growth, value, market neutral, small capitalisation, indexed, etc. Each of these approaches has its distinctive features, adherents and, in any particular financial environment, distinctive risk characteristics. For example, there is evidence that growth styles (buying rapidly growing earnings) are especially effective when the companies able to generate such growth are scarce; conversely, when such growth is plentiful, then there is evidence that value styles tend to outperform the indices particularly successfully.

PERFORMANCE MEASUREMENT

Fund performance is the acid test of fund management, and in the institutional context accurate measurement is a necessity. For that purpose, institutions measure the performance of each fund (and usually for internal purposes components of each fund) under their management, and performance is also measured by external firms that specialise in performance measurement. The leading performance measurement firms (e.g. Frank Russell in the USA) compile aggregate industry data e.g showing how funds in general performed against given indices and peer groups over various time periods.

In a typical case (let us say an equity fund), then the calculation would be made (as far as the client is concerned) every quarter and would show a percentage change compared with the prior quarter (e.g. +4.6% total return in US dollars). This figure would be compared with other similar funds managed within the institution (for purposes of monitoring internal controls), with performance data for peer group funds, and with relevant indices (where available) or tailor-made performance benchmarks where appropriate. The specialist performance measurement firms calculate quartile and decile data and close attention would be paid to the (percentile) ranking of any fund.

Generally speaking it is probably appropriate for an investment firm to persuade its clients to assess performance over a longer periods (e.g. 3 to 5 years) to smooth out very short term fluctuations in performance and the influence of the business cycle. This can be difficult however and, industrywide, there is a serious pre-occupation with short-term numbers and the effect on the relationship with clients (and resultant business risks for the institutions).

An enduring problem is whether to measure before-tax or after-tax performance. After-tax represents the benefit to the investor, but investors tax positions vary. Before tax measurement can mislead, especially in regimens that tax realised capital gains (and not unrealised). A successful active manager, measured before tax, can thus produce a miserable after tax result. One possible solution is to report the after-tax position of some standard tax-payer.

Absolute Versus Relative Performance

In the USA and the UK, two of the world's most sophisticated fund management markets, the tradition is for institutions to manage client money relative to benchmarks. For example, an institution believes it has done well if it has generated a return of 5% when the average manager generates a 4% return.

Risk-adjusted Performance Measurement

Performance measurement should not be reduced to the evaluation of fund returns alone, but must also integrate other fund elements that would be of interest to investors, such as the measure of risk taken. Several other aspects are also part of performance measurement: evaluating if managers have succeeded in reaching their objective, i.e. if their return was sufficiently high to reward the risks taken; how they compare to their peers; and finally whether the portfolio management results were due to luck or the manager's skill. The need to answer all these questions has led to the development of more sophisticated performance measures, many of which originate in modern portfolio theory.

Modern portfolio theory established the quantitative link that exists between portfolio risk and return. The Capital Asset Pricing Model (CAPM) developed by Sharpe (1964) highlighted the notion of rewarding risk and produced the first performance indicators, be they risk-adjusted ratios (Sharpe ratio, information ratio) or differential returns compared to benchmarks (alphas). The Sharpe ratio is the simplest and best known performance measure. It measures the return of a portfolio in excess of the risk-free rate, compared to the total risk of the portfolio. This measure is said to be absolute, as it does not refer to any benchmark, avoiding drawbacks related to a poor choice of benchmark. Meanwhile, it does not allow the separation of the performance of the market in which the portfolio is invested from that of the manager. The information ratio is a more general form of the Sharpe ratio in which the risk-free asset is replaced by a benchmark portfolio. This measure is relative, as it evaluates portfolio performance in reference to a benchmark, making the result strongly dependent on this benchmark choice.

Portfolio alpha is obtained by measuring the difference between the return of the portfolio and that of a benchmark portfolio. This measure appears to be the only reliable performance measure to evaluate active management. In fact, we have to distinguish between normal returns, provided by the fair reward for portfolio exposure to different risks, and obtained through passive management, from abnormal performance (or outperformance) due to the manager's skill, whether through market timing or stock picking. The first component is related to allocation and style investment choices, which may not be under the sole control of the manager, and depends on the economic context, while the second component is an evaluation of the success of the manager's decisions. Only the latter, measured by alpha, allows the evaluation of the manager's true performance.

Portfolio normal return may be evaluated using factor models. The first model, proposed by Jensen (1968), relies on the CAPM and explains portfolio normal returns with the market index as the only factor. It quickly becomes clear, however, that one factor is not enough to explain the returns and that other factors have to be considered. Multi-factor models were developed as an alternative to the CAPM, allowing a better description of portfolio risks and an accurate evaluation of managers' performance. For example, Fama and French (1993) have highlighted two important factors that characterise a company's risk in addition to market risk. These factors are the book-to-market ratio and the company's size as measured by its market capitalisation. Fama and French therefore proposed a three-factor model to describe portfolio normal returns. Carhart (1997) proposed to add momentum as a fourth factor to allow the persistence of the returns to be taken into account. Also of interest for performance measurement is Sharpe's (1992) style analysis model, in which factors are style indices. This model allows a custom benchmark for each portfolio to be developed, using the linear combination of style indices that best replicate portfolio style allocation, and leads to an accurate evaluation of portfolio alpha.

SPECULATION

Speculation, in the narrow sense of financial speculation, involves the buying, holding, selling, and short-selling of stocks, bonds, commodities, currencies, collectibles, real estate, derivatives or any valuable financial instrument to profit from fluctuations in its price as opposed to buying it for use or for income via methods such as dividends or interest. Speculation or agiotage represents one of three market roles in western financial markets, distinct from hedging, long or short term investing and arbitrage.

SPECULATION AREAS

Convention-and especially satire-sometimes speculators comically as speculating in pork bellies (in which a real market and real speculators exist) and often "losing their shirts" or making a fortune upon small market changes. Speculation exists in many such commodities but, if measured by value, the most important markets deal in financial futures contracts and other derivatives which involve leverage that can transform a small market movement into a huge gain or loss.

Type of Speculators

Most non-professional traders lose money on speculation, while those who do make money tend to become professionals. Occasionally some dramatic event will occur such as the effort of the Hunt brothers to corner the silver market or the currency speculations of George Soros or the speculative trading of Nick Leeson, which caused the collapse of Barings Bank.

By some definitions, most long term investors, even those who buy and hold for decades, may be classified as speculators, excepting only the rare few who are not primarily motivated by eventually selling at a good profit. Some dedicated speculators are distinguished by shorter holding times, the use of leverage, by being willing to take short positions as well as long positions (in markets where the distinction can be reasonably made). A degree of speculation exists in a wide range of financial decisions, from the purchase of a house to a bet on a horse, this is what modern market economists call as Ubiquitous Speculation.

In Security Analysis, Benjamin Graham gave a definition of speculation in relation to investment: "An investment operation is one which, upon thorough analysis, promises safety of principal and a satisfactory return. Operations not meeting these requirements are speculative."

The Economic Benefits of Speculation

The service provided by speculators to a market is primarily that by risking their own capital in the hope of profit, they add liquidity to the market and make it easier for others to offset risk, including those who may be classified as hedgers and arbitrageurs.

For example, if a certain market-say in pork bellies-had no speculators, only producers (pig farmers) and consumers (butchers etc) would participate in that market. With fewer players in the market, there would be a larger spread between the current bid and ask price of pork bellies. Any new entrant in the market who wants to either buy or sell pork bellies will be forced to accept an illiquid market and market prices that have a large bid-ask spread, or might even find it difficult to find a co-party to buy or sell to. A speculator (e.g. a pork dealer) may exploit the difference in the spread and, in competition with other speculators, reduce the spread thus creating a more efficient market.

Another example of the value of speculators is the ability of a pig farmer to sell his pork on a futures exchange at a known price ahead of its production.

Some Side effects

Auctions are a method of squeezing out speculators from a transaction, but they have their own perverse effects; see winner's curse. The winner's curse is however not very significant to markets with high liquidity for both buyers and sellers, as the auction for selling the product and the auction for buying the product occur simultaneously and the two prices are separated only by a relatively small spread. This mechanism prevents the winner's curse phenomenon from causing mispricing to any degree greater than the spread.

Speculative purchasing can also create inflationary pressure, causing particular prices to increase above their "true value" (real value-adjusted for inflation) simply because the speculative purchasing artificially increases the demand. Speculative selling can also have the opposite effect, causing prices to artificially decrease below their "true value" in a similar fashion. In various situations price rises due to speculative purchasing cause further speculative purchasing in the hope that the price will continue to rise. This creates a positive feedback loop in which prices rise dramatically above the underlying "value" or "worth" of the items. This is known as an economic bubble. Such a period of increasing speculative purchasing is typically followed by one of speculative selling in which the price falls significantly, in extreme cases this may lead to crashes. Overall, the participation of speculators in financial markets tends to be accompanied by significant increase in short term market volatility. This is not necessarily a bad thing, as heightened level of volatility implies that the market will be able to correct perceived mis-pricings more rapidly and in a more drastic manner.

Etymology

The word "speculate" comes from the Latin word speculatus, which is the past participle of speculari , meaning to look ahead, to spy, and to examine. The word speculari derive from the name specula, from specere "to see", who was the Roman legionary that watch the legion's camp known as castrum. In this word we find the etimological significant of the contemporanean word, that implies the activity of looking at distant things, in the space and also in the time. From "specula" derive in late Latin the word "speculatio, speculationis", the activity of philosophical enquiring. The word is used now with this sense in philosophy, as the activity of theorizing without a solid factual base, as the modern financial speculator who take position in the market without a solid statistical base.

10

Rate of Return

In finance, rate of return (ROR) or return on investment (ROI), or sometimes just return, is the ratio of money gained or lost on an investment relative to the amount of money invested. The amount of money gained or lost may be referred to as interest, profit/loss, gain/loss, or net income/loss. The money invested may be referred to as the asset, capital, principal, or the cost basis of the investment.

ROI is also known as rate of profit. Return can also refer to the monetary amount of gain or loss. ROI is the return on a past or current investment, or the estimated return on a future investment. ROI is usually given as a percent rather than decimal value.

ROI does not indicate how long an investment is held. However, ROI is most often stated as an annual or annualized rate of return, and it is most often stated for a calendar or fiscal year. In this article, "ROI" indicates an annual or annualized rate of return, unless otherwise noted.

ROI is used to compare returns on investments where the money gained or lost--or the money invested-are not easily compared using monetary values. For instance, a $1,000 investment that earns $50 in interest obviously generates more cash than a $100 investment that earns $20 in interest, but the $100 investment earns a higher return on investment.

- $50/$1,000 = 5% ROI
- $20/$100 = 20% ROI

Since rates of return are percentages, negative rates cannot be averaged with positive rates for purposes of calculating monetary returns. However, it is common practice in finance to estimate monetary returns by averaging periodic rates of return; these estimations are most useful when the averaged periodic returns are all positive, all negative, or have low variances.

MEASURING RATE OF RETURN

The initial value of an investment does not always have a clearly defined monetary value, but for purposes of measuring ROI, the initial value must be clearly stated--along with the rationale for this initial value. The final value of an investment also does not always have a clearly defined monetary value, but for purposes of measuring ROI, the final value must be clearly stated--along with the rationale for this final value.

Return on investment is a rate of profit or income (realized or unrealized). The return is sometimes adjusted for taxes in geographical areas or historical times in which taxes consumed or consume a significant portion of profits or income. Taxes are an expense which may or may not be considered when calculating ROI. Similarly, a return may be adjusted for inflation to better indicate its true value in purchasing power.

CASH FLOW (INCOME STREAM)

Cash Flow Example on $1,000 Investment

	Year 1	Year 2	Year 3	Year 4
Dollar Return	$100	$55	$60	$50
ROI	10%	5.5%	6%	5%

ROI is a measure of cash (or potential cash) generated by an investment, or the cash lost due to the investment. It measures the cash flow or income stream from the investment to the investor. Cash flow to the investor can be in the form of profit, interest, dividends, or capital gain/loss. Capital gain/ loss occurs when the market value or resale value of the investment increases or decreases. Cash flow here does not include the return of invested capital. To the right is a simple example of cash flow on a $1,000 investment.

ANNUAL RETURNS

An Annual Rate of Return is the return on an investment over a one-year period, such as January 1st through December 31st, or June 3rd 2006 through June 2nd 2007. Each ROI in the cash flow example above is an annual rate of return. An Annualized Rate of Return is the return on an investment over a period other than one year (such as a month, or two years) multiplied or divided to give a comparable one-year return. For instance, a one-month ROI of 1% could be stated as an annualized rate of return of 12%. Or a two-year ROI of 10% could be stated as an annualized rate of return of 5%.

In the cash flow example above, the dollar returns for the four years add up to $265. The annualized rate of return for the four years is $265 ÷ ($1,000 x 4 years) = 6.625%.

ARITHMETIC RETURN

In mathematical terms, the arithmetic return is defined as the following: $ROI_{Arith} = \frac{V_f - V_i}{V_i}$

where

- Vi is the initial investment value and
- Vf is the final investment value

This return has the following characteristics:

- $ROI_{Arith} = +1.00 = +100\%$ when the final value is twice the initial value
- $ROI_{Arith} > 0$ when the investment is profitable
- $ROI_{Arith} < 0$ when the investment is at a loss
- $ROI_{Arith} = -1.00 = -100\%$ when investment can no longer be recovered

YIELD

In financial economics, the term yield indicates a rate of return that is based on compounding, reinvestment, and/or the changing market value of a security. Yield indicates that the value of the investment increases or decreases during the investment period. Effective annual rate (EAR) or Annual percentage yield (APY) indicates an annual yield from compound interest. The yield depends on the frequency of compounding.

Effective Annual Rate Based on Frequency of Compounding

Rate	Semi-Annual	Quarterly	Monthly	Daily	Continuous
1%	1.002%	1.004%	1.005%	1.005%	1.005%
5%	5.062%	5.095%	5.116%	5.127%	5.127%
10%	10.250%	10.381%	10.471%	10.516%	10.517%
15%	15.563%	15.865%	16.075%	16.180%	16.183%
20%	21.000%	21.551%	21.939%	22.134%	22.140%
30%	32.250%	33.547%	34.489%	34.969%	34.986%
40%	44.000%	46.410%	48.213%	49.150%	49.182%
50%	56.250%	60.181%	63.209%	64.816%	64.872%

LOGARITHMIC OR CONTINUOUSLY COMPOUNDED RETURN

Academics use in their research natural log return called logarithmic return or continuously compounded return. The continuously compounded return is asymmetric thus clearly indicating that positive and negative percent returns are not equal. A 10% return results in 9.53% continuously compounded return while a -10% results in -10.53%. This clearly indicates that the investment will result in a dollar amount loss corresponding to the difference between the absolute values of the two numbers: 1% (this is an approximate equality).

- V_i is the initial investment value
- V_f is the final investment value

$$ROI_{Log} = \ln\left(\frac{V_f}{V_i}\right).$$

- $ROI_{Log} > 0$ is profit
- $ROI_{Log} < 0$ is a loss

- Doubling occurs when $ROI_{Log} = \ln(2) = 69.3\%$

- Total loss occurs when $ROI_{Log} \to -\infty$.

ROI CALCULATIONS FOR VARIOUS USES

ROI values typically used for personal financial decisions include Annual Rate of Return and Annualized Rate of Return. For risk-free investments such as savings accounts or Certificates of Deposit, the personal investor considers the effects of reinvesting/compounding on increasing savings balances over time. For investments in which capital is at risk, such as stock shares, mutual fund shares and home purchases, the personal investor considers the effects of price volatility and capital gain/loss on returns.

Profitability ratios typically used by financial analysts to compare a company's profitability over time or compare profitability between companies include Gross Profit Margin, Operating Profit Margin, ROI ratio, Dividend yield, Net profit margin, Return on equity, and Return on assets. (Barron's Finance, 442-456.)

During capital budgeting, ROI values typically used within a company to select which risk-free projects to pursue in order to generate maximum return or wealth for the company's stockholders include Average rate of return, Payback period, Net present value, Profitability index, and Internal rate of return. (Barron's Finance, 151-163.).

In many countries, it is also important to consider the after-tax rate of return.

AFTER-TAX RETURNS

The after-tax rate of return is calculated by multiplying the rate of return by the tax rate, then subtracting that percentage from the rate of return.

- A return of 5% taxed at 15% gives an after-tax return of 4.25%

  0.05 x 0.15 = 0.0075

  0.05 - 0.0075 = 0.0425 = 4.25%

- A return of 10% taxed at 25% gives an after-tax return of 7.5%

  0.10 x 0.25 = 0.025

  0.10 - 0.025 = 0.075 = 7.5%

CASH OR POTENTIAL CASH RETURNS

Time Value of Money

Investments generate cash flow to the investor to compensate the investor for the time value of money.

A dollar in cash is worth less today than it was yesterday, and worth more today than it will be worth tomorrow. The main factors that are used by investors to determine the rate of return at which they are willing to invest money include:

- estimates of future inflation rates
- estimates regarding the risk of the investment (e.g. how likely it is that investors will receive regular interest/ dividend payments and the return of their full capital)
- whether or not the investors want the money available ("liquid") for other uses.

The time value of money is reflected in the interest rates that banks offer for deposits, and also in the interest rates that banks charge for loans such as home mortgages. The "risk-free" rate is the rate on U.S. Treasury Bills, because this is the highest rate available without risking capital.

The rate of return which an investor expects from an investment is called the Discount Rate. Each investment has a different discount rate, based on the cash flow expected in future from the investment. The higher the risk, the higher the discount rate (rate of return) the investor will demand from the investment.

Any investment with a return less than the annual inflation rate represents a loss of value, even though the return might well be greater than 0%. When ROI is adjusted for inflation, the resulting return is considered an increase or decrease in purchasing power. If an ROI value is adjusted for inflation, it's stated explicitly, such as "The return, adjusted for inflation, was 2%." Investors usually seek a higher rate of return on taxable investment returns than on non-taxable investment returns.

COMPOUNDING OR REINVESTING

Compound interest or other reinvestment of cash returns (such as interest and dividends) does not affect the discount rate of an investment, but it does affect the Annual Percentage Yield, because compounding/reinvestment increases the capital invested.

For example, if an investor put $1,000 in a 1-year Certificate of Deposit (CD) that paid an annual interest rate of 4%, compounded quarterly, the CD would earn 1% interest per quarter on the account balance. The account balance includes interest previously credited to the account.

Compound Interest Example

	1st Quarter	2nd Quarter	3rd Quarter	4th Quarter
Capital at the beginning of the period	$1,000	$1,010	$1,020.10	$1,030.30
Dollar return for the period	$10	$10.10	$10.20	$10.30
Account Balance at end of the period	$1,010.00	$1,020.10	$1,030.30	$1,040.60
Quarterly ROI	1%	1%	1%	1%

The concept of 'income stream' may express this more clearly. At the beginning of the year, the investor took $1,000 out of his pocket (or checking account) to invest in a CD at the bank. The money was still his, but it was no longer available for buying groceries. The investment provided a cash flow of $10.00, $10.10, $10.20 and $10.30. At the end of the year, the investor got $1,040.60 back from the bank. $1,000 was return of capital.

Once interest is earned by an investor it becomes capital. Compound interest involves reinvestment of capital; the interest earned during each quarter is reinvested. At the end of the first quarter the investor had capital of $1,010.00, which then earned

$10.10 during the second quarter. The extra dime was interest on his additional $10 investment. The Annual Percentage Yield or Future value for compound interest is higher than for simple interest because the interest is reinvested as capital and earns interest. The yield on the above investment was 4.06%.

Bank accounts offer contractually guaranteed returns, so investors cannot lose their capital. Investors/Depositors lend money to the bank, and the bank is obligated to give investors back their capital plus all earned interest. Since investors are not risking losing their capital on a bad investment, they earn a quite low rate of return. But their capital steadily increases.

RETURNS WHEN CAPITAL IS AT RISK

Average Returns

Example #1 Level Rates of Return				
	Year 1	**Year 2**	**Year 3**	**Year 4**
Rate of Return	5%	5%	5%	5%
Geometric Average	5%	5%	5%	5%
Capital at End of Year	$105.00	$110.25	$115.76	$121.55
Dollar Profit/(Loss)				$21.55
Compound Yield				5.4%

There are three common ways investment returns are calculated over multiple periods of time

- Arithmetic Average Rate of Return Arithmetic mean
- Geometric Average Rate of Return (Time-Weighted Average Return)
- Dollar-Weighted Average Return Internal rate of return

These calculations use averages of periodic percentage returns. None will accurately translate to dollar gains or losses if percent losses are averaged with percent gains. A 10% loss on a $100 investment is a $10 loss, and a 10% gain on a $100 investment is a $10 gain. When percentage returns on investments are calculated, they are calculated for a period of time-not based on original investment dollars, but based on the dollars in the investment at the beginning and end of the period. So if an investment of $100 loses 10% in the first period, the investment amount is then $90. If the investment then gains 10% in the next period, the investment amount is $99.

Example #2 Volatile Rates of Return, including losses				
	Year 1	**Year 2**	**Year 3**	**Year 4**
Rate of Return	50%	-20%	30%	-40%
Geometric Average	50%	9.5%	16%	-1.6%
Capital at End of Year	$150.00	$120.00	$156.00	$93.60
Dollar Profit/(Loss)				($6.40)
Compound Yield				-1.4%

A 10% gain followed by a 10% loss is a 1% dollar loss. The order in which the loss and gain occurs does not affect the result. A 50% gain and a 50% loss is a 25% loss. An 80% gain plus an 80% loss is a 64% loss. To recover from a 50% loss, a 100% gain is required. The mathematics of this are beyond the scope of this article, but since investment returns are published as "Average Returns", it's important to note that average returns do not always translate into dollar returns.

To the right and below are some examples of what can happen to a 4-year $100 investment with an Arithmetic Average Rate of Return of 5%.

Example #3 Highly Volatile Rates of Return, including losses				
	Year 1	**Year 2**	**Year 3**	**Year 4**
Rate of Return	-95%	0%	0%	115%
Geometric Average	-95%	-77.6%	-63.2%	-42.7%
Capital at End of Year	$5.00	$5.00	$5.00	$10.75
Dollar Profit/(Loss)				($89.25)
Compound Yield				-22.3%

CAPITAL GAINS AND LOSSES

Many investments carry significant risk that the investor will lose some or all of the invested capital. For example, investments in company stock shares put capital at risk.

A stock share is partial ownership of a company, and the value of the stock depends on many factors, including the likelihood that the company will pay a dividend (a distribution of profit to shareholders). When stock shares are first offered for sale, the company receives the capital from the stock purchaser and uses the capital to operate its business. Once stock shares are sold to investors, the investors can sell the shares to other investors. Publicly-traded companies' stock shares are bought and sold (traded) on the stock markets.

The value of a stock share depends on what someone is willing to pay for it at a certain point in time. Unlike capital invested in a savings account, the capital value (price) of a stock share constantly changes. If the price is relatively stable, the stock is said to have "low volatility." If the price often changes a great deal, the stock has "high volatility." All stock shares have some volatility, and the change in price directly affects ROI for stock investments. Stock returns are usually calculated for holding periods such as a month, a quarter or a year.

HOLDING PERIOD RETURN

The holding period return, an arithmetic return, is calculated:

Holding-Period Return = (Ending Price - Beginning Price + Cash Dividend) / Beginning Price.

Example: Stock with low volatility and a regular quarterly dividend				
End of:	**1st Quarter**	**2nd Quarter**	**3rd Quarter**	**4th Quarter**
Dividend	$1	$1	$1	$1
Stock Price	$98	$101	$102	$99
Quarterly ROI	-1%	4.08%	1.98%	-1.96%
Annual ROI				3%

To the right is an example of a stock investment of one share purchased at the beginning of the year for $100. At the end of the first quarter the stock price is $98. This is a capital loss. The stock share bought for $100 can only be sold for $98, which is the value of the investment at the end of the first quarter. The first quarter return is:

($98 - $100 + $1) / $100 = -1%

Since the final stock price is $99, the annual ROI is:

($99 ending price - $100 beginning price
+ $4 dividends)/ $100 beginning price = 3% ROI.

If the final stock price had been $95, the annual ROI would be:

($95 ending price - $100 beginning price
+ $4 dividends) / $100 beginning price = -1% ROI.

REINVESTMENT WHEN CAPITAL IS AT RISK: RATE OF RETURN AND YIELD

Example: Stock with low volatility and a regular quarterly dividend, reinvested				
End of:	**1st Quarter**	**2nd Quarter**	**3rd Quarter**	**4th Quarter**
Dividend	$1	$1.01	$1.02	$1.03
Stock Price	$98	$101	$102	$99
Shares Purchased	0.010204	0.01	0.01	0.010404
Total Shares Held	1.010204	1.020204	1.030204	1.040608
Investment Value	$99	$103.04	$105.08	**$103.02**
Quarterly ROI	-1%	4.08%	1.98%	-1.96%

Yield is the compound rate of return that includes the effect of reinvesting interest or dividends.

To the right is an example of a stock investment of one share purchased at the beginning of the year for $100.

- The quarterly dividend is reinvested at the quarter-end stock price.
- The number of shares purchased each quarter = ($ Dividend)/($ Stock Price).
- The final investment value of $103.02 is a 3.02% Yield on the initial investment of $100. This is the compound yield, and this return can be considered to be the return on the investment of $100.

To calculate the rate of return, the investor includes the reinvested dividends in the total investment. The investor received a total of $4.06 in dividends over the year, all of which were reinvested, so the investment amount increased by $4.06.

- Total Investment = Cost Basis = $100 + $4.06 = $104.06.
- Capital gain/loss = $103.02 - $104.06 = -$1.04 (a capital loss)
- ($4.06 dividends - $1.04 capital loss) / $104.06 total investment = 2.9% ROI

The disadvantage of this ROI calculation is that it does not take into account the fact that not all the money was invested during the entire year (the dividend reinvestments occurred throughout the year). The advantages are: (1) it uses the cost basis of the investment, (2) it clearly shows which gains are due to dividends and which gains/losses are due to capital gains/losses, and (3) the actual dollar return of $3.02 is compared to the actual dollar investment of $104.06.

For American income tax purposes, if the shares were sold at the end of the year, dividends would be $4.06, cost basis of the investment would be $104.06, sale price would be $103.02, and the capital loss would be $1.04.

Since all returns were reinvested, the ROI might also be calculated as a continuously compounded return or logarithmic return. The effective continuously compounded rate of return is the natural log of the final investment value divided by the initial investment value:

- V_i is the initial investment ($100)
- V_f is the final value ($103.02)

$$ROI_{Log} = \ln\left(\frac{V_f}{V_i}\right) = \ln\left(\frac{103.02}{100}\right) = 2.98\%$$

MUTUAL FUND RETURNS

Mutual Funds and Exchange Traded Funds (ETFs) hold portfolios of various companies' stock shares. When the companies pay a dividend, and when the fund trades shares, dividends and capital gains are distributed to the mutual fund shareholders. Mutual funds trade at the net asset value of the stock shares.

Total Returns

Mutual funds report total returns based on reinvestment factors. Reinvestment factors are based on total distributions (dividends plus capital gains) during each period.

Year 1 Reinvestment Factor

$$= \frac{\text{Year 1 Total Distribution}}{\text{Year 1 Share Price}} + 1$$

Year 2 Reinvestment Factor

$$= \frac{\text{Year 2 Total Distribution} \times \text{Year 1 Reinvestment Factor}}{\text{Year 2 Share Price}} + 1$$

Year 3 Reinvestment Factor

$$= \frac{\text{Year 3 Total Distribution} \times \text{Year 2 Reinvestment Factor}}{\text{Year 3 Share Price}} + 1$$

Year 4 Reinvestment Factor

$$= \frac{\text{Year 4 Total Distribution} \times \text{Year 3 Reinvestment Factor}}{\text{Year 4 Share Price}} + 1$$

Year 5 Reinvestment Factor

$$= \frac{\text{Year 5 Total Distribution} \times \text{Year 4 Reinvestment Factor}}{\text{Year 5 Share Price}} + 1$$

Total Return = ((Final Price x Last Reinvestment Factor)-Beginning Price) / Beginning Price

Average annual return (geometric)

Average Annual Return (geometric)

$$= \left[\left(1 + \frac{\text{Cumulative Return}}{100} \right)^{\text{Time in years}^{-1}} - 1 \right] \times 100$$

Example

Example: Mutual Fund with low volatility and a regular annual dividend, reinvested at year-end share price, initial share value $100					
End of:	**Year 1**	**Year 2**	**Year 3**	**Year 4**	**Year 5**
Dividend	$5	$5	$5	$5	$5
Capital Gain Distribution			$2		
Total Distribution	$5	$5	$7	$5	$5
Share Price	$98	$101	$102	$99	**$101**
Shares Purchased	0.05102	0.04950	0.06863	0.05051	0.04950
Shares Owned	1.05102	1.10053	1.16915	1.21966	1.26916
Reinvestment Factor	1.05102	1.05203	1.07220	1.05415	**1.05219**

- Total Return = (($101 x 1.05219) - $100) / $100 = 6.27% (net of expenses)
- Average Annual Return (geometric) = (((28.19)/100)+1)^(1/5)) - 1) x 100 = 5.09%

Using a Holding Period Return calculation, after 5 years, an investor who reinvested owned 1.26916 share valued at $101 per share ($128.19 in value). ($128.19-$100)/$100/5 = 5.638% yield. An investor who did not reinvest received a total of $27 in dividends and $1 in capital gain. ($27+$1)/$100/5 = 5.600% return.

Mutual funds include capital gains as well as dividends in their return calculations. Since the market price of a mutual fund share is based on net asset value, a capital gain distribution is offset by an equal decrease in mutual fund share value/price. From the shareholder's perspective, a capital gain distribution is not a net gain in assets, but it is a realized capital gain.

SUMMARY: OVERALL RATE OF RETURN

Rate of Return and Return on Investment indicate cash flow from an investment to the investor over a specified period of time, usually a year.

ROI is a measure of investment profitability, not a measure of investment size. While compound interest and dividend reinvestment can increase the size of the investment (thus potentially yielding a higher dollar return to the investor), Return on Investment is a percentage return based on capital invested.

In general, the higher the investment risk, the greater the potential investment return, and the greater the potential investment loss.

11

APPLIED INFORMATION ECONOMICS

INTRODUCTION

Applied Information Economics (AIE) is a specific decision analysis method developed by Douglas W. Hubbard. It builds on several methods from the decision theory and risk analysis including the use of the Monte Carlo method. However, unlike most modeling approaches with simulations, AIE incorporates the following:

1. *Calibrated Probability Assessment*: This is a method for training estimators and experts (who are relied on for the inputs in Monte Carlo methods) to be neutrally confident about their assigned probabilities. That is, their probabilities are neither over confident (too high) nor under confident (too low). A Monte Carlo model created with calibrated estimates is the best possible representation of the decision makers' current state of uncertainty.

2. *Computing the Value of Additional Information*: AIE uses information value calculations from decision theory such as the expected value of perfect information and the value of imperfect (partial) information. Often, this is done for a large number of uncertain variables in some type of decision model or business case. The result will reveal where efforts to reduce uncertainty by making further measurements are best spent.

3. *Empirical Methods Applied According to the Information Value of the Measurement*: This step is, in fact, the reason for the name of the method. Most Monte Carlo

modeling experts stop modeling after the first (uncalibrated) probability estimates from experts and there is usually little emphasis on further measurements with empirical methods. Since AIE computes the value of additional information, measurement can be selective and focused. This step often results in a very different set of measurement priorities than would otherwise have been used.

4. *Various Optimization Methods including Modern Portfolio Theory*: MPT and other methods are applied to determine ideal risk and return positions for a set of alternatives.

AIE also emphasizes an "everything that matters is measurable" philosophy in business. It focuses on potentially observable consequences of decisions and models them no matter how uncertain they first appear to be. Often the value of information calculations will show that simple intuitive measurement methods will suffice.

COMPARISON TO OTHER METHODS

Compared to other methods common in business decision making, AIE has several advantages:

- Unlike the accounting-style business case or cost benefit analysis, it does not rely entirely on point estimates of uncertain values. Since it uses the Monte Carlo method, uncertainty can be modeled explicitly.
- Unlike most decision-theory analysis of uncertain decisions, the AIE model starts with calibrating the estimators. This has a significant effect on reducing over-confidence and under-confidence of experts used for estimating the probabilities.
- The calculation of the value of information tends to greatly improve how and on what measurement efforts are spent.
- Unlike various "softer" methods-such as arbitrary and subjective weighted scores-AIE converts all values to economic terms so that powerful financial and economic optimization methods can be employed.

AIE does tend to be somewhat more elaborate than these alternatives. But this is alleviated by the availability of trained experts in the field. It also becomes more important to choose rigor over simplicity when the decisions being analyzed are much larger and riskier.

ADOPTION OF AIE

Developed and first used in 1995, AIE is relatively new compared to most decision making methods in business and government. However, as early as 1998, a reader survey conducted by Information Week in 1998 showed that 12% of respondents use AIE for IT metrics. Being a more quantitative method, the adoption may be more difficult than some methods. Yet, the theoretical rigour and practical successes have drawn strong proponents.

Very few people have sufficient training and experience in AIE to be able to conduct an analysis without supervision, but more continue to gain certification. College classes on AIE are taught at Wharton and other schools.

COMPOUND INTEREST

Compound interest is interest based not only on the original principal, but also on any unpaid interest that has been added to the principal. The more frequently interest is compounded, the faster the balance grows.

Interest rates must be comparable in order to be useful, and in order to be comparable, the interest rate and the compounding frequency must be disclosed. Since most people think of rates as a yearly percentage, many governments require financial institutions to disclose a (notionally) comparable yearly interest rate on deposits or advances. Compound interest rates may be referred to as Annual Percentage Rate, Effective interest rate, Effective Annual Rate, and by other terms.

When a fee is charged up front to obtain a loan, APR usually counts that cost as well as the compound interest in converting to the equivalent rate. These government requirements enable consumers to compare the actual cost of borrowing.

Compound interest rates may be converted to allow for comparison: for any given interest rate and compounding frequency, an "equivalent" rate for a different compounding frequency exists.

Compound interest may be contrasted with simple interest, where interest is not added to the principal (there is no compounding). Compound interest predominates in finance and economics, and simple interest is used infrequently (although certain financial products may contain elements of simple interest).

TERMINOLOGY

The effect of compounding depends on the frequency with which interest is compounded and the periodic interest rate which is applied. Therefore, in order to define accurately the amount to be paid under a legal contract with interest, the frequency of compounding (yearly, half-yearly, quarterly, monthly, daily, etc.) and the interest rate must be specified. Different conventions may be used from country to country, but in finance and economics the following usages are common:

Periodic Rate: the interest that is charged (and subsequently compounded) for each period. The periodic rate is used primarily for calculations, and is rarely used for comparison. The periodic rate is defined as the annual nominal rate divided by the number of compounding periods per year.

Nominal Interest Rate or Nominal Annual Rate: the annual rate, unadjusted for compounding. For example, 12% annual nominal interest compounded monthly has a periodic (monthly) rate of 1%.

Effective Annual Rate: the nominal annual rate "adjusted" to allow comparisons; the nominal rate is restated to reflect the effective rate as if annual compounding were applied.

Economists generally prefer to use effective annual rates to allow for comparability. In finance and commerce, the nominal annual rate may be the most frequently used. When quoted with the compounding frequency, a loan with a given nominal annual rate is fully specified (the effect of interest for a given loan scenario can be precisely determined), but cannot be compared to loans with different compounding frequency. Loans and finance may have other "non-interest" charges, and the terms above do not attempt to capture these differences. Other terms such as annual percentage rate and annual percentage yield may have specific legal definitions and may or may not be comparable, depending on the jurisdiction.

The use of the terms above (and other similar terms) may be inconsistent, and vary according to local custom, marketing demands, simplicity or for other reasons.

EXCEPTIONS

- Short Term Government debt have a different convention. Their interest is calculated as (100-P)/P where 'P' is the price paid. Instead of normalizing it to a year, the interest is prorated by the number of days 't': (365/t)*100.
- Corporate Bonds are most frequently payable twice yearly. The amount of interest paid (each six months) is the disclosed interest rate divided by two (multiplied by the principal). The yearly compounded rate is higher than the disclosed rate.
- Canadian mortgage loans are generally semi-annual compounding with monthly (or more frequent) payments.
- U.S. mortgages generally use monthly compounding (with corresponding payment periods).
- Economists and certain techniques for, e.g., valuation of derivatives may use continuous compounding, where the maximum (bordering on infinite) frequency of compounding is used. Continuous compounding allows for the use of certain mathematical approaches that are more elegant and easier to compute.

MATHEMATICS OF INTEREST RATES

Simple Formulas

Formulas are presented in greater detail at time value of money. In the formulas below, i or r are the interest rate, expressed as a true percentage (i.e. 10% = 10/100 = 0.10). FV and PV represent the future and present value of a sum. These are the most basic formulas required by a new student:

$$FV = PV(1+i)^n$$

The above calculates the future value, (FV), of an investment, (PV), accruing at a fixed interest rate of i% for n periods. Also a=p(1+r/t)^nt can be used.

$$PV = \frac{FV}{(1+i)^n}$$

The above calculates what present value (PV) would be needed to produce a certain future value (FV) if interest of i% accrues for n periods.

$$i = \left(\sqrt[n]{\left(\frac{FV}{PV}\right)} - 1\right) \text{ or } \left(\left(\frac{FV}{PV}\right)^{\left(\frac{1}{n}\right)} - 1\right),$$

The above two formulas are the same and calculate the compound interest rate i% achieved if an initial investment of PV returns a value of FV after n accrual periods.

Translating Different Compounding Periods

Each time unpaid interest is compounded and added to the principal, the resulting principal is grossed up to equal P(1+i%).

(A) You are told the interest is 8% a year, with 2%(=8/4) interest charged every quarter. What is the equivalent annual rate?. Start with $100. At the end of one year it will be:

$100 (1+ .02) (1+ .02) (1+ .02) (1+ .02) = $108.24

We know that $100 invested at 8.24% will give you $108.24 at year end. So the equivalent rate is 8.24%. Using a financial calculator or a [table] is simpler still. Using the Future Value of a currency function, input

- PV = 100
- n = 4
- i = .02
- solve for FV = 108.24

(B) You know the equivalent annual interest rate is 4%, but it will be compounded quarterly. You need to find the interest rate that will be applied each quarter.

$100 (1+ .009853) (1+ .009853) (1+ .009853) (1+ .009853)

= $104

The mathematics to find the 0.9853% is discussed at Time value of money, but using a financial calculator or [table] is easier. Input

- PV = 100
- n = 4
- FV = 104
- solve for interest = 0.9853%

(C) You sold your house for a 60% profit. What was the annual return? You owned the house for 4 years, paid $100,000 originally, and sold it for $160,000.

$100,000 (1+ .1247) (1+ .1247) (1+ .1247) (1+ .1247)

= $160,000

Find the 12.47% annual rate the same way as B.) above, using a financial calculator or [table]. Input

- PV = 100,000
- n = 4
- FV = 160,000
- solve for interest = 12.47%

The Rule of 72

The Rule of 72 is a very simple way of illustrating the growth potential of compound interest. The rule says simply this:

$$\frac{72}{i} \approx n$$

where is the interest rate and is the number of time periods needed to double the principal.

For example, say a mutual fund grows at 12% average interest rate. According to the rule of 72, if money were invested in this mutual fund, then it would double every 6 $\left(\frac{72}{12}=6\right)$ years. This calculation deals only with the gross amount, taxes must be factored into growth if taxable vehicles (such as CD's, mutual funds, etc) are used.

However, the above Rule of 72 merely gives an approximation of the time needed to retain an investment before it doubles in value. The accurate calculation is as follows:

$$n=\frac{\ln 2}{\ln(1+i)}$$

PERIODIC COMPOUNDING

The amount function for compound interest is an exponential function in terms of time.

$$A(t)=A_0\left(1+\frac{r}{n}\right)^{n-t}$$

- n = Number of compounding periods per each t (time in years) (note that the total number of compounding periods is n.t)
- r = Nominal annual interest rate expressed as a decimal. e.g.: 6% = 0.06

As n increases, the rate approaches an upper limit of e^r. This rate is called continuous compounding.

Since the principal A(0) is simply a coefficient, it is often dropped for simplicity, and the resulting accumulation function is used in interest theory instead. Accumulation functions for simple and compound interest are listed below:

$$a(t)=1+tr$$

$$a(t)=\left(1+\frac{r}{n}\right)^{n-t}$$

Note: A(t) is the amount function and a(t) is the accumulation function.

FORCE OF INTEREST

In economics, the accumulation functions are often expressed in terms of e, the base of the natural logarithm. This facilitates the use of calculus methods in manipulation of interest formulas. This is called the force of interest.

The force of interest is defined as the following:

$$\delta_t = \frac{a'(t)}{a(t)}$$

$$a(n) = e^{\int_0^n \delta_t dt}$$

Note that this equation contains an ERROR given the previous equation. The below is a deemed correction.

$$a(n) = a(0)e^{\int_0^n \delta_t dt}$$

When the above formula is written in differential equation format, the force of interest is simply the coefficient of amount of change.

$$da(t) = \delta_t a(t)dt$$

The force of interest for compound interest is a constant for a given r, and the accumulation function of compounding interest in terms of force of interest is a simple power of e:

$$\delta = \ln(1+r)$$

$$a(t) = e^{t\delta}$$

Continuous Compounding

For interest compounded a certain number of times, n, per year, such as monthly or quarterly, the formula is:

$$a(t) = \left(1 + \frac{r}{n}\right)^{n-t}$$

Continuous compounding can be thought as making the compounding period infinitely small; therefore achieved by taking the limit of n to infinity. One should consult definitions of the exponential function for the mathematical proof of this limit.

$$a(t) = \lim_{n \to \infty}\left(1 + \frac{r}{n}\right)^{n-t}$$

$$a(t) = e^{r-t}$$

The amount function is simply

$$A(t) = A_0 e^{r.t}$$

A common mnemonic device considers the equation in the form

$$A = Pe^{r.t}$$

called 'PERT' where P is the principal amount, e is the base of the natural log, R is the rate per period, and T is the time (in the same units as the rate's period), and A is the final amount.

COMPOUNDING BASES

To convert an interest rate from one compounding basis to another compounding basis, the following formula applies:

$$r_2 = \left[\left(1 + \frac{r_1}{n_1}\right)^{\frac{n_1}{n_2}} - 1\right] \times n_2$$

where r_1 is the stated interest rate with compounding frequency n_1 and r_2 is the stated interest rate with compounding frequency n_2.

When interest is continuously compounded:

$$R = n \times \ln\left(1 + \frac{r}{n}\right)$$

where R is the interest rate on a continuous compounding basis and r is the stated interest rate with a compounding frequency n.

Another formula to calculate compound interest is $y = a.b^x$ where y is the money after interest is calculated, a is the initial deposit, b is the interest rate in a decimal form (divided by the number of compoundings if applicable), and x is the exponent of b which represents the time (multiplied by the number of compoundings if applicable).

History

If the Native American tribe that accepted goods worth 60 guilders for the sale of Manhattan in 1626 had invested the money in a Dutch bank at 6.5% interest, compounded annually, then in 2005 their investment would be worth over 700 billion (around US$820 billion), more than the assessed value of the real estate in all five boroughs of New York City.

Compound interest was once regarded as the worst kind of usury, and was severely condemned by Roman law, as well as the common laws of many other countries.

Richard Witt's book Arithmeticall Questions, published in 1613, was a landmark in the history of compound interest. It was wholly devoted to the subject (previously called anatocism), whereas previous writers had usually treated compound interest briefly in just one chapter in a mathematical textbook.

Witt's book gave tables based on 10% (the then maximum rate of interest allowable on loans) and on other rates for different purposes, such as the valuation of property leases. Witt was a London mathematical practitioner and his book is notable for its clarity of expression, depth of insight and accuracy of calculation, with 124 worked examples.

EFFECTIVE INTEREST RATE

The effective interest rate, effective annual interest rate, or simply effective rate is the interest rate on a loan or financial product restated from the nominal interest rate as an interest rate with annual compound interest.

Since an interest rate may be defined using different compounding terms (daily, monthly, annually, or other), the annual "cost" of interest between two different loans may not be comparable. The effective interest rate is used to make such loans more comparable by converting any loan into the equivalent annual rate.

The effective interest rate differs in two important respects from annual percentage rate: first, the effective interest rate generally does not incorporate one-time charges such as front-end fees or other "unusual" features; second, the effective interest rate is (generally) not a term defined by legal or regulatory authorities (as annual percentage rate is in many jurisdictions).

Annual Percentage Yield or effective annual yield is the analogous concept used for savings or investment products, such as a certificate of deposit. Since any loan is an investment product for the lender, the terms may be used to apply to the same transaction, depending on the point of view.

It is important to note that effective annual interest or yield may be calculated or applied differently depending on the circumstances, and the definition should be studied carefully. For example, a bank may refer to the yield on a loan portfolio after expected losses as its effective yield and include income from other fees, meaning that the interest paid by each borrower may differ substantially from the bank's effective yield.

Calculation

The effective interest rate is calculated as if compounded annually. The effective rate is calculated in the following way, where r is the effective annual rate, i the nominal rate, and n the number of compounding periods per year (for example, 12 for monthly compounding):

$$r = \left(1 + \frac{i}{n}\right)^n - 1$$

For example, a nominal interest rate of 6% compounded monthly is equivalent to an effective interest rate of 6.17%. 6% monthly is credited as 6%/12 = 0.5% every month.

After one year, the initial capital is increased by the factor (1+0.005)12 ≈ 1.0617. (n.b.: Percentage figures must always be divided by 100, as the percent sign is a notation convenience; e.g. 6% = 0.06).

When the frequency of compounding is increased upto the infinity the calculation will be:

$r = e^i - 1.$

NOMINAL INTEREST RATE

In finance and economics, nominal interest rate or nominal rate of interest refers to the rate of interest before adjustment for inflation (in contrast with the real interest rate); or, for interest rates "as stated" without adjustment for the full effect of compounding (also referred to as the nominal annual rate).

An interest rate is called nominal if the frequency of compounding (e.g. a month) is not identical to the basic time unit (normally a year).

Nominal and Real Interest Rates

The nominal interest rate (unadjusted for inflation) includes compensation for the lender's lost value due to inflation, whereas the real interest rate excludes inflation. The real interest rate therefore expresses the cost of borrowed funds after the expected erosion of the value of those funds due to the rise in the general price level. The relationship between real and nominal interest rates can be described in the equation:

- $(1 + r)(1 + i) = (1 + R)$ where r is the real interest rate, i is the inflation rate, and R is the nominal interest rate.
- A common approximation for the real interest rate is:

real interest rate = nominal interest rate -expected inflation

In this analysis, the nominal rate is the stated rate, and the real interest rate is the interest after the expected losses due to inflation. Since the future inflation rate can only be estimated, the ex ante and ex post (before and after the fact) real interest rates may be different; the premium paid to actual inflation may be higher or lower. In contrast, the nominal interest rate is known in advance.

Nominal and Effective Interest Rates

The nominal interest rate is the periodic interest rate times the number of periods per year; for example, a nominal annual interest rate of 12% based on monthly compounding means a 1% interest rate per month (compounded).

A nominal interest rate for compounding periods less than a year is always higher than the equivalent rate with annual compounding. A nominal rate without the compounding frequency is not fully defined: for any interest rate, the effective interest rate cannot be specified without knowing the compounding frequency and the rate.

Although some conventions are used where the compounding frequency is understood, consumers in particular may fail to understand the importance of knowing the effective rate.

Nominal interest rates are not comparable unless the compounding periods are the same; effective interest rates correct for this by "converting" nominal rates into annual compound interest.

In many cases, depending on local regulations, interest rates as quoted by lenders and in advertisements are based on nominal, not effective, interest rates, and hence may understate the interest rate compared to the equivalent effective annual rate.

The term should not be confused with simple interest (as opposed to compound interest). Simple interest is interest that is not compounded.

The effective interest rate is always calculated as if compounded annually.

The effective rate is calculated in the following way, where r is the effective rate, i the nominal rate, and n the number of compounding periods per year (for example, 12 for monthly compounding):

$$r = \left(1 + \frac{i}{n}\right)^n - 1.$$

EXAMPLES

Monthly Compounding

A nominal interest rate of 6% compounded monthly is equivalent to an effective interest rate of 6.17%. 6% monthly is credited as 6%/12 = 0.5% every month. After one year, the initial capital is increased by the factor (1+0.005)12 ≈ 1.0617.

Daily Compounding

A loan with daily compounding will have a substantially higher rate in effective annual terms. For a loan with a 10% nominal annual rate and daily compounding, the effective annual rate is 10.516%. For a loan of $10,000 (paid at the end of the year in a single lump sum), the borrower would pay $51.56 more than one who was charged 10% interest, compounded annually.

12

Exponential Growth

In economics, exponential growth (or geometric growth) occurs when the growth rate of a function is always proportional to the function's current size. Such growth is said to follow an exponential law (but see also Malthusian growth model). This implies for any exponentially growing quantity, the larger the quantity gets, the faster it grows. But it also implies that the relationship between the size of the dependent variable and its rate of growth is governed by a strict law, of the simplest kind: direct proportion. It is proved in calculus that this law requires that the quantity is given by the exponential function, if we use the correct time scale. This explains the name.

INTUITION

The phrase exponential growth is often used in nontechnical contexts to mean merely surprisingly fast growth. In a strictly mathematical sense, though, exponential growth has a precise meaning and does not necessarily mean that growth will happen quickly. In fact, a population can grow exponentially but at a very slow absolute rate (as when money in a bank account earns a very low interest rate, for instance), and can grow surprisingly fast without growing exponentially. And some functions, such as the logistic function, approximate exponential growth over only part of their range. The "technical details" section below explains exactly what is required for a function to exhibit true exponential growth.

But the general principle behind exponential growth is that the larger a number gets, the faster it grows. Any exponentially growing number will eventually grow larger than any other number which grows at only a constant rate for the same amount of time (and will also grow larger than any function which grows only subexponentially). This is demonstrated by the classic riddle in which a child is offered two choices for an increasing weekly allowance: the first option begins at 1 cent and doubles each week, while the second option begins at $1 and increases by $1 each week. Although the second option, growing at a constant rate of $1/week, pays more in the short run, the first option eventually grows much larger:

Week	0	1	2	3	4	5	6	7	8	9	10	11	12	13	14	15
Option 1	1c	2c	4c	8c	16c	32c	64c	$1.28	$2.56	$5.12	$10.24	$20.48	$40.96	$81.92	$163.84	$327.68
Option 2	$1	$2	$3	$4	$5	$6	$7	$8	$9	$10	$11	$12	$13	$14	$15	$16

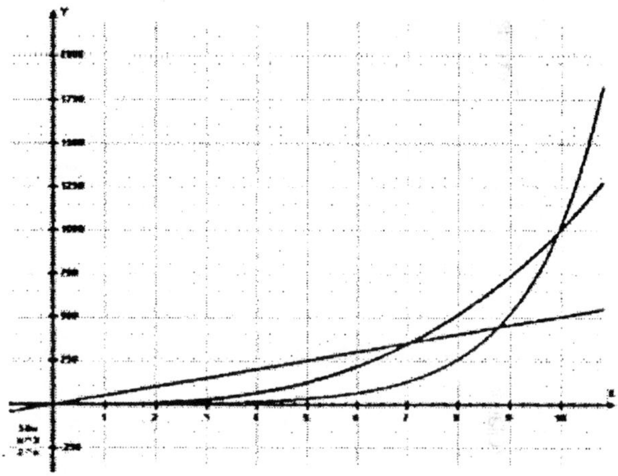

The graph illustrates how an exponential growth surpasses both linear and cubic growths.

We can describe these cases mathematically. In the first case, the allowance at week n is 2n cents; thus, at week 15 the payout is 215 = 32768c = $327.68. All formulas of the form kn, where k is an unchanging number greater than 1 (e.g., 2), and n is the amount of time elapsed, grow exponentially. In the second case, the payout at week n is simply n + 1 dollars. The payout grows at a constant rate of $1 per week.

This image shows a slightly more complicated example of an exponential function overtaking subexponential functions:

The red line represents 50x, similar to option 2 in the above example, except increasing by 50 a week instead of 1. Its value is largest until x gets around 7. The blue line represents the polynomial x^3. Polynomials grow subexponentially, since the exponent (3 in this case) stays constant while the base (x) changes. This function is larger than the other two when x is between about 7 and 9. Then the exponential function 2x (in green) takes over and becomes larger than the other two functions for all x greater than about 10.

Anything that grows by the same percentage every year (or every month, day, hour etc.) is growing exponentially. For example, if the average number of offspring of each individual (or couple) in a population remains constant, the rate of growth is proportional to the number of individuals. Such an exponentially growing population grows three times as fast when there are six million individuals as it does when there are two million.

Bank accounts with fixed-rate compound interest grow exponentially provided there are no deposits, withdrawals or service charges. Mathematically, the bank account balance for an account starting with s dollars, earning an annual interest rate r and left untouched for n years can be calculated as s(1 + r)n. So, in an account starting with $1 and earning 5% annually, the account will have $\$1\times(1+0.05)^1 = \$1.05$ after 1 year, $\$1\times(1+0.05)^{10} = \$1.62$ after 10 years, and $131.50 after 100 years. Since the starting balance and rate do not change, the quantity $\$1\times(1+0.05) = \$1.05$ can work as the value k in the formula k^n given earlier.

TECHNICAL DETAILS

Let x be a quantity growing exponentially with respect to time t. By definition, the rate of change dx/dt obeys the differential equation:

$$\frac{dx}{dt} = kx$$

where $k \neq 0$ is the constant of proportionality (the average number of offspring per individual in the case of the population). (See logistic function for a simple correction of this growth model where k is not constant). The solution to this equation is the exponential function $x(t) = x_0 e^{kt}$ -- hence the name exponential growth ('e' being a mathematical constant). The constant x_0 is the initial size of the population.

In the long run, exponential growth of any kind will overtake linear growth of any kind (the basis of the Malthusian catastrophe) as well as any polynomial growth, i.e., for all a:

$$\lim_{n \to \infty} \frac{x^0}{Ce^x} = 0.$$

There is a whole hierarchy of conceivable growth rates that are slower than exponential and faster than linear (in the long run). Growth rates may also be faster than exponential. The linear and exponential models are not merely simple candidates but are those of greatest occurrence in nature.

In the above differential equation, if $k < 0$, then the quantity experiences exponential decay.

CHARACTERISTIC QUANTITIES OF EXPONENTIAL GROWTH

The law of exponential growth can be written in different but mathematically equivalent forms, by using a different base. The most common forms are the following:

$$x(t) = x_0 e^{kt} = x_0 e^{t/r} = x_0 \times 2^{t/T} = x_0 \left(1 + \frac{r}{100}\right)^r,$$

where as in the example above x0 expresses the initial quantity (i.e. x(t) for t = 0).

The quantity k is called the growth constant; the quantity r is known as the growth rate (percent increase per unit time); t is the e-folding time; and T is the doubling time. Indicating one of these four equivalent quantities automatically permits calculating the three others, which are connected by the following equation (which can be derived by taking the natural logarithm of the above):

$$\kappa = \frac{1}{\tau} = \frac{\ln 2}{T} = \ln\left(1 + \frac{r}{100}\right).$$

A popular approximated method for calculating the doubling time from the growth rate is the rule of 70, i.e. $T \simeq 70/r$ (or better: $T \simeq 70/r + 0.03$).

LIMITATIONS OF EXPONENTIAL MODELS

As discussed above, an important point about exponential growth is that even when it seems slow on the short run, it becomes impressively fast on the long run, with the initial quantity doubling at the doubling time, then doubling again and again. For instance, a population growth rate of 2% per year may seem small, but it actually implies doubling after 35 years, doubling again after another 35 years (i.e. becoming 4 times the initial population), etc.

This implies that both the observed quantity and its time derivative will become several orders of magnitude larger than what was initially meant by the person who conceived the growth model. Because of this, some effects not initially taken into account will distort the growth law, usually moderating it as for instance in the logistic law. Exponential growth of a quantity placed in the real world (i.e. not in the abstract world of mathematics) is a model valid for a temporary period of time only.

For this reason, some people challenge the exponential growth model on the ground that it is valid for the short term only, i.e. nothing can grow indefinitely. For instance, a population in a closed environment cannot continue growing if it eats up all the available food and resources; industry cannot continue pumping carbon from the underground into the atmosphere beyond the limits connected with oil reservoirs and the consequences of climate change; etc.

Problems of this kind exist for every mathematical representation of the real world, but are specially felt for exponential growth, since with this model growth accelerates as variables increase in a positive feedback, to a point where human response time to inconvenience can be insufficient. On these points.

EXAMPLES OF EXPONENTIAL GROWTH

- Biology.
  * Microorganisms in a culture dish will grow exponentially, at first, after the first microorganism appears (but then logistically until the available food is exhausted, when growth stops).
  * A virus (SARS, West Nile, smallpox) of sufficient infectivity ($k > 0$) will spread exponentially at first, if no artificial immunization is available. Each infected person can infect multiple new people.
  * Human population, if the number of births and deaths per person per year were to remain at current levels (but also see logistic growth).
  * Many responses of living beings to stimuli, including human perception, are logarithmic responses, which are the inverse of exponential responses; the loudness and frequency of sound are perceived logarithmically, even with very faint stimulus, within the limits of perception. This is the reason that exponentially increasing the brightness of visual stimuli is perceived by humans as a smooth (linear) increase, rather than an exponential increase. This has survival value. Generally it is important for the organisms to respond to stimuli in a wide range of levels, from very low levels, to very high levels, while the accuracy of the estimation of differences at high levels of stimulus is much less important for survival.
- Computer technology
  * Processing power of computers. See also Moore's law and technological singularity (under exponential growth, there are no singularities. The singularity here is a metaphor.).

  * In computational complexity theory, computer algorithms of exponential complexity require an exponentially increasing amount of resources (e.g. time, computer memory) for only a constant increase in problem size. So for an algorithm of time complexity 2^x, if a problem of size x =10 requires 10 seconds to complete, then a problem of size x =11 will require 20 seconds, and x =12 will require 40 seconds. This kind of algorithm typically becomes unusable at very small problem sizes, often between 30 and 100 items (most computer algorithms need to be able to solve much larger problems, up to tens of thousands or even millions of items in reasonable times, something that would be physically impossible with an exponential algorithm). Also, the effects of Moore's Law do not help the situation much because doubling processor speed merely allows you to increase the problem size by one. E.g. if a slow processor can solve problems of size x in time t, then a processor twice as fast could only solve problems of size x+1 in the same time t. So exponentially complex algorithms are most often impractical, and the search for more efficient algorithms is one of the central goals of computer science.
  * Internet traffic growth.
  * Investment. The effect of compound interest over many years has a substantial effect on savings and a person's ability to retire.

- Physics
  * Avalanche breakdown within a dielectric material. A free electron becomes sufficiently accelerated by an externally applied electrical field that it frees up additional electrons as it collides with atoms or molecules of the dielectric media. These secondary electrons also are accelerated, creating larger numbers of free electrons. The resulting exponential growth of electrons and ions may rapidly lead to complete dielectric breakdown of the material.

  * Nuclear chain reaction (the concept behind nuclear weapons). Each uranium nucleus that undergoes fission produces multiple neutrons, each of which can be absorbed by adjacent uranium atoms, causing them to fission in turn. If the probability of neutron absorption exceeds the probability of neutron escape (a function of the shape and mass of the uranium), $k > 0$ and so the production rate of neutrons and induced uranium fissions increases exponentially, in an uncontrolled reaction.

- Multi-level marketing.

Exponential increases are promised to appear in each new level of a starting member's downline as each subsequent member recruits more people.

EXPONENTIAL STORIES

The surprising characteristics of exponential growth have fascinated people through the ages.

Rice on a Chessboard

A courtier presented the Persian king with a beautiful, hand-made chessboard. The king asked what he would like in return for his gift and the courtier surprised the king by asking for one grain of rice on the first square, two grains on the second, four grains on the third etc. The king readily agreed and asked for the rice to be brought. All went well at first, but the requirement for 2n - 1 grains on the nth square demanded over a million grains on the 21st square, more than a quadrillion on the 41st and there simply was not enough rice in the whole world for the final squares. (From Meadows et al. 1972, p.29 via Porritt 2005). For variation of this see Second Half of the Chessboard in reference to the point where an exponentially growing factor begins to have a significant economic impact on an organization's overall business strategy.

The Water Lily

French children are told a story in which they imagine having a pond with water lily leaves floating on the surface.

The lily population doubles in size every day and if left unchecked will smother the pond in 30 days, killing all the other living things in the water. Day after day the plant seems small and so it is decided to leave it to grow until it half-covers the pond, before cutting it back. They are then asked, on what day that will occur. This is revealed to be the 29th day, and then there will be just one day to save the pond. (From Meadows et al. 1972, p.29 via Porritt 2005)

CREDIT CARD INTEREST

Credit card interest is the principal way in which card issuers generate revenue. A card issuer is a bank that gives a consumer (the cardholder) a card or account number that can be used with various payees to make payments and borrow money from the bank simultaneously. The bank pays the payee and then charges the cardholder interest over the time the money remains borrowed. Banks suffer losses when cardholders do not pay back the borrowed money as agreed. As a result, optimal calculation of interest based on any information they have about the cardholder's credit risk is key to a card issuer's profitability. Banks check national and international credit bureau reports that identify the borrowing history of the card holder applicant with other banks, or take detailed interviews and documentation of the applicant's finances, before determining what interest rate to offer. Interest is criticized for being confusing to cardholders who also tend to lack self control and buy compulsively using whatever resources are provided to them, letting the bank profit on something that may not always be of true benefit. The response usually given in return is that consumers should educate themselves about how to make rational decisions regarding their power to purchase on credit card accounts.

INTEREST RATES

Interest rates vary widely. Some credit card loans are secured by real estate, and can be as low as 6 to 12% in the USA (2005). Typical credit cards have interest rates between 7 and 29.99% in the USA (2007), depending upon the borrower's credit history. Typical credit limits are $200 to $20,000 on unsecured loans, and can be any amount up to the equity in real estate ($1000 to $200,000 being a typical range) on a secured loan. Interest rates in developing countries are typically far higher, with rates of 150% per year not being uncommon. Brazil has even higher interest rates, about 50% over that of most developing countries, which average about 200%. A bank-issued Visa or Mastercard to a new account holder can have annual interest as high as 240%, even though inflation seems under control at around 6% per annum (Economist, May 2006). These accounts have typically very low credit limits (USD$40 to $400), and are used for convenience and quick payback. They also often offer a grace period with no interest until the due date.

Calculation of Interest Rates

Credit card holders should be aware that most US credit cards are quoted in terms of nominal APR compounded monthly, which is not the same as the effective annual rate (EAR). Despite the "Annual" in APR, it is not necessarily a direct reference for the interest rate paid on a stable balance over one year. The more direct reference for the one-year rate of interest is EAR. The general conversion factor for APR to EAR is EAR=(1+APR/n)^n-1, where n represents the number of compounding periods of the APR per EAR period. E.g., for a common credit card quoted at 12.99% APR compounded monthly, the one year EAR is (1+.129949/12)^12-1, or 13.78%. Note that a high US APR of 29.99% carries an effective annual rate of 34.48%.

Table 1 below, given by Prosper (2005), shows data from Experian, one of the 3 main US and UK credit bureaus (along with Equifax in the UK and Trans Union in the USA and internationally). (The data actually comes from installment loans [closed end loans], but can also be used as a fair approximation for credit card loans [open end loans]). The table shows the loss rates from borrowers with various credit scores. To get a desired rate of return, a lender would add the desired rate to the loss rate to determine the interest rate. Although borrowers certainly differ, a rational lender usually predicts that borrowers will behave as others from their credit score group have behaved in the past. Banks then compete on details by making analyses of how to use data such as this along with any other data they gather from the application and history with the cardholder, to determine an interest rate that will attract borrowers by remaining competitive with other banks and still assure a profit. Debt-to-income ratio (DTI) is another important factor for determining interest rates. The bank calculates it by adding up the borrower's obligated minimum payments on loans, and dividing by the cardholder's income. If it is more than a set point (such as 20% in this example) then loans to that applicant are considered a higher risk than given by this table. These loss rates already include incomes the lenders receive from payments in collection, either from debt collection efforts after default or from selling the loans to third parties for further collection attempts, at a fraction of the amount owed.

Table: Expected default loss rates for 2004 installment loans with given credit ratings and less than 20% DTI

Experian score	Expected annual loss rate (as % of loan balance)
760+ low risk	0.2
720-759	0.9
680-719	1.8
640-679	3.3
600-639	6.2
540-599	11.1
540 high risk	19.1
No credit rating	no data (the lender is on its own)

Interrelated Fees

Banks make many other fees that interrelate with interest charges in complex ways (since they make a profit from the whole combination), including transactions fees paid by merchants and cardholders, and penalty fees, such as for borrowing over the established credit limit, or for failing to make a minimum payment on time.

Banks vary widely in the proportion of credit card account income that comes from interest (depending upon their marketing mix). In a typical UK card issuer, between 80% and 90% of cardholder generated income is derived from interest charges. A further 10% is made up from default fees.

Laws

Usury: Many nations limit the amount of interest that can be charged (often called usury laws). Most countries strictly regulate the manner in which interest rates are agreed, calculated, and disclosed. Some countries (especially with Muslim influence) prohibit interest being charged at all (and other methods are used, such as an ownership interest taken by the bank in the cardholder's business profits based upon the purchase amount).

USA Truth in Lending Act. In the United States, there are four commonly accepted methods of charging interest, which are listed in the section below, "Methods of Charging Interest". These are detailed in Regulation Z of the Truth in Lending Act. There is a legal obligation on US issuers that the method of charging interest is disclosed and is sufficiently transparent to be fair. This is typically done in the Schumer Box, which lists rates and terms in writing to the cardholder applicant in a standard format. Regulation Z details four principal methods of calculating interest. For purposes of comparison between rates, the "expected rate" is the APR applied to the average daily balance for a year, or in other words, the interest charged on the actual balance left lent out by the bank at the close of each business day.

That said, there are not just four prescribed ways to charge interest i.e. those specified in Regulation Z. US issuers can charge interest according to any reasonable method to which the card holder agrees. The four (or arguably six) "safe-harbour" ways to describe and charge interest are detailed in Regulation Z. If an issuer charges interest in one of these ways then there is a shorthand description of that method in Regulation Z that can be used. If a lender uses that description, and charges interest in that way, then their disclosure is deemed to be sufficiently transparent and fair. If not, then they must provide an explanation of the method used. Because of the safe-harbour definitions, US lenders have tended to gravitate towards these methods of charging and describing the way interest is charged, because it is (i) easy and (ii) legal compliance is guaranteed. Arguably, the approach also provides flexibility for issuers, enhancing the profile of the way in which interest is charged, and therefore increasing the scope for product differentiation on what is, after all, a key product feature.

Pre-payment Penalties: Clauses calling for a penalty for paying more than the contracted regular payment were once common in another type of loan, the installment loan, and they are of great concern to governments regulating credit card loans. Today, in many cases because of strict laws, most card issues do not charge any pre-payment penalties at all. That means cardholders can "cancel" the loan at any time by simply paying it off, and be charged no more interest than that calculated on the time the money was borrowed.

Canceling Loans: Cardholders are often surprised in situations where the bank cancels or changes the terms on their loans. Most card issuers are allowed to raise the interest rate--within legal guidelines--at any time. Usually they have to give some notice, such as 30 or 60 days, in writing. If the cardholder does not agree to the new rate or terms, then it is expected that the account will be paid off. That can be difficult for a cardholder with a large loan who expected to make payments over many years. Banks can also cancel a loan, and request that all amounts be paid back immediately, usually by a clause in the contract, for any default on the contract, whatsoever, which could be as simple as a late payment or even a default on a loan to another bank if the contract states it.

Methods for Charging Interest

APR is the principal means of comparing credit products. Because interest is compounded on a monthly basis, to calculate charges on a credit card account the APR has to be de-compounded. Most major banks use the following methodology:

Increase the figure to the highest possible value while still meeting advertising requirements. e.g., if a card is advertised at a percentage rate of 17.9, then any value up to 17.949 will still be rounded down to 17.9, and thus still be correct. Once this number has been derived, it must be converted to a decimal multiplier - in this case the number would be 1.17949. To derive the monthly rate, obtain the twelfth root (i.e., raise to the power 1/12). This will provide you with a rate which, when compounded over a year, will equal the APR. At this point, it is important to round down-since the APR has already been maximised in order to make use of the highest rate possible, rounding any figures up might push the APR over the edge and onto a higher rate, leaving the card issuer liable for false advertising claims. This method is subject to change, depending on the bank in question, and is highly influenced by cardholder perceptions and bank strategy, sometimes with a value of simplicity for cardholders; other times with the effect of obfuscating the true interest rates charged.

Methods vary by country because of customs and laws. A brief summary of each of the four methods given under USA Regulation Z follows, this list followed by a few examples from other countries and some discussion of differences between the various methods:

Average Daily Balance: The sum of the daily outstanding balances is divided by the number of days covered in the cycle to give an average balance for that period. This amount is multiplied by a constant factor to give an interest charge. The resultant interest is the same as if interest was charged at the close of each day, except that it only compounds (gets added to the principal) once per month. It is the simplest of the four methods in the sense that it produces an interest rate approximating if not exactly equal the expected rate.

Adjusted Balance: The balance at the end of the billing cycle is multiplied by a factor in order to give the interest charge. This can result in an actual interest rate lower or higher than the expected one, since it does not take into account the average daily balance, that is, the time value of money actually lent by the bank. It does, however, take into account money that is left lent out over several months.

Previous Balance: The reverse happens: the balance at the start of the previous billing cycle is multiplied by the interest factor in order to derive the charge. As with the Adjusted Balance method, this method can result in an interest rate higher or lower than the expected one, but the part of the balance that carries over more than two full cycles is charged at the expected rate.

Two-Cycle Average Daily Balance: The sum of the daily balances of the previous two cycles is used, but interest is charged on that amount only over the current cycle. This can result in an actual interest charge that applies the advertised rate to an amount that does not represent the actual amount of money borrowed over time, much different that the expected interest charge. The interest charged on the actual money borrowed over time can vary radically from month-to-month (rather than the APR remaining steady). For example, a cardholder with an average daily balance for the June, July, and August cycles of $100, 1000, 100, will have interest calculated on 550 for July, which is only 55% of the expected interest on 1000, and will have interest calculated on 550 again in August, which is 550% higher than the expected interest on the money actually borrowed over that month, which is 100.

However, when analyzed, the interest on the balance that stays borrowed over the whole time period ($100 in this case) actually does approximate the expected interest rate, just like the other methods, so the variability is only on the balance that varies month-to-month. Therefore, the key to keeping the interest rate stable and close to the "expected rate" (as given by Average daily balance method) is to keep the balance close to the same every month. The strategic consumer who has this type of account either pays it all off each month, or makes most charges towards the end of the cycle and payments at the beginning of the cycle to avoid paying too much interest above the expected interest given the interest rate; whereas business cardholders have more sophisticated ways of analyzing and using this type of account for peak cash-flow needs, and willingly pay the "extra" interest to do better business.

Much confusion is caused by and much mis-information given about this method of calculating interest. Because of its complexity for consumers, advisors from Motley Fool (2005) to Credit Advisors (2005) advise consumers to be very wary of this method (unless they can analyze it and achieve true value from it). Despite the confusion of variable interest rates, the bank using this method does have a rationale; that is it costs the bank in strategic opportunity costs to vary the amount loaned from month-to-month, because they have to adjust assets to find the money to loan when it is suddenly borrowed, and find something to do with the money when it is paid back. In that sense, the two-cycle average daily balance can be likened to electric charges for industrial clients, in which the charge is based upon the peak usage rather than the actual usage. And, in fact, this method of charging interest is often used for business cardholders as stated above. These accounts often have much higher credit limits than typically consumer accounts (perhaps tens or hundreds of thousands instead of just thousands).

United Kingdom: The Daily Accrual method is commonly used in the UK. The annual rate is divided by 365 to give a daily rate. Each day, the balance of the account is multiplied by this rate, and at the end of the cycle the total interest accrued is billed to the account. The effect of this method is theoretically mathematically the same over one year as the Average Daily Balance method, because the interest is compounded monthly, but calculated on daily balances. Although a detailed analysis can be done that shows that the effective interest can be slightly lower or higher each month than with the Average Daily Balance method, depending upon the detailed calculation procedure used and the number of days in each month, the effect over the entire year provides only a trivial opportunity for arbitrage.

13

Exceptions, Differences between Methods, and Marketing

INTRODUCTION

In effect, differences in methods mostly act upon the fluctuating balance of the most recent cycle (and are almost the same for balances carried over from cycle to cycle. Banks and consumers are aware of transaction costs, and banks actually receive income in the form of per-transaction payments from the merchants, besides gaining a new loan, which is more business for the bank. Therefore, the interest charged in the most recent cycle interrelates with other incomes and benefits to the cardholder and bank, such as transaction cost, transaction fees to the bank, marketing costs for gaining each new loan (which is like a sale for the bank) and marketing costs for overall cardholder perception, which can increase market share. Ergo, the rate charged on the most recent cycle is largely a matter of marketing preference based upon cardholder perceptions, rather than a matter of maximizing the rate.

BANK FEE ARBITRAGE AND ITS LIMITS

In general, differences between methods represent a degree of precision over charging the expected interest rate. Precision is important because any detectable difference from the expected rate can theoretically be taken advantage of (through arbitrage) by cardholders (who have control over when to charge and when to pay), to the possible loss of profitability of the bank. However, in effect, the differences between methods are trivial except in terms of cardholder perceptions and marketing, because of transaction costs, transaction income, cash advance fees, and credit limits. While cardholders can certainly effect their overall costs by managing their daily balances (for example, by buying or paying early or late in the month depending upon the calculation method), their opportunities for scaling this arbitrage to make large amounts of money are very limited. For example, in order to charge the maximum on the card, to take maximum advantage of any aribtrageable difference in calculation methods, cardholders must actually buy something of that value at the right time, and doing so only to take advantage of a small mathematical discrepancy from the expected rate could be very inconvenient. That adds a cost to each transaction that obscures any benefit that can be gained. Credit limits limit how much can be charged, and thus how much advantage can be taken (trivial amounts), and cash advance fees are charged by banks partially to limit the amount of free movement that can be accomplished. (With no fee cardholders could create any daily balances advantageous to them through a series of cash advances and payments).

CASH RATE

Most banks charge a separate, higher interest rate, and a cash advance fee (ranging from 1 to 5% of the amount of cash taken) on cash or cash-like transactions (called "quasi-cash" by many banks). These transactions are usually the ones for which the bank receives no transaction fee from the payee, such as cash from a bank or ATM, casino chips, and some payments to the government (and any transaction that looks in the bank's discretion like a cash swap, such as a payment on multiple invoices). In effect, the interest rate charged on purchases is subsidized by other profits to the bank.'

DEFAULT RATE

Many banks since 2000 have a contractual default rate (in the US, 2005, ranging from 10% to 36%), which is typically much higher than the regular APR. The rate takes effect automatically if any of the listed conditions occur, which can include the following: one or two late payments, any amount overdue beyond the due date or one more cycle, any returned payment (such as an NSF check), any charging over the credit limit (sometimes including the bank's own fees), and--in some cases--any reduction of credit rating or default with another lender, at the discretion of the bank. In effect, the cardholder is agreeing to pay the default rate on the balance owed unless all the listed events can be guaranteed not to happen. A single late payment, or even a non-reconciled mistake on any account, could result in charges of hundreds or thousands of dollars over the life of the loan. These high effective fees create a great incentive for cardholders to keep track of all their credit card and checking account balances (from which credit card payments are made) and for keeping wide margins (extra money or money available). However, the current lack of provable "account balance ownership" in most credit card and checking account designs (studied between 1990 and 2005) make these kinds of "penalty fees" a complex problem, indeed.

VARIABLE RATE

Many credit card issuers give a rate that is based upon an economic indicator published by a respected journal. For example, most banks in the USA offer credit cards based upon the lowest US Prime Rate as published in the Wall Street Journal on the previous business day to the start of the calendar month. For example, a rate given as 9.99% plus the prime rate will be 16.99% when the prime rate is 7.00% (such as the end of 2005). These rates usually also have contractual minimums and maximums to protect the consumer (or the bank, as it may be) from wild fluctuations of the prime rate. While these accounts are harder to budget for, they can theoretically be a little less expensive since the bank does not have to accept the risk of fluctuation of the market (since the prime rate follows inflation rates, which affect the profitability of loans). A fixed rate can be better for consumers who have fixed incomes or need control over their payments budgets.

GRACE PERIOD

Many banks provide an exception to their normal method of calculating interest, in which no interest is charged on an ending statement balance that is paid by the due date. Banks have various rules. In some cases the account must be paid off for two months in a row to obtain the discount. If the required amount is not paid, then the normal interest rate calculation method is still used. This allows cardholders to use credit cards for the convenience of the payment method (to have one invoice payable with one check per month rather than many separate cash or check transactions), which allows them to keep money invested at a return until it must be moved to pay the balance, and allows them to keep the float on the money borrowed during each month. The bank, in effect, is marketing the convenience of the payment method (to receive fees and possible new lending income, when the cardholder does not pay), as well as the loans themselves.

PROMOTIONAL INTEREST RATE

Many banks offer very low interest, often 0%, for a certain number of statement cycles, on certain sub-balances ranging from the entire balance to purchases or balance transfers (used to pay off other accounts), or for buying certain merchandise in stores owned or contracted with by the lender. The cardholder gets lower interest, the payee gets more sales, and the bank gets a chance to increase income by having more money lent out, and possibly an extra marketing transaction payment from the payee or sales side of the business for helping to make the sale (in some cases as much as the entire interest payment, charged to the payee instead of the cardholder).

These offers are often complex, requiring the cardholder to work to understand the terms of the offer, and possibly to pay off the sub-balance by a certain date or have interest charged retro-actively, or to pay a certain amount per month over the minimum due (an "interest free" minimum payment) in order to pay down the sub-balance. Methods for communicating the sub-balances and rules on statements vary widely and do not usually conform to any standard. For example, sub-balances are not always reconcilable with the bank (due to lack of debit and credit statements on those balances), and even the term "cycle" (for number of cycles) is not often defined in writing by the bank. Banks also allocate payments automatically to sub-balances in various--often obscure--ways. For example, they may contractually pay off promotional balances before higher-interest balances (causing the higher interest to be charged until the account is paid off in full.) These methods, besides possibly saving the cardholder money over the expected interest rate, serve to obscure the actual rate charged by the bank. For example, consumers may think they are paying zero percent, when the actual calculated amount on their daily balances is much more.

REWARDS PROGRAMS

This is a popular name (2005) for offers from card issuers (started with Discover Card in 1985) to share transactions fees with the cardholder through various games and bonus programs. Cardholders typically receive one "point", "mile" or actual penny (1% of the transaction) for each dollar spent on the card, and more points for buying from certain types of merchants or cooperating merchants, and then can pay down the loan, or trade points for airline flights, catalog merchandise, lower interest rates, gift cards, or cash. The points can also be exchanged, sometimes, between cooperating programs of different banks, making them more and more currency-like. These programs represent such a large value that they are not-completely-jokingly considered a set of currencies. These combined "currencies" have accumulated to the point that they hold more value worldwide than US (paper) dollars, and are the subject of company liquidation disputes and divorce settlements (Economist, 2005).

They are criticized for being highly inflationary, and subject to the whims of the card issuers (raising the prices after the points are earned). Many cardholders use a card for the points, but later forget or decline to use the points, anyway. While opening new avenues for marketing and competition, rewards programs are criticized in terms of being able to compare interest rates by making it impossible for consumers to compare one competitive interest rate offer to another through any standard means such as under the USA Truth in Lending Act, because of the extra value offered by the bonus program, along with other terms, costs, and benefits created by other marketing gimmicks such as the ones cited in here.

FISHER EQUATION

The Fisher equation in financial mathematics and economics estimates the relationship between nominal and real interest rates under inflation. In finance, this equation is primarily used in YTM calculations of bonds or IRR calculations of investments. In economics, this equation is used to predict nominal and real interest rate behavior.

Let r_r denote the real interest rate, r_n denote the nominal interest rate, and let i denote the inflation rate.

The Fisher equation is the following:

$$rn = r_r + i$$

The equation can be used in either ex-ante (before) or ex-post (after) analysis.

This equation is named after Irving Fisher who was famous for his works on the theory of interest. This equation existed before Fisher, but Fisher proposed a better approximation which is given below. The estimated equation can be derived from the proposed equation

$$1 + r_n = (1 + r_r)(1 + i).$$

Derivation

From

$$1 + r_n = (1 + r_r)(1 + i)$$

follows

$$1 + r_n = 1 + r_r + i + r_r i$$

and hence

$$r_n = r_r + i + r_r i$$

Drop $r_r i$ because $r_r + i$ is much larger than $r_r i$:

$$r_n = r_r + i$$

is the result.

Example

The market rate of return on the 4.25% UK government bond maturing on 7 March 2036 is currently 3.81% per annum. Let's assume that this can be broken down into a real rate of exactly 2% and an inflation premium of 1.775% (no premium for risk, as government bond is considered to be "risk-free"):

1.02 x 1.01775 = 1.0381

This article implies that you can ignore the third term (0.02 x 0.01775 = 0.00035 or 0.035%) and just call the nominal rate of return 3.775%, on the grounds that is almost the same as 3.81%.

At a nominal rate of return of 3.81% pa, the value of the bond is £107.84 per £100 nominal. At a rate of return of 3.775% pa, the value is £108.50 per £100 nominal, or 66p more.

The average size of actual transactions in this bond in the market in the final quarter of 2005 was £10 million. So a difference in price of 66p per £100 translates into a difference of £66,000 per deal.

YIELD CURVE

In finance, the yield curve is the relation between the interest rate (or cost of borrowing) and the time to maturity of the debt for a given borrower in a given currency. For example, the current U.S. dollar interest rates paid on U.S. Treasury securities for various maturities are closely watched by many traders, and are commonly plotted on a graph such as the one on the right which is informally called "the yield curve." More formal mathematical descriptions of this relation are often called the term structure of interest rates.

The yield of a debt instrument is the annualized percentage increase in the value of the investment. For instance, a bank account that pays an interest rate of 4% per year has a 4% yield. In general the percentage per year that can be earned is dependent on the length of time that the money is invested. For example, a bank may offer a "savings rate" higher than the normal checking account rate if the customer is prepared to leave money untouched for five years. Investing for a period of time t gives a yield Y(t). This function Y is called the yield curve.

Y is often, but not always, an increasing function of t. Yield curves are used by fixed income analysts, who analyze bonds and related securities, to understand conditions in financial markets and to seek trading opportunities. Economists use the curves to understand economic conditions.

The yield curve function Y is actually only known with certainty for a few specific maturity dates, the other maturities are calculated by interpolation.

The Typical Shape of the Yield Curve

Yield curves are usually upward sloping asymptotically; the longer the maturity, the higher the yield, with diminishing marginal growth. There are two common explanations for this phenomenon. First, it may be that the market is anticipating a rise in the risk-free rate. If investors hold off investing now, they may receive a better rate in the future. Therefore, under the arbitrage pricing theory, investors who are willing to lock their money in now need to be compensated for the anticipated rise in rates-thus the higher interest rate on long-term investments.

However, interest rates can fall just as they can rise. Another explanation is that longer maturities entail greater risks for the investor (i.e. the lender). Risk premium should be paid, since with longer maturities, more catastrophic events might occur that impact the investment. This explanation depends on the notion that the economy faces more uncertainties in the distant future than in the near term, and the risk of future adverse events (such as default and higher short-term interest rates) is higher than the chance of future positive events (such as lower short-term interest rates). This effect is referred to as the liquidity spread. If the market expects more volatility in the future, even if interest rates are anticipated to decline, the increase in the risk premium can influence the spread and cause an increasing yield.

The opposite situation-short-term interest rates higher than long-term-also can occur. For instance, in November 2004, the yield curve for UK Government bonds (i.e. the bonds which the UK Government issues to borrow money-see gilts) was partially inverted. The yield for the 10 year bond stood at 4.68% but only 4.45% on the thirty year bond. The market's anticipation of falling interest rates causes such incidents. Negative liquidity premiums can exist if long-term investors dominate the market, but the prevailing view is that a positive liquidity premium dominates, so only the anticipation of falling interest rates will cause an inverted yield curve. Strongly inverted yield curves have historically preceded economic depressions.

The yield curve may also be flat or hump-shaped, due to anticipated interest rates being steady, or short-term volatility outweighing long-term volatility.

Yield curves move on a daily basis, reflecting the market's reaction to news. A further "stylized fact" is that yield curves tend to move in parallel (i.e., the yield curve shifts up and down as interest rate levels rise and fall).

TYPES OF YIELD CURVE

There is no single yield curve describing the cost of money for everybody. The most important factor in determining a yield curve is the currency in which it is denominated. The economic situation of the countries and companies using each currency is a primary factor in determining the yield curve. For example the sluggish economic growth of Japan throughout the late 1990s and early 2000s has meant the yen yield curve is very low (rising from virtually zero at the three month point to only 2% at the 30 year point). By contrast the British pound curve ranges from 4-5% along its curve.

Different institutions borrow money at different rates, depending on their creditworthiness. The yield curves corresponding to the bonds issued by governments in their own currency are called the government bond yield curve (government curve). Banks with high credit ratings (Aa/AA or above) borrow money from each other at the LIBOR rates. These yield curves are typically a little higher than government curves. They are the most important and widely used in the financial markets, and are known variously as the LIBOR curve or the swap curve. The construction of the swap curve is described below.

Besides the government curve and the LIBOR curve, there are corporate (company) curves. These are constructed from the yields of bonds issued by corporations. Since corporations have less creditworthiness than governments and most large banks these yields are typically higher. Corporate yield curves are often quoted in terms of a "credit spread" over the relevant swap curve. For instance the five-year yield curve point for Vodafone might be quoted as LIBOR +0.25%, where 0.25% (often written as 25 basis points or 25bps) is the credit spread.

Normal Yield Curve

From the post-Great Depression era to the present, the yield curve has usually been "normal" meaning that yields rise as maturity lengthens (i.e., the slope of the yield curve is positive). This positive slope reflects investor expectations for the economy to grow in the future and, importantly, for this growth to be associated with a greater expectation that inflation will rise in the future rather than fall.

This expectation of higher inflation leads to expectations that the central bank will tighten monetary policy by raising short term interest rates in the future to slow economic growth and dampen inflationary pressure. It also creates a need for a risk premium associated with the uncertainty about the future rate of inflation and the risk this poses to the future value of cash flows. Investors price these risks into the yield curve by demanding higher yields for maturities further into the future.

However, a positively sloped yield curve has not always been the norm. Through much of the 19th century and early 20th century the US economy experienced trend growth with persistent deflation, not inflation. During this period the yield curve was typically inverted, reflecting the fact that deflation made current cash flows less valuable than future cash flows. During this period of persistent deflation, a 'normal' yield curve was negatively sloped.

Steep Yield Curve

Historically, the 20-year Treasury bond yield has averaged approximately two percentage points above that of three-month Treasury bills. In situations when this gap increases (e.g. 20-year Treasury yield rises relatively higher than the three-month Treasury yield), the economy is expected to improve quickly in the future. This type of curve can be seen at the beginning of an economic expansion (or after the end of a recession). Here, economic stagnation will have depressed short-term interest rates; however, rates begin to rise once the demand for capital is re-established by growing economic activity.

Flat or Humped Yield Curve

A flat yield curve is observed when all maturities have similar yields, whereas a humped curve results when short-term and long-term yields are equal and medium-term yields are higher than those of the short-term and long-term. A flat curve sends signals of uncertainty in the economy. This mixed signal can revert back to a normal curve or could later result into an inverted curve. It cannot be explained by the Segmented Market theory discussed below.

Inverted Yield Curve

An inverted yield curve occurs when long-term yields fall below short-term yields. Under this abnormal and contradictory situation, long-term investors will settle for lower yields now if they think the economy will slow or even decline in the future. An inverted curve may indicate a worsening economic situation in the future. In addition to potentially signaling an economic decline, inverted yield curves also imply that the market believes inflation will remain low. This is because, even if there is a recession, a low bond yield will still be offset by low inflation.

However, technical factors, such as a flight to quality or global economic or currency situations, may cause an increase in demand for bonds on the long end of the yield curve, causing long-term rates to fall. This was seen in 1998 during the Long Term Capital Management failure when there was a slight inversion on part of the curve.

Theory

There are four main economic theories attempting to explain how yields vary with maturity. Two of the theories are extreme positions, while the third attempts to find a middle ground between the former two.

Market Expectations (Pure Expectations) Hypothesis

$$\left(1+i_{it}\right)^{n}=\left(1+i_{st}^{year1}\right)\left(1+i_{st}^{year2}\right)...\left(1+i_{st}^{yearn}\right)$$

This hypothesis assumes that the various maturities are perfect substitutes and suggests that the shape of the yield curve depends on market participants' expectations of future interest rates. These expected rates, along with an assumption that arbitrage opportunities will be minimal, is enough information to construct a complete yield curve. For example, if investors have an expectation of what 1-year interest rates will be next year, the 2-year interest rate can be calculated as the compounding of this year's interest rate by next year's interest rate. More generally, rates on a long-term instrument are equal to the geometric mean of the yield on a series of short-term instruments. This theory perfectly explains the stylized fact that yields tend to move together. However, it fails to explain the persistence in the shape of the yield curve.

Liquidity Preference Theory

The Liquidity Preference Theory, an offshoot of the Pure Expectations Theory, asserts that long-term interest rates not only reflect investors' assumptions about future interest rates but also include a premium for holding long-term bonds, called the term premium or the liquidity premium. This premium compensates investors for the added risk of having their money tied up for a longer period, including the greater price uncertainty. Because of the term premium, long-term bond yields tend to be higher than short-term yields, and the yield curve slopes upward.

Addition: It is not actually liquidity that is of concern but maturity risk, that is, the risk until maturity is higher on longer term investments.

Market Segmentation Theory

This theory is also called the segmented market hypothesis. In this theory, financial instruments of different terms are not substitutable. As a result, the supply and demand in the markets for short-term and long-term instruments is determined independently. Prospective investors would have to decide in advance whether they need short-term or long-term instruments. Due to the fact that investors prefer their portfolio to be liquid, they will prefer short-term instruments to long-term instruments. Therefore, the market for short-term instruments will receive a higher demand. Higher demand for the instrument implies higher prices and lower yield. This explains the stylized fact that short-term yields are usually lower than long-term yields. This theory explains the predominance of the normal yield curve shape. However, because the supply and demand of the two markets are independent, this theory fails to explain the observed fact that yields tend to move together (i.e., upward and downward shifts in the curve).

In an empirical study, 2000 Alexandra E. MacKay, Eliezer Z. Prisman, and Yisong S. Tian found segmentation in the market for Canadian government bonds, and attributed it to differential taxation.

For a brief period in the last week of 2005, and again in early 2006, the US Dollar yield curve inverted, with short-term yields actually exceeding long-term yields. Market segmentation theory would attribute this to an investor preference for longer term securities, particularly from pension funds and foreign investors who prefer guaranteed longer term yields.

Preferred Habitat Theory

The Preferred Habitat Theory states that in addition to interest rate expectations, investors have distinct investment horizons and require a meaningful premium to buy bonds with maturities outside their "preferred" maturity, or habitat. Proponents of this theory believe that short-term investors are more prevalent in the fixed-income market and therefore, longer-term rates tend to be higher than short-term rates, for the most part, but short-term rates can be higher than long-term rates occasionally. This theory represents a middle ground between the Market Segmentation Theory and the Market Expectations Theory. Moreover, it seems to explain both the persistence of the normal yield curve shape and the tendency of the yield curve to shift up and down while retaining its shape.

Historical Development of Yield Curve Theory

On 15 August 1971, U.S. President Richard Nixon announced that the U.S. dollar would no longer be based on the gold standard, thereby ending the Bretton Woods system and initiating the era of floating exchange rates.

Floating exchange rates made life more complicated for bond traders, including importantly those at Salomon Brothers in New York.

By the middle of the 1970s, due to the prodding of the head of bond research at Salomon, Marty Liebowitz, traders began thinking about bond yields in new ways. Rather than think of each maturity (a ten year bond, a five year, etc.) as a separate marketplace, they began drawing a curve through all their yields. The bit nearest the present time became known as the short end--yields of bonds further out became, naturally, the long end.

Academics had to play catch up with practitioners in this matter. One important theoretic development came from a Czech mathematician, Oldrich Vasicek, who argued in a 1977 paper that bond prices all along the curve are driven by the short end (under risk neutral equivalent martingale measure), and accordingly by short-term interest rates.

The mathematical model for Vasicek's work was given by an Ornstein-Uhlenbeck process, and has since been discredited because the model predicts a positive probability that the short rate becomes negative and is inflexibile in creating yield curves of different shapes.

Vasicek's model has been superseded by many different models including the Hull-White model (which allows for time varying parameters in the Ornstein-Uhlenbeck process), the Cox-Ingersoll-Ross model, which is a modified Bessel process, and the Heath-Jarrow-Morton framework.

There are also many improvements on each of these models, but see the article on short rate model. Another modern approach is the LIBOR Market Model, introduced by Brace, Gatarek and Musiela in 1997 and advanced by others later.

Construction of the Full Yield Curve from Market Data

Typical inputs to the money market curve

Type	Settlement date	Rate (%)
Cash	Overnight rate	5.58675
Cash	Tomorrow next rate	5.59375
Cash	1m	5.625
Cash	3m	5.71875
Future	Dec-97	94.24
Future	Mar-98	94.23
Future	Jun-98	94.18
Future	Sep-98	94.12
Future	Dec-98	94.00
Swap	2y	6.01253
Swap	3y	6.10823
Swap	4y	6.16
Swap	5y	6.22
Swap	7y	6.32
Swap	10y	6.42
Swap	15y	6.56
Swap	20y	6.56
Swap	30y	6.56

A list of standard instruments used to build a money market yield curve.

The usual representation of the yield curve is a function P, defined on all future times t, such that P(t) represents the value today of receiving one unit of currency t years in the future. If P is defined for all future t then we can easily recover the yield (i.e. the annualized interest rate) for borrowing money for that period of time via the formula

$$y(t) = \left(\frac{1}{P(t)}\right)^{\frac{1}{t}} - 1$$

The significant difficulty in defining a yield curve therefore is to determine the function P(t). P is called the discount factor function.

Yield curves are built from either prices available in the bond market or the money market. Whilst the yield curves built from the bond market use prices only from a specific class of bonds (for instance bonds issued by the UK government) yield curves built from the money market uses prices of "cash" from today's LIBOR rates, which determine the "short end" of the curve i.e. for t = 3m, futures which determine the mid-section of the curve (3m = t = 15m) and interest rate swaps which determine the "long end" (1y = t = 60y).

In either case the available market data provides with a matrix A of cash flows, each row representing a particular financial instrument and each column representing a point in time. The (i,j)-th element of the matrix represents the amount that instrument i will pay out on day j.

Let the vector F represent today's prices of the instrument (so that the i-th instrument has value F(i)), then by definition of our discount factor function P we should have that F = A*P (this is a matrix multiplication). In actual fact noise in the financial markets means it is not possible to find a P that solves this equation exactly, and our goal becomes to find a vector P such that

$$A * P = F + \varepsilon$$

where e is as small a vector as possible (where the size of a vector might be measured by taking its norm, for example).

Note that even if we can solve this equation, we will only have determined P(t) for those t which have a cash flow from one or more of the original instruments we are creating the curve from. Values for other t are typically determined using some sort of interpolation scheme.

Practitioners and researchers have suggested many ways of solving the A*P = F equation. It transpires that the most natural method-that of minimizing e by least squares regression-leads to unsatisfactory results. The large number of zeroes in the matrix A mean that function P turns out to be "bumpy".

In their comprehensive book on interest rate modelling James and Webber note that the following techniques have been suggested to solve the problem of finding P:

1. Approximation using Lagrange polynomials
2. Fitting using parameterised curves (such as splines, the Nelson-Siegel family or the Svensson family of curves). Van Deventer, Imai and Mesler summarize three different techniques for curve fitting that satisfy the maximum smoothness of either forward interest rates, zero coupon bond prices, or zero coupon bond yields
3. Local regression using kernels
4. Linear programming

In the money market practitioners might use different techniques to solve for different areas of the curve. For example at the short end of the curve, where there are few cashflows, the first few elements of P may be found by bootstrapping from one to the next. At the long end, a regression technique with a cost function that values smoothness might be used.

14

CAPITAL BUDGETING

INTRODUCTION

Capital budgeting (or investment appraisal) is the planning process used to determine a firm's long term investments such as new machinery, replacement machinery, new plants, new products, and research and development projects.

Many formal methods are used in capital budgeting, including the techniques such as

- Net present value
- Profitability index
- Internal rate of return
- Modified Internal Rate of Return, and
- Equivalent annuity.

These methods use the incremental cash flows from each potential investment, or project. Techniques based on accounting earnings and accounting rules are sometimes used-though economists consider this to be improper-such as the accounting rate of return, and "return on investment." Simplified and hybrid methods are used as well, such as payback period and discounted payback period.

NET PRESENT VALUE

Each potential project's value should be estimated using a discounted cash flow (DCF) valuation, to find its net present value (NPV)-(see Fisher separation theorem). This valuation requires estimating the size and timing of all of the incremental cash flows from the project. These future cash flows are then discounted to determine their present value. These present values are then summed, to get the NPV. See also Time value of money. The NPV decision rule is to accept all positive NPV projects in an unconstrained environment, or if projects are mutually exclusive, accept the one with the highest NPV.

The NPV is greatly affected by the discount rate, so selecting the proper rate-sometimes called the hurdle rate-is critical to making the right decision. The hurdle rate is the minimum acceptable return on an investment. It should reflect the riskiness of the investment, typically measured by the volatility of cash flows, and must take into account the financing mix. Managers may use models such as the CAPM or the APT to estimate a discount rate appropriate for each particular project, and use the weighted average cost of capital (WACC) to reflect the financing mix selected. A commcn practice in choosing a discount rate for a project is to apply a WACC that applies to the entire firm, but a higher discount rate may be more appropriate when a project's risk is higher than the risk of the firm as a whole.

INTERNAL RATE OF RETURN

The internal rate of return (IRR) is defined as the discount rate that gives a net present value (NPV) of zero. It is a commonly used measure of investment efficiency.

The IRR method will result in the same decision as the NPV method for independent (non-mutually exclusive) projects in an unconstrained environment, in the usual cases where a negative cash flow occurs at the start of the project, followed by all positive cash flows. In most realistic cases, all independent projects that have an IRR higher than the hurdle rate should be accepted. Nevertheless, for mutually exclusive projects, the decision rule of taking the project with the highest IRR-which is often used-may select a project with a lower NPV.

In some cases, several zero NPV discount rates may exist, so there is no unique IRR. The IRR exists and is unique if one or more years of net investment (negative cash flow) are followed by years of net revenues. But if the signs of the cash flows change more than once, there may be several IRRs. The IRR equation generally cannot be solved analytically but only via iterations.

One shortcoming of the IRR method is that it is commonly misunderstood to convey the actual annual profitability of an investment. However, this is not the case because intermediate cash flows are almost never reinvested at the project's IRR; and, therefore, the actual rate of return is almost certainly going to be lower. Accordingly, a measure called Modified Internal Rate of Return (MIRR) is often used.

Despite a strong academic preference for NPV, surveys indicate that executives prefer IRR over NPV, although they should be used in concert. In a budget-constrained environment, efficiency measures should be used to maximize the overall NPV of the firm. Some managers find it intuitively more appealing to evaluate investments in terms of percentage rates of return than dollars of NPV.

EQUIVALENT ANNUITY METHOD

The equivalent annuity method expresses the NPV as an annualized cash flow by dividing it by the present value of the annuity factor. It is often used when assessing only the costs of specific projects that have the same cash inflows. In this form it is known as the equivalent annual cost (EAC) method and is the cost per year of owning and operating an asset over its entire life-span.

It is often used when comparing investment projects of unequal life-spans. For example if project A has an expected lifetime of 7 years, and project B has an expected lifetime of 11 years it would be improper to simply compare the net present values (NPVs) of the two projects, unless the projects could not be repeated.

The use of the EAC method implies that the project will be replaced by an identical project.

Alternatively the chain method can be used with the NPV method under the assumption that the projects will be replaced with the same cash flows each time. To compare projects of unequal length, say 3 years and 4 years, the projects are chained together, i.e. four repetitions of the 3 year project are compare to three repetitions of the 4 year project. The chain method and the EAC method give mathematically equivalent answers. The assumption of the same cash flows for each link in the chain is essentially an assumption of zero inflation, so a real interest rate rather than a nominal interest rate is commonly used in the calculations.

REAL OPTIONS

Real options analysis has become important since the 1970s as option pricing models have gotten more sophisticated. The discounted cash flow methods essentially value projects as if they were risky bonds, with the promised cash flows known. But managers will have many choices of how to increase future cash inflows, or to decrease future cash outflows. In other words, managers get to manage the projects-not simply accept or reject them. Real options analysis try to value the choices-the option value-that the managers will have in the future and adds these values to the NPV.

Ranked Projects

The real value of capital budgeting is to rank projects. Most organizations have many projects that could potentially be financially rewarding. Once it has been determined that a particular project has exceeded it's hurdle, then it should be ranked against peer projects (e.g.-highest IRR to lowest IRR). The highest ranking projects should be implemented until the budgeted capital has been expended.

COMPOUND ANNUAL GROWTH RATE

Compound Annual Growth Rate (CAGR) or cumulative annual growth rate is another term for the rate of return or interest rate variable in the formula Present value of a dollar and Future value of a dollar discussed at time value of money. It measures the rate of change in a value between two points in time (t and t0). These equations are basic to the concept of compound interest.

$$\mathrm{CAGR}(t_0,t)=\left(\frac{V(t)}{V(t_0)}\right)^{\frac{1}{t=t_0}}-1$$

In business, CAGR is used to describe the growth over a period of time of some element of the business, usually revenue, although other measures may be used (such as the number of units delivered, registered users, etc.). CAGR is not an accounting term, but remains widely used, particularly in growth industries. CAGR is preferable to applying more simplistic terms, such as "business doubled in three years", as it properly accounts for the effect of compounding.

Example

A company may double its sales (an increase of 100%) over a period of four years. Applying the formula above, the CAGR is approximately 18.9% (not 25% per year):

$$\text{CAGR} = \left(\frac{200}{100}\right)^{\frac{1}{4}} - 1 = 0.1892 = 18.92\%$$

Note: the actual sales figures may be used for calculation, or (as above) normalized values that retain the same mathematical proportion.

EXPECTED RETURN

The expected return is the weighted-average most likely outcome in gambling, probability theory, economics or finance.

Discrete Scenarios

In gambling and probability theory, there is usually a discrete set of possible outcomes. In this case, expected return is a measure of the relative balance of win or loss weighted by their chances of occurring.

For example, if a fair die is thrown and numbers 1 and 2 win ¤1, but 3-6 lose ¤0.5, then the expected gain per throw is

$1 \times 1/3 - 0.5 \times 2/3 =$ ¤0:

the game is thus fair.

CONTINUOUS SCENARIOS

In economics and finance, it is more likely that the set of possible outcomes is continuous (a numerical or currency value between 0 and infinity). In this case, simplifying assumptions are made about the distribution of possible outcomes. Either a continuous probability function is constructed, or a discrete probability distribution is assumed

INTERNAL RATE OF RETURN

The internal rate of return (IRR) is a capital budgeting method used by firms to decide whether they should make long-term investments.

The IRR is the annualized effective compounded return rate which can be earned on the invested capital, i.e. the yield on the investment.

A project is a good investment proposition if its IRR is greater than the rate of return that could be earned by alternative investments (investing in other projects, buying bonds, even putting the money in a bank account). Thus, the IRR should be compared to an alternative cost of capital including an appropriate risk premium.

Mathematically the IRR is defined as any discount rate that results in a net present value of zero of a series of cash flows.

In general, if the IRR is greater than the project's cost of capital, or hurdle rate, the project will add value for the company.

Method

To find the internal rate of return, find the IRR that satisfies the following equation:

$$\text{Initial Investment} = \sum_{t=1}^{N} \frac{C_t}{(1+\text{IRR})^r}$$

Example

(i = interest rate in percent)

Internal Rate of Return (IRR)

where NPV = 0 = -100 + 30/[(1+i)^1] + 35/[(1+i)^2] + 40/[(1+i)^3] + 45/[(1+i)^4]

IRR = i,

IRR = 17.09%

Year	Cash Flow
0	-100
1	+30
2	+35
3	+40
4	+45

Net Present Value (NPV)

Thus using IRR = i = 17.09%,

NPV = -100 + 30/[(1+i)^1] + 35/[(1+i)^2] + 40/[(1+i)^3] + 45/[(1+i)^4]

NPV = 0

(This calculation is condensed.)

PROBLEMS WITH USING IRR

As an investment decision tool, the calculated IRR should not be used to rate mutually exclusive projects, but only to decide whether a single project is worth investing in. In cases where one project has a higher initial investment than a second mutually exclusive project, the first project may have a lower IRR (expected return), but a higher NPV (increase in shareholders' wealth) and should thus be accepted over the second project. A method called marginal IRR can be used to adapt the IRR method to this case.

The IRR method should not be used in the usual manner for projects that start with an initial positive cash inflow, for example where a customer makes a deposit before a specific machine is built, resulting in a single positive cash flow followed by a series of negative cash flows (+ - - - -). In this case the usual IRR decision rule needs to be reversed.

If there are multiple sign changes in the series of cash flows, e.g. (- + - + -), there may be multiple IRRs for a single project, so that the IRR decision rule may be impossible to implement. Examples of this type of project are strip mines and nuclear power plants, where there is usually a large cash outflow at the end of the project.

In general, the IRR can be calculated by solving a polynomial. Sturm's Theorem can be used to determine if that polynomial has a unique real solution. Importantly, the IRR equation cannot be solved analytically (i.e. in its general form) but only via iterations.

A critical shortcoming of the IRR method is that it is commonly misunderstood to convey the actual annual profitability of an investment. However, this is not the case because intermediate cash flows are almost never reinvested at the project's IRR; and, therefore, the actual rate of return (akin to the one that would have been yielded by stocks or bank deposits) is almost certainly going to be lower. Accordingly, a measure called Modified Internal Rate of Return (MIRR) is used, which has an assumed reinvestment rate, usually equal to the project's cost of capital.

Despite a strong academic preference for NPV, surveys indicate that executives prefer IRR over NPV. Apparently, managers find it intuitively more appealing to evaluate investments in terms of percentage rates of return than dollars of NPV. However, NPV remains the "more accurate" reflection of value to the business.

In addition if the NPV of one project is higher than another and the other project has a higher IRR then the cross over point method can be used to solve this dispute.

Cross Over Point > RR = Accept project with higher NPV and if the Cross Over Point < RR = Accept project with higher IRR

15

Rate of Profit

In economics and finance, the profit rate is the relative profitability of an investment project, of a capitalist enterprise, or of the capitalist economy as a whole. It is similar to the concept of the rate of return on investment.

In Marxian political economy, the rate of profit (r) would be measured as

r = (surplus-value)/(capital invested).

where surplus-value corresponds to unpaid labor in the production process or to profits, interest, and rent (property income).

HISTORICAL COST VS. MARKET VALUE

The rate of profit depends on the definition of capital invested. Two measurements of the value of capital exist: capital at historical cost and capital at market value. Historical cost is the original cost of an asset at the time of purchase or payment. Market value is the re-sale value, replacement value, or value in present or alternative use.

To compute the rate of profit, replacement cost of capital assets must be used to define the capital cost. Assets such as machinery cannot be replaced at their historical cost but must be purchased at the current market value. When inflation occurs, historical cost would not take account of rising prices of equipment. The rate of profit would be overestimated using lower historical cost for computing the value of capital invested.

On the other side, due to technical progress, products tend to become cheaper. This in itself should raise rates of profit, because replacement cost declines.

A PRISONER'S DILEMMA

If, however, firms achieve higher sales per worker the more they invest per worker, they will try to increase investments per worker as long as this raises their rate of profit. If some capitalists do this, all capitalists must do it, because those who do not will fall behind in competition.

This, however, means that replacement cost of capital per worker invested, now calculated at the replacement cost necessary to keep up with the competition, tends to be increased by firms more so than sales per worker before.

This squeeze, that investments per worker tend to be driven up by competition more so than before sales per worker have been increased, causes the tendency of the rate of profit to fall. Thus, capitalists are caught in a prisoner's dilemma or rationality trap.

This "new" rate of profit (r'), which tends to fall, would be measured as

r' = (surplus-value)/(capital to be invested for the next period of production in order to remain competitive).

RETURN ON ASSETS

The Return on Assets (ROA) percentage shows how profitable a company's assets are in generating revenue.

ROA can be computed as:

ROA = EBIT / Total Assets = (Earnings Before Interest and Taxes / Sales) * (Sales / Assets)

This number tells you "what the company can do with what it's got", i.e. how many dollars of earnings they derive from each dollar of assets they control. It's a useful number for comparing competing companies in the same industry. The number will vary widely across different industries. Return on assets gives an indication of the capital intensity of the company, which will depend on the industry; companies that require large initial investments will generally have lower return on assets.

Usage

Return on assets is an indicator of how profitable a company is before leverage, and is compared with companies in the same industry. Since the figure for total assets of the company depends on the carrying value of the assets, some caution is required for companies whose carrying value may not correspond to the actual market value.

Return on assets is a common figure used for comparing performance of financial institutions (such as banks), because the majority of their assets will have a carrying value that is close to their actual market value.

Return on assets is one of the elements used in financial analysis using the Du Pont Identity.

RETURN OF CAPITAL

Return of capital (ROC) refers to payments back to "capital owners" (shareholders, partners, unitholders) that exceed the growth (net income/taxable income) of a business. It should not be confused with return on capital which measures a 'rate of return'.

The ROC effectively shrinks the firm's equity in the same way that all distributions do. It is a transfer of value from the company to the owner. In an efficient market, the stock's price will fall by an amount equal to the distribution. Most public companies pay out only a percentage of their income as dividends. In some industries it is common to pay ROC.

- Real Estate Investment Trusts (REITs) commonly make distributions equal to the sum of their income and the depreciation (capital cost allowance) allowed for in the calculation of that income. The business has the cash to make the distribution because depreciation is a non-cash charge.

- Oil and gas royalty trusts also make distributions that include ROC equal to the drawdown in the quantity of their reserves. Again, the cash to find the O&G was spent previously, and current operations are generating excess cash.
- Private business can distribute any amount of equity that the owners need personally.
- Structured Products (closed ended investment funds) frequently use high distributions, that include returns of capital, as a promotional tool. The retail investors these funds are sold to rarely have the technical knowledge to distinguish income from ROC.
- Public business may return capital as a means to increase the debt/equity ratio and increase their leverage (risk profile). When the value of real estate holdings (for example) have increased, the owners may realize some of the increased value immediately by taking a ROC and increasing debt. This may be considered analogous to cash-out refinancing of a residential property.
- When companies spin off divisions and issue shares of a new, stand-alone business, this distribution is a return of capital.

TAX CONSEQUENCES

There will be tax consequences that are specific to individual countries. As examples only:

- Governments may want to prevent the shrinking of the business base of their economy, so they may tax withdrawals of capital.
- Governments may want to stimulate the exploration for O&G. They may allow companies to "flow-through" the exploration expense to the shareholders so it can be redeployed.
- REITs may also flow through the depreciation expense they do not need to shareholders. It may be decades before the property is sold and taxes payable. It is better

to give the excess cash and the tax write-off to the shareholders.

- Since the ROC shrinks the business and represents a return of the investors' own money, the ROC payment received may not be taxed as income. Instead it may reduce the cost base of the asset. This results in higher capital gains when the asset is sold, but defers tax.

Misconceptions

It is wrong to think that the concept of ROC is only a tax issue. It is an economic measure. But the measurement of ROC resulting from accounting financial statements will be different from the tax man's ROC.

While accountants try to measure the economic reality (in theory at least), governments may allow businesses to expense the cost of capital assets faster, in order to stimulate investments. This difference in the speed of expensing will result in different ROC values.

It is wrong for the investor to think of the ROC as income. Income is a measure of how much "better off" you are now than you were then. The ROC simply transfers assets from the business to the investor. As the investor benefits from the payment, the business shrinks, and the investor's interest in that business shrinks. An example is the only way to illustrate this.

Example

You start a delivery business with one employee and one contract. Your initial investment of $12,000 goes to buy a vehicle.

- The contract is for four years and pays you $7,000 each year.
- The employee is paid $2,000 each year.
- Gas to run the vehicle will cost $1,000 each year.
- With perfect foresight the accountant knows the vehicle will die at the end of the four years, so he expenses it at $3,000 each year.

At the end of each year:

- Cash flow will be $4,000 (= 7,000-2,000-1,000). It is paid out to you.
- Net income will be $1,000 (= 7,000-2,000-1,000-3,000).
- The ROC is $3,000 (= cash received - net income) (= 4,000-1,000).

At the end of four years:

- You have received cash payments of $16,000 (= 4,000*4).
- Total ROC payments equal $12,000 (= 3,000*4).
- Total income payments equal $4,000 (= 1,000*4).
- Your initial investment has been 100% recovered by the ROC (= 12,000-12,000).
- Your vehicle is now dead and worth nothing.
- Without it, you need to repeat your investment in order to keep operating, so the business is worth nothing.

CONCLUSIONS

- Cash flows do not measure income. They measure only cash flows.
- Depreciation, depletion and amortization cannot be ignored as "non-cash expenses". They are valid allocations of a one-time cash flow over the time period that the asset helps generate revenues.
- In the process of normalizing rates of return between different investment opportunities, ROC should not be included in the consideration of 'income' or 'dividends'.

Time Value of Money

Some people dismiss ROC (treating it as income) with the argument that the full cash is received and reinvested (by the business or by the shareholder receiving it). It thereby generates more income and compounds. Therefore ROC is not a "real" expense.

There are several problems with this argument.

- No one is arguing that the income earned on the full cash flow reinvested is not additional real income.
- If the original asset purchase had not been made, its cash cost would have been invested and earning returns in that same way.
- If you consider that depreciation is an allocation of the original cost of the asset, then you must agree that time-value-of-money considerations make the original cost HIGHER than the sum of the subsequent ROC expenses not realized until many years in the future.
- If you consider that depreciation measures the amount of cash that must be retained in order to finance the eventual replacement asset, then you must agree that the cost of that replacement will have increased in cost in the interim by inflation for that asset. Inflation is the basis for the time-value-of-money.

BIBLIOGRAPHY

Adams, T.F.M. : *A Financial History of the New Japan*, Kodansha International Ltd., Lokyo, 1972.

Anna J. Schwartz: *A Monetary History of the United States 1867-1960,* Princeton, Princeton University Press, 1963.

Arrow, Kenneth J.: *Social Choice and Individual Values,* New York, Wiley, 1951.

Ashok, Vasant: *Indian Economy in the World Setting,* Bombay, Himalaya, 1988.

Barro, Robert J., : *Economic Growth.* McGraw-Hill, 1995.

Behari, Madhuri: *Indian Economy since Independence: Chronology of Events,* Delhi, D.K. Publications, 1983.

Bhagwati, Jagdish: *India in Transition: Freeing the Economy,* Oxford, Clarendon Press, 1993.

Bhuleshkar, Vasant: *Indian Economy in the World Setting,* Bombay, Himalaya, 1988.

Box, George: *Time Series Analysis, Forecasting, and Control,* Holden Day, San Francisco, 1976.

Brent, R.P.: *Algorithms for Minimization Without Derivatives,* Englewood Cliffs, NJ: Prentice-Hall, 1972.

Campbell, J.Y., Lo, A.W.: *The Econometrics of Financial Markets,* Princeton University Press, 1996.

Chandhok, H.L.: *The Economy: Annual Time Series Data,* New Delhi, Living Media India, 1990.

Chandler, Alfred: *The Visible Hand: The Managerial Revolution in American Business,* Cambridge, Harvard University Press, 1977.

Chaudhuri, Pramit: *The Indian Economy: Poverty and Development,* New York, St. Martin's Press, 1979.

Chiang, Alpha C.: *Fundamental Methods of Mathematical Economics,* McGraw-Hill, 1984.

Cooley, Thomas F.: *Frontiers of Business Cycle Research,* Princeton University Press, 1995.

Cox, D.R.: *Theoretical Statistics,* London, Chapman & Hall. 1974.

Dahiya, L.N.: *Dynamics of Economic Life in Rural India*, Delhi, Gian, 1991.

Das, Kishore: *Economic History of Mughal India: An Annotated Bibliography, 1526-1875*, Calcutta, Santiniketan, 1991.

Davidson, Russell: *Estimation and Inference in Econometrics,* Oxford University Press, 1993.

Derrick, William R.: *Complex Analysis and Applications,* Belmont, CA: Wadsworth, 1984.

Desai, Vasant: *A Study of Rural Economics: A Systems Approach,* Bombay, Himalaya, 1983.

Devaney, Robert L.: *A First Course in Chaotic Dynamical Systems,* Addison-Wesley, 1992.

Dhingra, C.: *The Indian Economy: Resources, Planning, Development, and Problems,* Delhi, Sultan Chand, 1983.

Downs, Anthony: *An Economic Theory of Democracy,* New York, Harper and Row, 1957.

Durrett, Richard: *Probability: Theory and Examples,* Duxbury Press, 1996.

Ehrenberg, Ronald: *Modern Labor Economics,* Harper Collins, 1994.

Enders, Walter: *Applied Econometric Time Series,* John Wiley and Sons, 1995.

Friedman, Milton: *A Monetary History of the United States 1867-1960,* Princeton, Princeton University Press, 1963.

Goldsmith, W.: *The Financial Development of India, 1860-1977,* New Haven, Yale University Press, 1983.

Goyal, S.K.: *Agricultural Prices and Its Impact on the Indian Economy: A Case Study of Haryana,* New Delhi, Classical, 1992.

Greene, William H.: *Econometric Analysis,* MacMillan Publishing Company, 1993.

Greer, Douglas F.: *Industrial Organization and Public Policy,* MacMillan Publishing Company, 1992.

Gwilym Jenkins: *Time Series Analysis, Forecasting, and Control,* Holden Day, San Francisco, 1976.

Hart, Oliver: *Firms, Contracts, and Financial Structure,* Clarendon Press, Oxford, 19ᵒ5.

Hayek, F. A.: *Denationalisation of Money - the Argument Refined,* The Institute of Economic Affairs, Great Britain, 1976.

Hinkley D.V. : *Theoretical Statistics,* London, Chapman & Hall, 1974.

Hoshii, Iwao: *A Financial History of the New Japan*, Kodansha International Ltd., Lokyo, 1972.

Huang, Chi-fu: *Foundations of Financial Economics,* Prentice-Hall, 1988.

Ishwar, C.: *The Indian Economy: Resources, Planning, Development, and Problems*, Delhi, Sultan Chand, 1983.

Jha, P.R.: *Agriculture and Economic Development,* New Delhi, Ashish, 1988.

Joshi, Vijay: *India: Macroeconomics and Political Economy, 1964-1991*, Washington, World Bank, 1994.

Kenneth Rogoff: *Foundations of International Macroeonomics,* The MIT Press, 1996.

Kishore, K.: *Economic History of Mughal India: An Annotated Bibliography, 1526-1875*, Calcutta, Santiniketan, 1991.

Kreps, David M: *A Course in Microeconomic Theory,* Princeton University Press, 1990.

Landes, David S.: *The Unbound Prometheus,* Cambridge University Press, 1969.

Little, I.M.D.: *India: Macroeconomics and Political Economy, 1964-1991*, Washington, World Bank, 1994.

Long, Clarence: *Wages and Earnings in the United States, 1860-1890,* Princeton, Princeton University Press, 1960.

MacKinley, A.C.: *The Econometrics of Financial Markets,* Princeton University Press, 1996.

Maddala, G.S.: *Limited-Dependent and Qualitative Variables in Econometrics,* Cambridge University Press, 1983.

Milica, Zarkovic: *The Political Economy of Discontinuous Development: Regional Disparities and Inter-regional Conflict,* New York, Praeger, 1991.

Mongia, J.N.: *India's Economic Development Strategies, 1951-2000 A.D.*. New Delhi, Allied, 1986.

Nozick, Robert: *Anarchy, State, and Utopia,* New York, Basic Books, 1974.

Obstfeld, Maurice: *Foundations of International Macroeonomics,* The MIT Press, 1996.

Penson, J.B., O. Capps, C.R. Rosson III: *Introduction to Agricultural Economics,* Prentice Hall, NJ, 1996.

Peter H. Lindert: *American Inequality: A Macroeconomic History,* New York, Academic Press, 1980.

Pranab, K.: *The Political Economy of Development in India,* Delhi, Oxford University Press, 1984.

Priestly, M. B.: *Spectral Analysis and Time Series,* Academic Press, Ltd, 1981.

Raj, K.N.: *New Economic Policy*, Delhi, Oxford University Press, 1986.

Ray, S.K.: *Indian Economy*, New Delhi, Prentice-Hall, 1987.

Robert H. Litzenberger: *Foundations of Financial Economics,* Prentice-Hall, 1988.

Robert Smith: *Modern Labor Economics,* Harper Collins, 1994.

Romer, David: *Advanced Macroeconomics,* McGraw-Hill, 1996.

Sargent, Thomas J.: *Dynamic Macroeconomic Theory,* Harvard University Press, 1987.

Sargent, Thomas J.: *Macroeconomic Theory,* New York, Academic Press, 1979.

Sinha, R.K.: *Economic Development since Independence*, New Delhi, Deep and Deep, 1988.

Tirole, Jean: *The Theory of Industrial Organization,* MIT Press, 1988.

Tomasson, F.: *India's Persistent Dilemma: The Political Economy of Agrarian Reform*, Boulder, Colorado: Westview Press, 1994.

Williamson, Jeffrey G.: *American Inequality: A Macroeconomic History,* New York, Academic Press, 1980.

Williamson, Jeffrey: *Did British Capitalism Breed Inequality?,* Allen and Unwin, Winchester, 1985.

Xavier Sala-i-Martin: *Economic Growth.* McGraw-Hill, 1995.

INDEX

A

B

C

❑❑❑